To
Marilyn
Olson,

whose research
helped to correct
some of the dots on
the map of Matt's
life.

Thank you and good luck,

Alex Poulsen

Chasing Dillinger

*Police Captain Matt Leach,
J. Edgar Hoover and the Rivalry
to Capture Public Enemy No. 1*

ELLEN POULSEN *and*
LORI HYDE

Exposit
Jefferson, North Carolina

Photographs are from the collection of the author
unless credited otherwise.

ISBN (print) 978-1-4766-7465-0 ∞
ISBN (ebook) 978-1-4766-3312-1

LIBRARY OF CONGRESS CATALOGUING DATA ARE AVAILABLE

BRITISH LIBRARY CATALOGUING DATA ARE AVAILABLE

Front cover image of Dillinger, photographed in Tucson, January 1934
(author collection); Matt Leach's hallmark photo, reproduced
in a spate of 1930s detective magazines (courtesy James Stack)

Printed in the United States of America

Exposit is an imprint of McFarland & Company, Inc., Publishers

Exposit
Box 611, Jefferson, North Carolina 28640
www.expositbooks.com

To my dad,
Frederick G. Wilcox.
Without him, I would never have ventured
down this path to find the history.
—Lori Hyde

In memory of Rick Mattix,
1930s crime writer, historian
and friend to us both.
—Ellen Poulsen

Table of Contents

Part IV. The Landowner

Acknowledgments

As this project came to its conclusion, it became obvious that collecting the final material was going to involve a lot of people. Many of our friends and associates stepped up with the help that was needed to clarify information and identify subjects in photos. For the last-minute call to arms, we thank everyone who stood by with a good sense of humor through requests for photos, permissions, and quotes.

We wish to thank everyone who helped to motivate us and keep this project going, most notably Chicago native and Dillinger expert Tom Smusyn, whose vast contributions made this book possible. Tom never wants recognition, but the numerous citations from the "Smusyn Collection" speak volumes about the help he provided.

Special thanks to the late Sandy Jones for showing us the best photos and for making us laugh.

We deeply appreciate the generosity of Matt Leach's nephews, James Stack, the late Richard Leach and John Leach for sharing their recollections—with special thanks to Jim Stack for the use of his private collection of newspaper articles, documents and photos.

We also owe a debt of gratitude to author Marilyn Olsen, who generously allowed us the use of her research papers on Matt Leach and the history of the Indiana State Police (ISP). We wish to thank Steve McShane and the staff of the Calumet Regional Archives, Sergeant Noel Houze of the Indiana State Police, and James Knight of the Halverson Funeral Home in Somerset, Pennsylvania. We also wish to thank the staff of the Lake County Vital Records Department in Lake Superior Court; the staff of the East Chicago Indiana Public Library; Vicki Casteel and the staff of the Indiana State Library; the staff of the University of Texas at Austin, Harry Ransom Division; and Debra Brookhart of the American

Legion. Special appreciation goes to Andy Dowdle, who has compiled accurate source material on the Dillinger gang arrests in Tucson and the arresting officers. Thank you especially to Philip D. Hart, staff writer, *Serb World, U.S.A.*, who clarified the correct spelling of Matt Leach's father's name in the face of many different versions found in public records.

We owe a special thanks to our friend William "Bill" Helmer, who coined the title of this book and who provided much assistance and moral support. Thank you to Walter "Butch" Smith, who helped to identify an image of Detective Harvey Hire by showing us a picture from his private family photo collection. Thank you to Jim Emerson, who let us into the Crown Point County Jail after hours and gave us the grand tour. Special thanks to Tom Hunt, who led us to McFarland & Co. and the Exposit Books imprint. We owe a debt of gratitude to Susan Kilby of McFarland for her kindness and patience.

We wish to thank the following researchers and writers for their friendship and help with research and checking, or for having done groundwork in the past that provided the research for this book. They are notably Sarah Bahr, Bob Bates, Stan Benjamin, John Binder, Vanessa Binek, Claude Cazanave, Estella Cox, Russ Felt, the late Ernie Hudson, the late Rick Mattix, Steve Sato, Tom Pryor, and Larry Wack. To anyone whose name does not appear in this list of researchers, writers and readers who contributed to this book, we have appreciated your friendship throughout this project.

Preface

As co-authors of this book, we share the equivalent of a life term of research into the 1930s Midwest crime wave. We are both linked to Indiana State Police Captain Matt Leach because we share his historical resolve that the John Dillinger saga—the chase, the aftermath—warrants a deep study.

We hail from different regions of the United States. Lori grew to adulthood in the state of Indiana, where she learned to shoot and cuss, while her father kept the Hoosier folk tradition alive by relating tales of the outlaw John Dillinger. I grew up in Brooklyn, where a dollar-bin hardcover about Dillinger, purchased in a storefront in the shadow of the elevated train, triggered her interest in the outlaw.

We have each retained an early fascination with the 1930s crime wave. This interest in the snaggle-faced bank robber and his confederates extends to the cops who alternately chased him and cajoled him, and ultimately killed him.

When we met in person recently at the county jail in Crown Point, Indiana, we toured the empty prison, followed Dillinger's trail out the door, and smiled for pictures in the spot where Dillinger reached out to his prosecutor and hugged him for the camera.

The Crown Point meeting occurred after years of correspondence. Lori had piqued my interest in Indiana State Police Captain Matt Leach through her article on Leach that appeared in *On the Spot: The History of Crime and Law Enforcement During the Twenties and Thirties.* Through letters and e-mails, we had agreed that Captain Leach was one character of the Dillinger saga who had not gotten fair treatment, either in literature or in life. Leach remained the outcast who gave all and netted nothing in return. It seemed ludicrous that this profile survived

1

when everyone else from the 1930s crime saga, from Ma Barker to Melvin Purvis, had undergone some tweaking. Matt Leach was still being depicted as he had been back in the 1930s, when his reputation had tarnished into mythology.

As researchers, we were familiar with the published books on John Dillinger—many of whose authors remain our friends—and we knew from our reading that Leach's role in the story warranted a second look. The development of this book began with that thought. The seminal researcher, writer and editor of *On the Spot,* the late Rick Mattix, to whom this book is dedicated, endorsed the book idea. He connected us with some of the people whose words and insights appear within these pages.

We were fortunate to receive the research assistance of the family members of Matt Leach. The captain was close to his sisters and brothers, and their grown children have been immensely helpful with recollections, documents and photos. The availability of genealogy websites helped to document the oral histories. There are always gaps in family history, and this book has tried to avoid conjecture in such cases.

Interstate travel has helped to lend this book a personal voice. Individually we have gone to Leach's home town, his grave site, and the stretch of road where he was killed. We have seen the cities and counties that received Leach and his uniformed entourage, either in hostility (Lake County, Tucson) or in trust (Chicago). Along the way, we have visited libraries, archives and vital records depositories.

We knew at the start that there would be questions to stifle and frustrate us. This book details our studied conclusions when no easy answers appeared. During the presentation of this work, we silently honored the memory of Eugene Teague and Paul Minneman, the fallen Indiana State Police officers killed in attempts to capture the Dillinger and Brady gangs during Matt Leach's tenure in the ISP.

Books generally present stylistic challenges. We wanted to present our subject both as his intimates knew him and as the public perceived him. Our dilemma was that Matt Leach was a gregarious public figure throughout the Dillinger years of the 1930s. In contrast, his private life was a cocoon watched over by his family members and fellow legionnaires.

As a way of separating these dual facets of his life, we refer to Matt

Leach in two distinct ways within this book. We call him "Matt" through-out the chapters that cover his years as a private citizen and soldier.

During his term in the Indiana State Police, Matt Leach subjugated his personal relationships. He was consumed with his identity as "Dillinger's nemesis." In these sections of the book, we refer to him by his last name only, in keeping with the public figure.

This tale of Matt Leach's stunning fame and shocking downfall should not be viewed as a decaying monument to a bygone era. It is our intention that the crevices of Matt Leach's career will reveal a new aspect of the Depression-era crime wave. The officers and federal agents who composed the closed circle of 1930s gangbusters, whose covert deals, techniques and machinations helped end the machine-gun reign of ter-ror, played a role that affected the outcomes. They too had their stories.

Introduction:
The Infinite Chase

In these days when bank robber John Dillinger is a blockbuster from the past, the name Matt Leach is barely remembered. His exclusion from history is a travesty.

In the months when Dillinger was an unknown ex-con, Leach initiated the Dillinger mania. As he became a national public enemy ripping through five states, Dillinger remained an obsession that kept the lawman forever locked in the chase. After Dillinger's death, the quest went into Leach's mind, where it anchored itself. It followed him, like a vindictive ghost, to the hour of his death.

The captain of the Indiana State Police from 1933 to 1937, Leach had much in common with John Dillinger. Their childhoods were marked by the disappearance of one of their parents; Dillinger's mother died when he was three years old, and Leach's father left the family in Serbia to pave the way for life in America.

In youth, each joined the armed services, albeit for distinct reasons. Their careers would be played through the opposite poles of the criminal justice system. In this capacity each man stood out from his peers, sporting a photographic expression of pride. Both the cop and the criminal carried the burden of their egos like a gunnysack through their respective civil and criminal careers. They each died violently, the bank robber in a bloodied Chicago alley, Leach on a rain-slicked highway. Dillinger's end catapulted him into history. Leach would die twenty years later in pursuit of a disembodied Dillinger. When he died, his manuscript disappeared. The accident wiped out Leach's dream of publishing his version of the secrets behind Dillinger's death.

Dillinger's death was illustrious compared to that suffered by Matt

Leach. The gangster's fabled fate in a burst of FBI bullets has outlasted Leach's death on the Pennsylvania turnpike. Throughout the manhunt and its aftermath, Leach remained in the shroud of obscurity thrown over him by the FBI.

After Dillinger violated the federal Dyer Act in March 1934, by driving a stolen motor vehicle over the Indiana state line, the FBI claimed jurisdiction. Although a raft of federal anti-crime laws had been sent to Congress, Dillinger's only federal offense at this time was interstate car theft. The FBI's first strategic attempt to gain a footing in the Dillinger chase was to grill the man who knew everything. Matt Leach opened his doors to the FBI, at that time known as the Division of Investigation, and offered his own brand of Hoosier hospitality to the federal agents. The FBI helped themselves to his files, then shut him out of the chase. Leach lost his equilibrium and throughout the Dillinger quest never regained it. With the exception of a handful of Indiana journalists who printed his insights and quotes, he became irrelevant to the chase. This didn't stop him from acting as a watchdog to police agencies that remained on the case.

It isn't known whether Dillinger, in the frantic months after the Crown Point escape with a wooden pistol, figured out that Leach was no longer his most dogged bounty hunter. We don't know if the bank robber ever analyzed the politics of his violation of the Dyer Act in law enforcement circles, but the entry of the FBI to the case meant that Matt Leach was subtly blacklisted.

No other law enforcement figure, including Captain John Stege of Chicago's Dillinger Squad, would be punched out of the insider's ring. Only Melvin Purvis, special agent in charge of the Chicago office, would be forced to resign over his excessive press coverage.

Once the Dillinger hunt was controlled by the towering FBI, Leach would have been wise to restrict himself to Indiana cases. As he was being kicked upstairs, Leach should have seen that the view was nice enough. He lacked the foresight to save himself from the symbolic beheadings that Hoover levied on disfavored agents and non–FBI police officers.

Leach would dive into a jurisdictional dispute that morphed into a bitter conflict with J. Edgar Hoover. Just when it got personal is not really known. Professional rivalry grew into personal enmity when

Leach came forward and disputed the FBI's telling of the events. Yet the animosity between Leach and the FBI had started months before Dillinger hit the pavement outside of the Biograph.

In 1934, when first confronted with Captain Leach, Hoover assumed that the captain would stick to local police work and leave the interstate investigations to the FBI. By the time that Dillinger was killed, however, Hoover had reevaluated the Indiana lawman, accepting the fact that Leach would never respect the limitations of the state line. Hoover had yet to understand the power to which Leach had ascended under Governor McNutt's patronage system. It must have seemed odd to Hoover, a despotic administrator, to witness a state agency where an underling had inordinate power.

The climax of the fighting between Leach and the FBI happened in the days after Dillinger's death. Captain Leach was the first official to publicly challenge this, the FBI's most hallowed achievement. While the FBI took all the credit for Dillinger's shooting death in the alley of Chicago's Biograph Theater on July 22nd, 1934, Leach began telling the inside story to his press connections.

Secrets pocked the Dillinger killing. Leach was about to reveal the stark facts behind the official version of the shooting: Dillinger's hideout was laid out in detail to the FBI in a Chicago hotel room by two East Chicago, Indiana, officials, Captain Timothy O'Neill and Sergeant Martin Zarkovich. The latter brought his old friend, the notorious Gary vice figure Anna Sage, with whom Dillinger was living at the time he was killed.[1]

Leach was the cheese who stood alone. The leaks were immediately buried beneath the FBI's official version, which prevailed for decades to come. So completely whitewashed was the story that in 1964, author Fred J. Cook wrote of Dillinger, "Mention the names of ... Matt Leach and Sergeant Martin Zarkovich, and it's almost a cinch the reaction will be a bewildered 'Who were they?'"[2]

Leach had put himself on the line to no avail. At the time of his startling charges of East Chicago's corruption surrounding Dillinger's death, his bravado had earned him a controversial reputation. His was the single voice in the dark fog of East Chicago and the death of two police officers, whose unexplained double murders were inexorably linked to Dillinger yet never explained to anyone's satisfaction.

To avenge the leaks, Hoover would authorize a watch on Leach's every move from 1934 to 1937. When the FBI was able to officially challenge Leach three years later over his handling of the Brady case, the federal agents brought their case history to the table. In spite of Dillinger's death having been the origin of Leach's opposition to the FBI, they carefully left the name of "Dillinger" out of the proceedings. Leach would not let them get away with the omission and he brought it up himself.

The name of Dillinger was, by 1937, a relic of the frontier days when the FBI was still the Division of Investigation within the Department of Justice. The Indiana state laws mandating cooperation between the FBI and the Indiana State Police didn't go into effect until after Dillinger's death. The resolutions of the Indiana General Assembly of 1935 crystallized the gray area of "lack of cooperation" into tangible obstruction of the work of the FBI.

That did not stop Leach, nor did it eliminate his own counterclaims against the FBI. Leach remained vehement in his accusations of unprofessional conduct and lack of department courtesy.

The first altercation between Leach and the FBI had occurred in March of 1934 when agents went to Mooresville, Indiana, to tour Dillinger's hometown without notifying Leach of their activities. Leach had brought a formal complaint before Governor McNutt, and accused the Bureau of "deliberately seeking to confuse state and local law enforcement agencies for the purpose of advancing the ambition of Mr. Hoover."[3]

Hoover had blocked Leach from the Dillinger case at the zenith of the chase, but excluding Leach handicapped the search for the bank robber. The director ignored Leach at a point when all intelligence was urgently needed. What Hoover failed to grasp, in his righteous refusal to bring a rival in on the attack, was that Leach approached his job in the same way as Hoover did.

While Leach was close in narcissistic temperament to fellow Hoosier John Dillinger, he was closer yet to Hoover. These two officials had more in common, with respect to their prey, than either cared to admit. They bore a united approach to their jobs, two heads acting as one.

Neither Hoover nor Leach ever left his post. Hoover did travel, but never considered his trips as time off from work. At the time Leach was fired he had never taken a vacation, outside of an American Legion trip to post–World War I Europe in 1927. These men had personal lives that never interfered with their careers. Hoover developed a closeted relationship with Clyde Tolson, his second in command. Leach was married at the time of the Dillinger chase, but the marriage later ended in divorce.

In childhood, both Hoover and Leach stuttered. Each found a way around the potential speech defect—Hoover by developing a rapid speech pattern, Leach by using it to his advantage while interrogating prisoners, eliciting their sympathy. Leach publicly joked about his speech impediment to avoid being defined by the physical handicap.

Both men rose from humble origins within the rank and file of the police circles in which each worked. Leach had taken giant steps into his post of captain of the Indiana State Police by sandwiching himself between Indiana governor Paul V. McNutt and his director of Public Safety, Albert George Feeney. They jointly appointed Leach to head their reform administration's state police, which had been consigned to Feeney's Division of Public Safety in the wake of the 1932 election.

Hoover was sponsored by President Woodrow Wilson's cabinet appointee, Attorney General A. Mitchell Palmer, with whom Hoover had instigated the notorious Palmer Raids.

The similarity ends, however, in the sharp-edged separation of each official from his mentor. Hoover had a habit of turning former friends into enemies, and his federally sanctioned autonomy allowed it. But Leach worked in the State of Indiana in the early 1930s, where power remained contingent upon the favoritism of one's early backers. His forced abdication occurred when they could no longer support him. By the time their support could have salvaged his career, Governor McNutt was no longer the governor. Governor Maurice Clifford Townsend had reappointed Leach after his 1936 election. Townsend had grandfathered Leach in his steady position through gritted teeth; Townsend was aware that Leach had campaigned for his opponent in the primaries.

The ambivalence between Leach and Townsend was a far cry from Leach's friendship with McNutt, which bore the emotional provenance of their glory days in the American Legion. Leach was a military man. This was a value to which Hoover never subscribed. He adhered to his own personal code of nationalism, but declined the option of making the ultimate sacrifice for his country. While both Hoover and Leach embodied rigorous traits of service, this calling motivated them in different ways.

The May 1917 Selective Service Act mandated that males aged 21–30 must register for the draft. The age range was later changed to include men aged 18–45. For different reasons, the Selective Service Act would not directly affect either man. Leach joined the U.S. National Guard in 1915 and volunteered for service in World War I. In his native Washington, D.C., Hoover was an active member of his high school's Reserve Officers' Training Course (ROTC). His military aspirations ended in 1917, after he was hired as a Justice Department clerk. Despite provisions written into the Selective Service Act that limited "dodging" of the draft, Hoover was able to avoid military service because his new job offered him exempt status.

Hoover stayed cloistered within the Bureau, cleaving to his task with the surety of a born civil servant. Leach, an extravert, made friends. The war years would help Leach to form his identity and would ease him into the fraternity of the American Legion. It remained with him throughout his life. It would embrace him in the dark days of 1937, providing him with meaningful enterprise after he was fired.

If the era of the 1930s Midwest crime wave has become known as that of the public enemy, one fact remains. Both Leach and Hoover had become obsessed with John Dillinger. It was Dillinger the bank robber, and only Dillinger, who lit the spark beneath each lawman. Hoover ended up consigning the outlaw to the status of a trophy. Leach left his job with Dillinger an unsatisfied craving, an obsession that would follow him to the fatal highway crash, twenty-one years after Dillinger's death.

What stands out about Matt Leach's role in the Dillinger saga is not that he lacked the clout to stand up to the FBI, or that he was always one step behind Dillinger. Leach was one of the first lawmen, along with Pinkerton detective Forrest Huntington, to realize the impact that Dillinger and the members of his gang were going to have on the national scene. He was the embodiment of the law, trailing the gang through as many Midwestern states as would willingly allow him jurisdiction—and that meant mainly Ohio, Illinois, and reluctantly, Wisconsin and Arizona.

J. Edgar Hoover, posing for target practice with an aide, ca. 1930s.

While the director of the FBI stayed in Washington, Leach was kinetic, his interstate movements often rivaling that of the bandits themselves. He was a character, preening for cameras in his stiff, three-piece suits and folded handkerchiefs, with hands clasped purposefully. He cut a good figure. Life as an immigrant, struggling to read, write and speak in English, had taught him to always look the part of the prosperous American. Ironically, his gangster foes had the same gentleman's approach to clothes.

By the time the era of the public enemy ended with the death or imprisonment of the headline-grabbing desperadoes, Matt Leach had made enemies—bona fide, solid enemies. The rifts formed after his associates failed to understand—or simply refused to accept—his astonishing temperament. These bad relationships festered. Yet there was a window where Leach had an opportunity to turn the situation around.

Times changed with the end of the public enemy era. The nation's culture progressed out of the sad days of the NRA eagle and the bread lines. The Bureau of Investigation and the Division of Investigation of Dillinger's bygone era had taken a new name: the Federal Bureau of Investigation. It had built itself up around Dillinger's noir shooting death at the Biograph Theater in Chicago.

New headline-grabbing mobsters, such as New York's Murder Inc., came to prominence as the nation packed the Depression-era crime wave into mothballs. Those who were officially involved in the Dillinger case were reinventing the controversial roles they'd once played.

The death of Dillinger forced everyone to change—everyone except Matt Leach. He couldn't govern his officers in cooperation with the federal government, didn't recognize that this was essential for the welfare of his own department. For three years after Dillinger's death, Leach continued to have altercations with the FBI. Some of these cases were sensational, like the "Head and Hands" murder of a retired Cincinnati fire captain, Harry R. Miller. The grizzly tabloid affair was a battleground where Leach accused Indiana field agents of hindering his investigation by intentionally losing files he'd handed over. They then joined with Indiana police board attorneys and charged Leach with violating the constitutional rights of the "Head and Hands" suspects in order to get confessions. Leach's rebuttal was that his actions had resulted in arrests of suspects who were duly tried and convicted. Leach publicly defended his actions while privately grappling with the issue of the suspects' guilt or innocence. He later admitted that he believed his case had lacked evidence. In this admission, he proved that he had evolved from a hot-headed gangbuster into a tarnished detective. By that time, his career was over. The veteran police captain was dismissed by the Indiana State Police Board at the behest of the FBI. Insiders knew it was Hoover's move to set a precedent and establish his authority over state and civil police.

To the majority of readers, Matt Leach had never stood for any case except Dillinger. Visually, Leach remains forever posed before a quaint, vintage telephone. In the public mind he will continue to stutter, to interfere and to play the man that Dillinger hated. Yet a deeper examination will reveal a self-educated student of the criminal mindset who met the public enemy face to face, who stood up to Hoover, and who died knowing more about Dillinger than anyone who came before or after.

Prologue

By the late–Depression year of 1937, FBI director J. Edgar Hoover had cobwebs littering his campaign against the thirties desperadoes. This was surprising considering that by then, every bank robber, safe cracker and kidnapping gang from the 1930s Midwest crime wave had been killed or jailed within the lichened walls of Alcatraz. Hoover's office practices were orderly as a file cabinet yet fueled by his dirty, street-fighting nature. He liked to settle scores. In this respect, he resembled the criminals he vilified.

This time the enemy was another law enforcer.

September 4th, 1937, dawned like any other day at the Indianapolis Statehouse. In his basement office, Matt Leach, captain of the Indiana State Police, arrived at his desk. As always, he was dressed impeccably, groomed as though he were headed to a formal affair. This was how he presented himself to the world. It was a world that often involved news photos and publicity—and he was at the ready.

Leach had heard rumors that he was going to be asked to resign. This was nothing new to the captain, who had weathered the political storms of hiring and firing in Indiana since the 1920s. Leach knew that the present circumstances did not involve the tired cycle of politics and patronage. This time, it was personal. Leach had always had rivals within his home state of Indiana. These conflicts he'd been able to control. While Leach thought the self-governing nature of Indiana was solvent, he knew he had strong enemies in Washington in the newly empowered Federal Bureau of Investigation.

Hoover had never forgiven Matt Leach for making public announcements challenging the FBI's role in the 1934 killing of bank robber John Dillinger. The captain had leaked the bombshell that the FBI agents helped steal cash from the bandit's stiffening body. This put the FBI on the level of grave robbers when put before the general public. The worst of the leaks, in the eyes of the exclusionist director, was that the FBI had needed help from a local police department in East Chicago to catch Dillinger.

Although he knew the FBI had branded him as an obstructionist, Matt Leach had never cowered before the federal agency. Even after the Indiana Legislature had drafted Chapter 299 of the Acts of the Indiana General Assembly of 1935, Leach refused to back down. This legislation mandated cooperation between the Indiana State Police and the FBI, and made it an offense for a state or city official to interfere with the federal agency. Leach had disregarded this legislation, treating it like a discarded rough draft. The new law was the old law as far as he was concerned. It reiterated what he'd learned in the heated days when the FBI visibly entered the Dillinger case, in March of 1934. In that tumultuous period after Dillinger's "wooden gun" escape from the Crown Point County Jail, during which time the outlaw had stolen a county car and crossed the line from Indiana to Illinois, the federal agency took all of Leach's files and made his investigations its own. Then they tossed him aside, deriding him, challenging him, tailing him and harassing his officers.

Now they were getting Leach fired. Because the news was leaked to him by a member of the police board, Leach had time to write a statement. As he went about his business that September morning in 1937, the statement adorned his desk like an interloper among the day's paperwork. When the superintendent of the state police, Donald F. Stiver, walked into his office, Leach expected the worst. Stiver then handed Leach a memorandum: the missive asking him to resign. Springing into a flight or fight reaction, Leach refused. Stiver then told him he was fired, that his replacement had been chosen, that he could pack up his kit bag and leave. This confrontation ended the career of Matt Leach.

Captain Matt Leach, headline maker, pundit, self-proclaimed spokesperson and defender of the governor of Indiana during the Dillinger era three years earlier, had been a flamboyant force. Now, it hardly mattered that Leach's replacement, Captain Walter Eckert, was bland as soap, because nobody would ever compare to the antics of Matt Leach, the first captain of the Indiana State Police.

During the years of his service to the ISP, Leach had always defined himself as a loyal bastion of Governor Paul V. McNutt's administration. The first year of McNutt's governance had been marred by the exploits of Dillinger, whose parole McNutt had signed and who had instigated the most notorious prison escape in Indiana's recent history. Matt Leach had served as McNutt's figurehead, mouthpiece and fall guy. It earned him the governor's gratitude and unfailing protection. Leach became controversial when he started leaking information to the press during the Dillinger hunt. His habit of involving the press angered other policemen and created distrust among policing agencies. Throughout it all, Leach never truly realized that his controversial practices had a four-year shelf life. McNutt, Leach's protector, was mandated to serve only one term under Indiana law.

Leach's fiery tenure lasted until 1937. When it ended in his office that morning in September, he meekly packed his artifacts of the Dillinger years into a cardboard box. Thus demeaned, he left his office in the basement of the Indianapolis Statehouse. His mind, active as always, went over the names of the reporters he would call. On this day, as on every day for the preceding four years, Leach called the press. He released his statement, which was published in the Indianapolis dailies. In his statement he defended his own position. He said he would not resign and leave the post vacant for his successor, that he would demand a full hearing before the Indiana State Police Board:

> I have refused today to resign as Captain of the Indiana State Police as requested by the State Police Board on the complaint of J. Edgar Hoover, Director of the Federal Department of Justice.
>
> My sole reason for refusing to resign is the record of our department through the period of going on five years, in which I have been the active head of the State Police.

The Indiana State Police Board had fired him officially for his mishandling of the case of fugitive Al Brady and his gang. This gang of murdering thieves went simply by "The Brady Gang." They had briefly tried to elevate themselves in stature by calling themselves "The New Dillingers." It was this allusion to Dillinger that exploded with the force of a misfired rifle. The Indiana State Police Board, in accusing Leach of mishandling the case, charged the captain with leaking information to the newspapers about Brady without the authorization of the police superintendent. When Leach appeared for his hearing two weeks later, he was expecting a blue wall of support by his department colleagues. Instead, the captain was met by a contingent of agents of the Federal Bureau of Investigation. Four of them were set to testify against him.

At the same time, regional dailies opined that the firing was an outrage that challenged Indiana's history of independence from federal meddling, that Leach's problems with the FBI stemmed from a letter he'd written to Governor McNutt back in 1934 that challenged the Division's methods of hunting the Dillinger gang in Indiana. This appeared to be at the heart of Leach's termination at the behest of the FBI. Insiders knew that Leach was fired not because of Brady but because of Dillinger. It was the Depression-era outlaw and the jurisdictional wars that sprang from him that had been at the root of the feud between Leach and the Division of Investigation.

The FBI agents who followed Hoover's directives and harassed Leach never realized that Leach felt entitled to Dillinger by virtue of a relationship that he'd built with the bank robber over the past several months. Leach had built a dangerous crosswalk in becoming a visible nemesis to Dillinger and his gang. No FBI agent could replicate the intimate relationship that Leach had forged with the Dillinger gang. No police officer or FBI agent was prepared to believe that a lawman could become obsessed with a criminal and not have it interfere with the job. So Leach lost credibility with other police agencies just as he gained it with the gang he so desperately wanted to catch.

During the months when the Dillinger gang members known as the Terror Gang ran between Chicago, Indianapolis, Ohio, Tennessee, Florida and finally Arizona, Leach never personally arrested any of them. He forged his strategies behind the scenes while Dillinger, Harry Pierpont, Charles Makley, John Hamilton and Russell Clark remained at large. This distance between the lawman and his prey was as symbolic as it was physical. Leach became an apparition in the minds of the Terror Gang. He haunted their dreams; he followed them on levels higher than the roads and cities they travelled through. Yet he couldn't get close to who they were, never really figured them out. To him they were merely criminals, subjects he could read about in his books on criminal psychology.

Dillinger gang member Harry Pierpont was caustically realistic about the separation of criminal and lawman. "They call us morons, rappers," he said bitterly to his moll Mary Kinder in the weeks before his execution. When Leach did exchange words with members of the gang, they were shackled and jailed. But for the steel bars that protected Leach when he met the gang face to face, they found him to be the most dreaded cop. Gang associate Pearl Elliott, Dillinger himself and even trigger man Harry Pierpont vowed to get revenge on him.

After Dillinger's death, the FBI watched Leach's every move. While aware that he was the object of surveillance by the FBI, Leach did not bury himself in a rubber-gun detail. He didn't hide behind a desk in the basement of the Statehouse, safely within the city of Indianapolis. The captain moved forward, visible as ever, and embraced a new era of law enforcement supposedly devoid of politics and patronage. Leach's mistake was to choose what he wanted to keep while discarding what he didn't like.

Times had changed since Leach was under the protection of Governor Paul V. McNutt, when he had served as the first captain of the ISP in the arid spring of 1933. Years later, by 1937, Leach's raw hunger for Indiana's sovereignty had grown. His mistake was to overemphasize the Brady Gang's centricity to Indiana in an era when states no longer operated in a vacuum. That had angered other police departments, but they had maintained silence. Not so with the FBI. The agency was not about to play games of department courtesy when that had never been a feature of their mission before.

In 1936, Leach had allowed himself to overstate the importance of what should have been the routine police work of investigating the whereabouts of the Brady Gang. Rather than stay in Indiana, Leach insisted on traveling to Baltimore, Maryland, to investigate the Bradys. In doing so he left himself wide open, so to speak. His conduct in and around Baltimore, as he travelled back and forth from Indianapolis, created the basis for the FBI's allegations against him: that he leaked information to the press and that he had tampered with FBI witnesses.

Hoover's use of the Brady case in firing Leach had ironic overtones. The director had no vested interest in the outcome of this gang of low-level robbers and murderers. He had already made his reputation on the backs of John Dillinger, the Barkers, Charles "Pretty Boy" Floyd, Machine Gun Kelly and Alvin Karpis. He did, however, need to prevent another crime wave and the glamorization of a group of thugs. As he saw it, Leach and his press releases regarding Brady would bring about the elevation of this new gang of desperadoes to notoriety. Leach had done an amazing thing in bringing Dillinger to the attention of the general public. If he did it once, he could do it again—unless he was stopped in his tracks.

The machine-gunning Brady and his minuscule gang became Hoover's excuse for starting an action against Leach. When the FBI was able to officially challenge Leach over his handling of the Brady case, they had a lot of ammunition. The FBI had enumerated Leach's every move from 1934 to 1937, and brought its case history to the table. In spite of the antagonism between the two administrators, Hoover insisted that the Brady Gang incident was the only cause of the firing.

During the September 17th hearing, during which Leach fought to keep his job, his strident pose appeared anxious next to the unemotional FBI agents. Leach had maintained his headline-grabbing style developed during the Dillinger case. Calm was a demeanor Leach never would assume. Some onlookers had always believed he lacked the objectivity expected in a detective. Rule of law meant lack of prejudice, bias and sympathy, at least while on the record. And this was on the record. It would blight Leach's last stand.

In the six-hour hearing, Leach learned that the police board had filed an exhaustive list of allegations against him. They charged him with revealing police secrets, obstructionism and acting in a manner unbecoming a police officer. In spite of the Dillinger case having been the origin of Leach's opposition to the FBI, the agents who testified deliberately left the name of "Dillinger" out of the proceedings. That removed the specter of a vendetta being at the core of the proceedings. It was an easy act and omission. The irony of the situation, as it came to its ugly head in September of 1937, was that the former principals of the Dillinger case, the people whose names were slated for history books, would carefully avoid mentioning Dillinger in discussing Leach's track record of alleged noncooperation.

At the hearing of September 17th, Leach sought to sway public opinion. He charged the FBI with obstructing him by claiming that they had withheld information from him and the Indiana State Police. That became a moot point with devastating results. Unknown to him, the

Indiana State Police had already obtained the disputed Brady files. The FBI had handed them over as part of the deal to get him fired.

This spoke directly to the outcome of the hearing. Leach was outnumbered by the federal agents and police board members who said that he had to go. It must have wounded his pride to listen to the charges, which accused him of conducting himself in a manner unbecoming a police officer, and failing to achieve greater success in preventing and detecting crimes and apprehending criminals. As he sat there, a sagging, unreliable witness in his own defense, he knew the terrible truth: He was not only fired; his legacy was going to be eradicated. As he sat there, a sagging, unreliable witness in his own defense, he knew the terrible truth. His legacy was going to be eradicated.

PART I

The Dreamer

CHAPTER 1

Destination: Gary, Indiana

In order to understand the man who has come to be known as Matt Leach, you must understand the place of his birth.—Philip Hart

Matija Licanin spent his first day on Ellis Island under a classification that puzzled his exhausted mother. Even though he'd just turned twelve, Matija was being called an "alien held for special inquiry." He sat with Mila, his mother, in the detention area. There they ate and slept with other hopefuls not met by someone in New York. They were the ones whose arrival from Hamburg was an anonymous affair.

It was 1906, a time when Ellis Island officials viewed women traveling without men as potential streetwalkers. Although she listed herself as married, Mila had traveled under her maiden name of Ljubicic. The intake guards, bastions of America's gateway, had the power to accept or reject an immigrant. The presence of a child only intensified their scrutiny of Mila Ljubicic. With no English, Mila had trouble explaining that she and the boy were joining Vujo Licanin.

Vujo was Mila's husband and the father that Matija had never had a chance to know. Vujo had picked up a drinking problem in America, along with enough money to pay for their passage. With his sporadic work record, he'd somehow paved their way through his tithe of hard work over the past decade.

While she desperately waited at Ellis Island, Mila was understandably grateful for her first taste of American food. She was happy that her son could eat while they waited like criminals. During three August days in New York Harbor, they huddled like the tired masses of the famous slogan. Frightened and tentative, Mila had no way of knowing

whether they would be met by Vujo or held indeterminately in detention. There was even the possibility that the uniformed men at Ellis
Island would send her or her boy back home. Finally, their release onto
the Battery-bound ferry ended their unhappy experience at Ellis Island.[1]

It was the edge of summer, and the trip had severed Matija's ties to
his own life in Serbia. For a twelve-year-old boy, that life could have
included a blossoming friendship with a girl, other boys to hang out
with, a sense of immortality in a world existing only for his development.
In America, other kids his age were reluctantly preparing for that grand
tradition, going back to school. Not so for Matija. Even if he could speak
English, the school system wasn't top priority. The land of opportunity—a mere catchphrase for laborers such as his father—conjured up
weekly wages, not the unpaid idleness of a classroom education. In the
mentality of the Licanin family and Serbs like them, America was for
work. That was the sole purpose of the family's entry to the United
States, which had kicked off when the economy in their own region had
faltered in the late 1880s.

On the manifest of the Hamburg steamer *Patricia,* Mila and Matija
were boilerplate stamped as Croatian.[2] It was a popular misnomer
attached to many arrivals from the former Austria-Hungry region. In
reality, they were Serbs who came from the Croatian region but who were
not ethnic Croatians. While always referring to themselves as Serbian,
the Licanin family hailed from the Austria-Hungarian section of Vrginmost, Kordun. The name Licanin literally meant "the One from Lika."[3]

Matija, in his native land, would have gone through his life as a
"Lichan," or one born in Lika. For most Americans unschooled in the
geography of Matija's homeland, the term Austria-Hungary was easier
to understand.[4]

Sometime after 1880, the men of Kordun had launched a mass
immigration to the United States. Their region had been a neutral land
strip, utilized for fighting foreign enemies. Kordun stood in a trail of
fortified cities known as Austria's military frontier. For over three hundred years, from 1537 to the late 1800s, it was a free zone whose inhabitants served as a militia guarding a border in exchange for land and
autonomy. The region evolved into a quasi-military territory where
women kept pistols in the house and men never left home without a
gun. It was called *Cordon militaire,* or the military border. Since feudal

The SS *Patricia*, shown here ca. 1906, ushered young Matt and his mother into America as Serbian immigrants.

times, the Military Frontier had defended the Austrian Empire against Turks, Prussians, the French, Italians and Russians. By 1870, a decade before Matija's birth, the European political systems had changed and rendered the Military Frontier obsolete. Feeling threatened by the change in their social fabric, men like Vujo left for America.

The inhabitants of the Military Frontier, skilled in warfare for generations, now headed for a different battle. Factory work beckoned. It would give them a way to earn a living utilizing their physical strength. The backbreaking work offered by the steel mills of the American Midwest paid well. This work gave the new man a chance to learn English and still work. With the mass exodus from the region, Lika soon resembled a ghost town, devoid of the very men who had made it a paramilitary stronghold over centuries.[5]

Vujo joined the great wave that took place between 1880 and 1900. Amid the deserted cottages of Vrginmost, Matija was born on August 1st, 1894.[6] During that period, Vujo left for the United States. Twelve years would pass before he would see his wife and child come to America.

Matija, who would become a first-generation American, started his life in Lika and absorbed the values inherent in the region. Though the Military Frontier was defunct, its attitudes were not. He would grow to manhood with a rabid thirst for warfare and police work. That was his birthright, along with the melancholy nature that passed through the generations of men who had served as frontiersmen on the border.

When Matija settled into his life in the United States, Lika faded into memory as that familiar catchphrase, the old country. It was a thing to forget. All the frontier bravado and ethnicity now hobbled him in the melting pot of the Midwest. "No speak English," he heard, and the phrase humiliated him. His language was the Illyrian Serbian-Croatian tongue of the borderland. He didn't like hearing his mother ridiculed, either. So he quickly learned English. It was especially important that he learn to speak quickly, because Mila was slow to learn and needed his help to talk to the landlord and the grocer. The imperative to speak a strange language in record time contributed to the speech problems that would plague his adult life.

Vujo was moving between Youngstown, Ohio, and Steelton near Harrisburg, Pennsylvania, at the time that Mila and Matija joined him. Matija was the first child born to Mila and the only one of her four children to be born in Austria-Hungary. Once she joined Vujo, she bore him two children in rapid succession. Her son Mosije, called Marshall, was born in 1906. Milan, called Mahlon, was born after Marshall, in 1910.[7] Matija, although foreign-born and much older, would remain close to his brothers throughout his life. With his brothers, he shared a growing hatred for Vujo, whose drunken rages they witnessed. Matija and Marshall, the two oldest boys, tried to stop Vujo from acting aggressively toward their mother.[8]

By 1910, the growing Licanin family followed the migration westward to the industrial complex spearheaded by U.S. Steel and several other steel mills settling on the north shore of Indiana. With an abundance of jobs available for its growing population of steelworkers, Gary's attractions lured the family. There they put down roots as they settled into the rhythms of daily life. Millie cooked the veal, lamb, pork and plum dishes that had been the staple of life in Europe. They went to local markets and socialized among their neighbors. While some friends went to the Serbian Orthodox Church, St. Sava, the Licanin clan felt religion was a private affair. Except for Vujo, who drifted around, the family believed that Gary was a fertile place in which to live and work.

The year 1910 saw Matija become a big brother twice. As well as his baby brother, Mahlon, Matija welcomed the child who would forever be his baby sister. Mildred's parenthood was officially attributed to Mila Ljubicic, still using her maiden name, and Vujo Licanin, whose name was misspelled by every public record worker he encountered. The misunderstandings surrounding his name, which ranged from Vugo, to Vuko, to Vujo, finally caused him to consider a more American-sounding name. He liked the sound of "Louis."

Gary was a new town, a boom town, swelling with jobs, businesses and economic growth. Built over sand and swamp, it boasted beaches for swimming and a downtown area for shopping and businesses. In its future lay one-family homes that would arise during the postwar period of the late forties and fifties. In the 1910s, apartment houses provided housing for the mill employees. In that sense, it was the ultimate factory town, with a mill providing stability for its families. Sometime after 1911, Mila and Vujo moved to 2194 Broadway.[9]

In 1912, after one unsuccessful attempt, Vujo achieved his goal of American citizenship. What should have been a family affair was shrouded in confusion. Vujo's bid for Americanization influenced Mila to start going by the popular name of "Millie." Under laws in place at the time, Millie would have been naturalized along with Vujo. Strangely, she kept listing herself as a noncitizen in census records. This may point to the fact that she was uninformed of her rights as a citizen. The only one of their children to be born in Europe, Matija, would now be considered a naturalized American. Vujo's naturalization would have resulted in the automatic citizenship of Matija. Yet as an adult, Matt Leach would say that he was naturalized in the army.[10]

As new Americans, the family lived in the spirit of the time, which was to leave the old country across the waves. His four children were dependent and he needed acceptance among the mill bosses, so Vujo adopted a solution for his Serbian name. He informally called himself Louis in the hope of avoiding prejudice. Although the family members would adopt the Americanized "Leach" between 1922 and 1925, Vujo would retain his surname of Licanin. Vujo soon left and moved to Youngstown, Ohio.[11] He was causing misery during his drunken episodes. While much of this was witnessed by Matija and his siblings, the violence was diffused by relatives and friends. They were clannish out of necessity. The ties bound them to their dreams and helped preserve the gloss of life in Gary.

Sometime between 1912 and 1915, Matija's name changed to Mathew, with one "t." He was also sometimes listed as having the middle initial "L," although this seems to be some mistake as any middle name remained a mystery. It isn't known whether the young man liked his new name, but it is noteworthy that he never used it.

In a burst of independence, he assumed a cheeky American shortcut, which took the first syllable of his birth name. "Matt" retained the cadence and resonance of the original Matija. It must have helped the developing young man, still an adolescent, to make this difficult adjustment. Throughout his life, he would never use "Mathew," not in official papers nor in being addressed. "Matt" would appear on all his documents. In adopting an American name with traces of his birthright, the youth made the first in a series of moves to reflect his developing sense of self.

As Vujo briefly moved to Youngstown, the newly minted "Matt" took responsibility as head of the household. It was hard to make ends meet in the apartment on Broadway. He didn't have a clear path to manhood. Mila, who was now Millie, yet struggling with English, was dependent on Matt. The wellspring of jobs at U.S. Steel hadn't invoked the American dream for Vujo, who was drifting through Indiana, Ohio and Pennsylvania. It is noteworthy that with all the jobs that the Gary Works had to offer, Vujo left town to find work. He sometimes worked as a security guard, sometimes tended bar in local saloons. That made it very easy for him to drink to excess.

"[The children] would hide from their father," said Matt's nephew, Jim Stack. "They would hide in the coal bins and listen while he pulled the old woman by the hair."[12]

In this troubled environment, Matt perfected his knowledge of the English language and transitioned out of his Serbo-Croatian linguistic pattern. His difficulties with this process were partially to blame for an affliction that caused him to speak in a rambling manner. "He didn't stutter," said Jim Stack. "He just kept on talking."[13] The impediment often made him an object of scorn. As an adult, he found to his dismay that his way of speaking gave his enemies something to ridicule.

Matt's education terminated at the end of the fifth grade. It was an

Gary, Indiana, was a young factory town. Matt Leach found work at American Bridgeworks, shown here ca. 1910 (Calumet Regional Archives).

occurrence that was not uncommon for that era.[14] He became a wage earner early on.

Matt worked in U.S. Steel subsidiary American Bridge Company Works, which was popularly called the American Bridgeworks. The job lasted for a year, as Matt learned enough to call himself an electrician. He also worked at one point in Rockford, Illinois, as a wood finisher in a furniture factory.[15]

Perhaps he disliked the monotony of factory life, or maybe it was restlessness. He could not stay there. For Matt, the only child in the family who was old enough to go out on his own, the choice left him in a quandary. He had the responsibility of taking care of his mother in the periods when Vujo didn't work or left town. This financial burden was a weight, the millstone around Matt's neck.

Shortly before his twenty-first birthday, Matt found a way to escape

American Bridgeworks Co's Works, Gary, Ind.

American Bridgeworks, shown here ca. 1910, stood for Gary, Indiana: bright, colorful and productive (Calumet Regional Archives).

the drudgery while ensuring a paycheck for his mother. He lied about his age by giving a false date of birth and listing himself as twenty-two years old. On July 19th, 1915, the one-hundred-fifty-four-pound Matt was mustered into Company P, 1st Infantry of the Indiana National Guard. He was savvy enough to avoid listing his ethnicity as "Serbian," given the connotations of the outbreak of the First World War in Serbia the year before. He wrote instead, the more benign term of "Austrian." He was accepted into full military service in spite of a physical defect: his left hand was missing its middle finger. Almost a year later, on June 23rd, Private 1st Class Leach signed a six-year oath. He would prove to be a valuable asset to the armed forces.[16]

In 1916, the federal government was sending Indiana National Guardsmen to the Mexican border to serve with General John J. Pershing. Matt was sent to the border in the expedition into Mexico chasing Francisco "Pancho" Villa, who attacked the U.S. military at Columbus, New Mexico. By the end of this campaign in 1917, Matt had earned the rank of corporal.

As though fueled by adrenaline, Matt once again mobilized himself for battle. In 1917, on three separate dates, able-bodied men enlisted in the armed forces in preparation for the American entry into World War I. During this campaign, Vujo signed up.[17] For the Licanin family, enlistment in the armed services was a natural path, a reminder of the old Military Frontier.

Matt was assigned to the 150th Field Artillery Regiment, 42nd (Rainbow) Division, and Co. F of the 151st Infantry under Colonial George Healy, the 38th (Cyclone) Division. On October 5th, 1918, he left for Europe. In England and France, under the American Expeditionary Forces (AEF), he made sergeant 1st class and became a teacher, instructing his men in the use of the bayonet. Although he was there long enough to see some warfare, his tenure on the front did not last too long. Two months later, on December 19th, 1918, in preparation for demobilization, Indiana's infantry went home.

Matt's honorable discharge took place on January 8th, 1919.[18] Matt left the service and moved back in with his mother and Vujo, now himself an ex-serviceman going by the name of "Louis." Matt's father worked his usual shift in a saloon, as the family settled into an apartment at 1054 Grant.[19]

Matt's younger brother, Marshall, was picking up jobs in Gary as a boxer at the Gary YMCA. Matt, Marshall and Mahlon weren't little boys anymore, hiding behind the coal bin while their father beat up their mother. One day, during a violent episode, Matt pushed Vujo up against the wall. Marshall remained behind him, ready to jump in at a moment's provocation. With the tension mounting, Millie and Vujo moved back to Steelton, Pennsylvania. Millie continued to live with him under her maiden name. They remained in Steelton through the early part of the 1920s. As ambivalent as he must have been to have his mother living alone with his father, Matt now had some freedom from supporting her. The move emancipated Matt from his parents.

Like many men, Matt made the leap from military service to a job at home that resembled the armed forces. He applied to the Gary Police Department. The circumstances of his employment were unusual. On January 31st, 1922, Gary mayor Roswell O. Johnson, whom the Gary Police Department yearbook described as "a man of mature years, sound judgment and winning personality,"[20] decided to lower the ax on his staff. He called a special meeting of the Board of Public Safety. Under Johnson, the pink slips fell like confetti. He brazenly fired fourteen members of the police force and hired fourteen men to replace them.

In an attempt to acknowledge Gary's diversity, the 1934 Gary Police yearbook stated, "Gary police with its personnel composed of all the different nationalities to be found in Gary except the Orient, can handle any language on the face of the globe except Japanese and Chinese, two classes of people who very seldom get into jail."[21]

With a large population of Serbian people living in Gary, the police force wanted patrolmen like Matt who could straddle two cultures. Matt was one of the newly hired. Perhaps the first time he saw his name published in a newspaper was when he was listed by the *Gary Post-Tribune* as having been familiar with police work. This was not bad for a novice; Matt was honing his self-promotion skills.[22]

Gary's mayor, R. O. Johnson, shown with family, ca. 1910 (Calumet Regional Archives).

Matt left the armed forces comfortable with civilian life yet carrying the aura of military deportment. He was tall and slim with a thirty-four-inch chest. At one-quarter inch below six feet, he was handsome in a uniform. His image was slightly marred by the missing left middle finger.[23] That shortened left hook didn't stop him from getting the job.

Being a Gary police officer meant that Matt was part of the history of the town itself. The department took pride in having risen out of the sand and swamp that was the locale before 1906. The first lawmen of Gary were club-wielding tough-guys. Their job was to curb the violence-prone construction workers who hung around the town. Brothels and after-hours places were everywhere. When the first police department formed in 1907, its members sported copper stars, high derby hats and handlebar mustaches. With no clerical personnel, records weren't kept.

When Matt was hired, the Gary Police Department was a fledgling fraternity, fifteen years young and subject to the ebb and flow of mass firing and rehiring. Under the administration of Mayor Johnson, the department included a boy's truancy division, vice and tavern squads, a dog wagon, auto and pawnshop detail and a drunk-control unit. The Bertillon method of identification was still in effect, which depended upon physical description as a means of identifying suspects.[24]

Being on the job leant a measure of security to Matt, whose mother didn't last long with Vujo in Pennsylvania. By 1923, Millie was separated from her husband and living with Matt in an apartment at 1218 Ellsworth Place.[25] In this simple setting, Matt's job was his livelihood for the first few years under Chief William A. Forbis.[26]

In 1925, Matt got married. Marion Brancis, his twenty-one-year-old

Matt Leach, Gary Police Department, ca. 1920s (courtesy James Stack).

bride, was a second-generation Serbian whose parents came from Austria. She was born in Chicago and had moved to Gary as a young woman. Matt was marrying a woman who bore a level of sophistication as a Chicago native and also as a divorcée. Marion had been married and quickly divorced at the age of 19. She was declared Mrs. Matt Leach by a Crown Point justice of the peace on February 27th, 1925. Her groom listed his occupation as police officer. On the application for a marriage license, Matt listed his birth date as September 17th, 1894. Either he was never told his exact birth date or he never remembered it correctly. He had a habit of changing his date of birth on official forms. It appears that Vujo was now going by his American name, because Matt listed his father's name as Louis, a steel worker residing in Gary.[27]

It was a time when couples didn't often acquire their own apartment when they married, due to insufficient income or savings for rent. The couple lived for a short time at the Ellsworth Place apartment with Matt's mother, father, brothers and sister, before moving into the family home at 1176 Jackson Street with a full roster of relatives. The Leach family lived here for at least five years, with some extended family members joining them as others moved out. Matt's mother, his brother Mahlon, and his sister Mildred lived with Matt and Marion in this family home.[28] If it sounds crowded, it was the glue that held them together; Matt's siblings would remain loyal to each other throughout their lives.

The 1920s were the years of two rising stars in the Leach family. It was an exciting time for them, crowded as they were in their apartment. The young sons were being covered in the newspapers and making strides in civic duty as well as on the sports scene. Matt spent his spare time promoting the boxing career of Marshall, who was moving up from his matches at the local Y and into the Gary Golden Gloves. By 1919, Marshall played for the Gary High School Athletic Association against Ted Ross, a South Chicago middleweight.[29] "Marshall became a professional boxer," Jim Stack recalled. "He had 43 bouts, with a record of 28 wins, 10 losses and 5 draws."[30] Matt used his newly honed administrative skills to manage Marshall's boxing career. The boxer's press coverage sounded like it had been drafted by Matt, who was now developing his talent for generating publicity.

Marshall was a tough, no-nonsense man who later joined the Marines. Born in 1906, he was half a generation younger than Matt.

Having developed a passion for boxing, Matt's brother took to pugilism before the age of twenty. Starting as a featherweight at the Gary YMCA team, he put on weight, becoming a lightweight and later, a welter. Fighting in ten-round bouts, he faced George Nichols in Buffalo and held to draw. Marshall's banner year was 1929, when he engaged in 26 bouts. As a pro whom Matt had christened "the Steel City Middleweight," Marshall battled Italian Jack Herman of Cleveland in 1929.[31]

As Marshall's career hit its apex, Matt began issuing statements to the press. It amazed him to see his words in print. Just a few years earlier, he was little Matija, the alien they'd kept on Ellis Island, the kid who couldn't speak English. Now, his words were being read in the newspaper, and it was his brother they were reading about. This gave him his first real taste of the power of the press.

Things were happening to Marshall's career, however, that were not being reported. The dark side of boxing was the threat of mobsters, losses, and physical injury. Matt enjoyed the vicarious publicity but endured none of the pain of Marshall's career. Matt did not neglect his own job as he rose to the rank of sergeant. On June 1st, 1927, he was named acting lieutenant. Matt was now first assistant to Captain John R. Smith and had 75 men working under him—desk sergeants, drivers, motorcycle patrol and patrolmen.[32]

While living in the cramped quarters of an extended family, both Marshall and Matt publicly positioned themselves as men's men, untethered by domestic ties. In spite of their working-class apartments with the shared bathrooms and lack of privacy, each became locally famous in his way.

Even as he helped others, Matt was shrewd enough to know that he needed a power base from which to rise out of a city cop's lifestyle. He joined the American Legion. The veterans' organization had started in Paris in 1919 to provide fellowship to homebound men recovering from the Great War. Here Matt forged the connections necessary to rise in professional stature. He became an asset to Legion officials, one of whom would someday serve as governor of Indiana. With the Legion, Matt sailed to Paris in 1927 for a heralded convention called the American Legion Pilgrimage or Second American Expeditionary Force. During this memorable voyage, the legionnaires visited the battle sites and memorials of their war experience. For Matt, an immigrant, the voyage marked the first time he'd traveled internationally as a vacationer. The experience added to his knowledge of the world and lent to him a European air of sophistication.[33]

As Matt and Marshall grew and changed with the times, the Gary Police Force failed to make great strides toward progressive policing. It did, however, take on the new science of identification called fingerprinting to replace the old Bertillon system. The new miracle of modern policing made for good publicity for the department.

The reality was widespread gaming in the saloons and hotels on Washington Street. The syndicate-operated vice parlors catered to hundreds of customers, operating with open police and political support, which stretched all the way to the Lake County seat. Bookies and madams were familiar characters. Police corruption ran rampant.[34] The Torrio-Capone gang in Chicago brought gambling to Gary through Thomas Johnson. His supervision of gambling resulted in the epidemic of gambling and bootlegging in the town.[35] So pervasive was bootlegging that Matt, now a patrol lieutenant, was arrested in a crackdown. Along with patrolman Roy Keele, who would later figure in the Dillinger story as the ex-husband of Dillinger's girlfriend Polly Hamilton Keele, Matt was arrested in a bootlegging shakeup when he was accused of failing to deliver whiskey to a police warehouse.[36] On January 1st, 1930, Matt's career hit the tin ceiling. The promotions ended. He was fired.[37]

In a police department that thrived on mass firings and rehiring, it made sense that he would leave the way he'd entered back in 1922. The patronage system that brought him into the Gary Police Department ushered him out in the same inexplicable way.

CHAPTER 2

Statehouse Room 126

Words just fail to express my appreciation of all the things you have
done.—Paul V. McNutt, governor of Indiana 1933–1937, in a 1932
letter to Matt Leach

The Depression visited hard times on the Leach family. "They lived
a very poor life," said Jim Stack. "My mother had to wear the same dress
to school for a whole year."[1] With Matt fired, nothing felt secure.

Changes were also occurring in Marshall's fighting career. From
June of 1929 to February of 1931, he had straight wins. Marshall went on
to box until 1932, when he took a job with the Gary Police Department.[2]

As soon as Matt lost his rank as a Gary police lieutenant and was
fired, November arrived with an election and a new regime. The mass
firings once again upset the local economy. It was a tentative holiday
season for the many breadwinners losing their jobs. New Year's Day,
1930, signaled an end to the prosperous twenties.

The firing of Matt from his job, over a missing truckload of Cana-
dian ale, was a ploy. Gary was the outpost of the Chicago mob's bootlegging and gambling operations. The firing was an excuse for another
one of Mayor Johnson's safety board firings and rehirings.[3]

The casual manner in which the dismissals were conducted should
have been easy for Matt to handle. They were a part of Indiana's civil
service experience. Remembering that he was originally appointed to
the Gary force to replace a dismissed officer, Matt reasoned that the
same system that got him axed could push him ahead. But he knew he'd
have to do things right. For Matt, that meant the equivalent of modern
networking. He tracked down everyone with the power to help him. It
paid off when, two months after he was fired, he came back as an automobile license inspector in Indiana's northern counties. This appointment

lasted less than two months. When he lost that job, Matt scrambled to find another post in law enforcement. It seemed that Gary's new administration, under Superintendent Stanley Bucklind, had no place for him. Matt then went to a county sheriff named Joe Kyle, requesting a new assignment. On February 18th he was appointed deputy sheriff, a job-sharing position he held alongside a police officer named William Linn.[4]

In leaving the city limits of Gary's jurisdiction, Matt now had a chance to expand his visibility around Lake County. Using his new territory wisely, he began looking crosswise toward the Indiana State Legislature. Since the war, Matt had been active in the Gary American Legion post. Also a member of the Gary Elks, Matt was a fixture in the local fraternal organizations. It was through the American Legion that Matt clawed his way into the inner circle of Paul Vories McNutt. It was no easy task.

The future governor of Indiana was, in the years 1928 to 1929 when Matt befriended him, national commander of the American Legion and commander of the American Legion Department of Indiana.[5] In that era, a man of McNutt's socioeconomic level would pay little attention to a Serbian immigrant. But Matt, never daunted by a social inferiority complex, stood out. He knew that failure to make himself known to McNutt would force him back into the steel mills or worse—it could result in ruin now that the Depression had hit. He did not want to be stuck crouched at the bridge, stifled by the troll of unemployment. So Matt worked at getting noticed. Through his long-winded exchanges, he came to the attention of McNutt.

Like Matt, McNutt used the American Legion to build his professional power base. A distinguished man who had been an intellectually gifted child, Paul McNutt was always thought of as a winner. He was born into an affluent and cultured family. He was upheld by his teachers and respected by his fellow students. At Indiana University, McNutt participated in extracurricular activities, so many that he could have been called an overachiever. Upon graduation, he went to Harvard Law School. While a practicing lawyer and assistant law professor, he entered service in World War I through campus recruitment in 1917.

McNutt's direction was clear by 1925. He was acting in his appointment as dean of the Indiana University Law School. He had already drafted new corporation laws for Indiana and was founder of the *Indiana*

Law Journal. He showed expertise in the blending of politics and law that would later
mark his administration.[6]

More crucial was an ap-
pointment that started him on
his quest for political standing.
Many of the legionnaires joined
the McNutt for Governor clubs.
Matt joined McNutt's team and
actively campaigned for him.
His future gubernatorial aide,
Pleas Greenlee, an Elk who was
already in politics and clerked
in the Indiana House of Representatives in the 1931 session,
held the position of club secretary. During McNutt's candidacy in 1932, Matt positioned
himself with Greenlee as part of
a fraternal double team of Elks
and legionnaires.[7] Matt cam-

**Governor Paul V. McNutt, ca. 1930s (cour-
tesy Indiana State Library).**

paigned for McNutt in a riotous way. One time, Matt disrupted a meeting
held for Frank Mayr, Jr., the Democratic secretary of state. Matt was not
there as a booster for Mayr, who opposed the candidacy of McNutt. In a
move designed to draw attention away from Mayr and toward McNutt as
a candidate, Matt jumped out of his seat and shouted in favor of McNutt.[8]

These antics paid dividends. McNutt won the election and Matt
won McNutt's favor. Matt must have known he was in the inner circle
when he received a letter of gratitude from McNutt in 1932. The words
reflect a personal fondness for Matt:

> Dear Matt: I told you how I felt about the fine work you have done in my
> behalf and how much I appreciate it. This acknowledges your telegram
> which touches me very deeply. Words just fail to express my appreciation
> of all the things you have done—Paul.[9]

McNutt served as commander of the American Legion post in
Bloomington before being elected to the post of department commander

of the Indiana Department of the American Legion in 1927. While there, he increased the department's membership by one third. Matt was a help to McNutt in this project with his kinetic energy and willingness to make speeches. McNutt won the gubernatorial seat in the 1932 land-slide election. With Democrats filling state jobs and Republicans leaving in droves, McNutt appointed Matt to work as the principal doorkeeper of the Indiana House of Representatives. This use of political generosity generated a lot of anger within Lake County. In the Depression, jobs were in short supply. Some of the open positions were listed: stenogra-pher, page, assistant doorkeeper—they were honest jobs. Many officials around the area would hold a grudge and whisper that the governor was putting his own friends in jobs that lesser representatives had prom-ised to others.

Although Matt was the administration's choice, his placement pushed several candidates out. Outside of the fraternal organizations of the Elks and the American Legion, as well as the police department in Gary, nobody had heard of him.

Matt got his doorkeeper job thanks to an impending Indiana law that would be packaged into an executive order within the next two years. Called the Government Reorganization Act of 1933[10] and infor-mally based on a state-wide spoils system that had functioned in political backrooms for years, it would vest McNutt with the authority to hire and fire all state employees. Because the position of doorkeeper didn't come with an apt job description, and possibly to quell the noise sur-rounding Matt's appointment there, the Indiana House of Representa-tives wrote a decree and vested Matt with an award for his service. They weren't able to say it was a long and faithful career because Matt's service amounted to a matter of weeks. Simply put, they thanked him:

> WHEREAS: said Mat Leach [*sic*], of Gary, is a man of noble sentiment, silver tongue, compelling industry and unimpeachable honesty.
> …This humble servant of the most noble Indiana House of Representa-tives, has long and faithfully performed his many duties; guarded well the inner and outer doors of the temple; scrutinized all who wished to enter their sacred portals….[11]

The political naysayers now had to deal with a doorkeeper elevated to sainthood. Nobody knew how serious the appointment was. Five weeks later, the doorkeeper got his reward for the years of working for the local Democratic campaign. McNutt crowned Leach the head of the Indiana State Police. If grudges had been formed over the gatekeeper position, the appointment to head the ISP went over like a lead balloon. In the crucial year ahead, Matt would have little support and much opposition. While dogged by the whispers of favoritism, McNutt was bathing in a swirl of victory confetti. He appointed Matt Leach captain of the newly restructured Indiana State Police by February's end. Officially, Matt got the job on March 14th, 1933.[12]

In appointing Leach, McNutt was doing what came naturally to an Indiana politician, rubbing salt into the wounds of the factions that had opposed his candidacy. Grover C. Garrett, the outgoing captain of the ISP, was a bastion of the defeated administration along with Mayr. McNutt set about restructuring the twin agencies of corrections and law enforcement that had existed under Garrett. Needing to validate the reform rhetoric of his campaign, McNutt signed an executive order that placed the police and criminal bureaus and also the fire marshal department under the umbrella called the Division of Public Safety. He appointed Albert G. Feeney to head the new division.[13]

Feeney, who would later serve as the mayor of Indianapolis, was a Notre Dame all–American center who played on the Ramblers with Knute Rockne. He was appointed with the approval of Fredrick Van Nuys, a Democrat and winner of the 1932 election to the U.S. Senate. Superintendent Feeney would work in an embattled fashion until 1935 with Pleas E. Greenlee, who was known unofficially as McNutt's "patronage secretary."

Greenlee acted as a front man for McNutt's hiring decisions. He had risen in the new administration in the way that Matt had, through the ascending network of legionnaires who had served in World War I. He had commanded his local legion post twice as a district commander. After the war, he went into newspaper work blended with business when he bought the Michigan City *Dispatch*, a formidable news source. He came up against Al Feeney through differences of opinion that started almost immediately. Matt tried to stay neutral as the two men argued privately.

Feeney wanted mainly to establish the state police radio broadcasting system, and had a plan to obtain the money from the business community and banking organizations. From then on, the Indiana State

Police would always include the banner, "As Reorganized by Gov. Paul V. McNutt."[14]

Matt went into Room 126 of the Indiana Statehouse, which served as both the district and general headquarters. He received an annual salary of $3,000.[15] This was markedly higher than the compensation earned by new recruits, who had to go to school to learn the job while paying for their own guns and uniforms.

It was an exciting time for Matt as he and Marion moved out of the apartment in Gary. With Matt's sister Mildred working as a stenographer, Marion working as an enumerator for the federal census-taking bureau, and Marshall still earning money as a pugilist, the family was surviving.[16]

Matt and Marion moved into an apartment at 850 North Penn, Indianapolis, where they lived for a short time. It must have felt liberating for the couple to be able to live away from their extended family. As much as the Leach family was a loving and supportive clan, the couple was not used to having much privacy.[17]

With the transfer to Indianapolis, Matt took the opportunity afforded by his salary increase to outfit himself for press appearances and photographs. At 1933 prices, a

Leach's hallmark photograph, dated 1933, reproduced detective magazines of the 1930s (courtesy James Stack).

man could buy a suit for less than ten dollars. Matt purchased broadcloth shirts and striped ties, belts of leather with shiny buckles, and tidy Dobbs straw hats, which could be gotten for sixty-nine cents. His tall physique, with no extra fat around the middle, complemented his new clothing. In that era, socializing was a dress-up affair and nobody went without a shirt and tie.

The social circle of Mr. and Mrs. Matt Leach extended to the Serbian Americans around Indianapolis who formed the grapevine from Gary. In contrast, Governor McNutt's parties, diligently reported in the pages of the Indianapolis Sunday photo

Indiana Captain Matt Leach, neatly pressed and fastidious, ca. 1930s (courtesy James Stack).

inserts, never included the Leaches or, for that matter, Al Feeney, Pleas Greenlee or any other public safety appointee.

The couple could go to the movies and see a Laurel and Hardy film for the price of twenty-five cents. They could visit the Indianapolis Apollo Theater and see Irene Dunne or Janet Gaynor. There was nightlife and fun for the taking. Yet it seems that the career-obsessed Matt was not making recreation and leisure a priority. He was photographed playing golf, but with other officials. If he smoked a cigarette, it was while giving an interview.

Matt had to lower his social expectations from his legionnaire circle of elites and get to know his fellow officers, male and female. For the first time, he was working with a policewoman of rank. He met with Marie M. Grott, the chief clerk of the Indiana Crime Bureau. Grott would later distinguish herself as a fingerprint and identification expert, attaining the rank of Crime Bureau head. She would go on to travel with the Leach entourage to Tucson and serve as an escort to captured Dillinger gang member Mary Kinder from Tucson, Arizona, to Indianapolis. In spite of her bold accomplishments, the press focused mainly on her sex. At one point described as "comely," she was a woman before her time. On a personal note, Grott, like Leach, had left her mother in her hometown of Michigan City to live in Indianapolis.[18]

There were other seasoned officers to meet. Detective Harvey Hire would later be appointed by Feeney's successor, Donald F. Stiver, to head the detective force of twenty officers. There was a former sergeant turned detective, Arthur "Art" Keller. Lieutenant Chester L. Butler would be involved in the Dillinger hunt, with tragic consequences. There was the usual firing and rehiring. One officer was temporarily let go, and later rehired. He was Joseph E. Stack, future husband of Matt's sister, Mildred.[19]

In place, by 1933, was McNutt's executive order that grouped the State Fire Marshal, State Motor Police, Bureau of Criminal Identification and Investigation into the Division of Public Safety, with a reorganization of the Highway Commission going on at the same time. In the spirit of reorganization, Matt began his own reinvention of the Indiana State Police. Much of it started as a continuation of past political rhetoric. The true reforms, such as radio cars or new motorcycles, were not forthcoming.[20]

Then came the publicity. A storm of interest was fanned by the sterling new governor. He held press conferences twice a day during meetings of the General Assembly. Matt, who had enjoyed the glare of the spotlight back in the twenties as Marshall's boxing manager, was garrulous with the reporters. One correspondent, William "Tubby" Toms, an *Indianapolis News* reporter, quoted Matt extensively. As the years passed, their professional relationship would grow into a lifetime friendship. It all added up to good public relations for Matt and also for Toms, who often got the inside scoop on steamy crime stories.[21]

As possibly the first police officer to have human interest stories written about him, Matt Leach announced sanctimoniously that there would be no graft, no gossip, no smoking a cigar while in uniform, and no keeping company with persons of questionable character.[22] Because press reporting on the local level was rarely investigative, no one bothered to mention that the captain had been fired in Gary in a bootlegging sweep.

The fluff articles captured what those persons who were intimate to Matt knew in their hearts. Philip Hart, who interviewed Mildred Stack, Matt's sister, summed it up: "You can't understand Matt Leach's psyche unless you understand the people [of the Military Frontier]. That's the way they think. You don't bribe them. Leach set the policies. He was really clean. He was a tough law enforcement guy."[23]

The newly minted Captain Leach was being quoted every day in the papers, and reporters were lending to the straitlaced policeman a sense of humor. They called the ISP a "gallant force, not swashbuckling, but … like a picked troop."[24] This was an era when the average reader knew what the term "swashbuckling" meant; it was an allusion to the popular actor Errol Flynn in his movie roles as Robin Hood and Captain Blood. As such, this phrase was a compliment to a uniformed officer, suggestive of force and bravery.

The reporters were dazzled by Captain Leach, even writing antidotes depicting a human interest slant to the usual quotes and headlines. One story reported that the police chief had mistakenly locked himself in his office.[25] Between the lines the reader was expected to chuckle, as Matt Leach was hardly a bumbler.

The more tangible accomplishment of the reorganization was the implementation of the barracks system. Although it would later be criticized as wasteful, the system was, in its origins, an efficient use of manpower. A barracks was opened to patrol the Calumet region in Northern Indiana at Tremont. It was slated to house a radio station. What wasn't loudly broadcast was that there wasn't enough money being pumped into the new ISP. The Tremont Barracks was erected to save taxpayer money, situated as it was between Gary and Michigan City. At the time, there was still no radio system within the police cars.

"Albert Feeney … is working on … a police radio and hopes to have a radio sending and receiving, established at the barracks soon," Matt told newspapers hungry for quotes and material. "When this is accomplished the state police in this region will be linked with the Michigan state police and the Chicago police, both of whom operate their own radio stations. Plans are being worked out whereby the state troopers will be able to close all roads in this vicinity in case of a bank robbery and to stop every car on the highways."

Al Feeney's job would be to get the federal permission for a new radio transmitter to commence operation. He wanted eight police cars to be installed with receiving sets, ostensibly for use during heavy traffic during the 1933 and 1934 World's Fair, "A Century of Progress," in Chicago.[26] It seemed like a frivolous intention, considering that bank robberies were on the increase and that kidnapping had escalated in Kansas City and St. Paul under the criminal hands of the Barker-Karpis gang and the band of outlaws surrounding George "Machine Gun" Kelly.

Compared to this burgeoning crime wave, World's Fair traffic concerns were trivial. The subject matched the playful reputation that newspapers were laying on Matt Leach. Through all the foolish press he garnered in the spring of 1933, Matt did not forget his benefactor. His devotion to McNutt made him a loyal defender of the gubernatorial seat in the upcoming year. McNutt failed to deliver on the radios, which weren't installed in police cars in time to stop the crime wave heading their way.[27]

The months of January through May of 1933 were a honeymoon period for the new administration. These Depression-era politicians were still in a 1920s mindset where nothing had a consequence and everything could be changed. The mentality of mass firings culminated in the dismissal of numerous prison guards at the Indiana State Penitentiary at Michigan City and the hiring of new, inexperienced men. McNutt was especially criticized for firing Warden Walter H. Daly, who was considered a career expert in penology, and replacing him with Louis E. Kunkel, a criminal attorney and politician with no prison experience.

The ensuing backlash later resulted in a reversal of patronage appointments. Al Feeney, Governor McNutt and Matt Leach at one point joined hands and declared that the state, from now on, would be hiring only policemen and not politicians.[28] It was a case of too little, too late.

CHAPTER 3

Clemency

Mishandled Paroles—America's Shame!—*Look* magazine, Feb. 1, 1937

There was a smudge obscuring Indiana's new deal for law enforcement. The town of East Chicago was Gary's evil twin. It provided a second home to the local prostitution, bootlegging and gambling houses.

Wide open since Prohibition, the town was conveniently close to the actual city of Chicago. In its appearance East Chicago was suburban, a classic bedroom community. Depending on the political direction, vice establishments switched their locations between Gary and East Chicago. They set up shop where they could operate without too much police interference. The elements that made East Chicago an attractive spot for vice were a cut-'em-loose judicial bench, a corrupted police department and deep-pocketed politicians.

East Chicago was fraught with the political tension of wet versus dry factions. In 1922 its embattled mayor, Frank Callahan, ran on the dry ticket only to resign after one term because of the "local liquor problem." Callahan had been a double threat, bringing dry judges into power with him. Yet his efforts failed during his one term in office. He threw up his hands in a public declaration of surrender, blaming revolving door courtrooms with too many loopholes. In a statement he charged, "It is practically impossible under the present state law to obtain a fair share of convictions."

Callahan's biggest social impact occurred during 1922, his election year. His dry agenda pushed many of the vice operators out of East Chicago and over to Gary. This provided the factory town with an outlet for gambling and prostitution. A vice strip sprung up along the presidentially

49

named streets of Washington, Adams and Jefferson. It remained that way during the years that Leach served in the Gary Police Department.[1]

When lawlessness became too apparent, the federal government intervened. The 1921 case of bootlegging boss William "Big Bill" Subotich is an example. After he was arrested by the federal dry forces, the local bench suspended his jail sentence. It took a federal grand jury to enforce sentencing. Although he was initially sent to Crown Point County Jail and allowed to wear his silk shirts, a federal judge took offense at this slap on the wrist. Subotich was then mandated by the federal government to serve time in the Putnamville penal farm. The newspapers made a veiled reference to political misfeasance when it reported that Subotich had "missed all the fun of the East Chicago election" while serving his sentence.[2]

All of this was no surprise to Leach. As a police detective and lieutenant in Gary for eight years, the captain was aware of the vice operators on Subotich's payroll, including Anna Sage, aka Katie Brown, who would later make history as the noxious "Woman in Red."

Leach's press releases conveniently omitted mention of East Chicago. The town was under Lake County's jurisdiction. Robert Estill was the Lake County prosecutor who expressed strong opposition to Leach's appointment to the job of legislative gatekeeper. Estill would be condemned that year by the local press for speculative misconduct allegations. The *Gary Post Tribune* reported that Estill ran Chicago syndicate mobster Lawrence "Dago" Mangano out of Gary. The Chicago mobster had allegedly opened a gambling den in Sage's Kostur Hotel at 13th and Washington. The paper hinted Estill's backers were local syndicate members who viewed Dago Mangano as an interloper.[3] It is possible that Estill blamed Leach for leaking this fabricated story, which placed Estill among Gary's gambling factions. Estill vehemently opposed Leach's appointment and encouraged his minions to do the same. Estill's inner circle, from the higher echelon of the East Chicago Police Department to the hired hands at Crown Point, stuck with him and ostracized Leach.

Eight years on the Gary Police Department had taught Leach to play politics. This strategy included the old adage of keeping friends close but enemies closer. He declined to comment on East Chicago in his garrulous press conferences. While he knew all of Gary's vice operators in the 1920s, Leach was slow to grasp that a new crime wave was coming in the spring of 1933. When an escaped convict from Chicago named Jimmie Williams met bank robber Eddie Bentz in East Chicago, their meeting launched a series of events.

Jimmie Williams was an escaped convict who was later known as Baby Face Nelson. His given name of Lester Gillis had been left with his family on Chicago's west side, where they lived. He was desperate to put together a team for a robbery when he arrived in East Chicago. Once there he went to a shop that dealt in bank job accessories. Nelson had met Eddie Bentz through his own underworld contacts in Chicago that branched into the Capone and Touhy gangs. Through Bentz or perhaps through other confederates, Nelson met two recently paroled men from the Indiana prison system. They were John Herbert Dillinger and Homer Van Meter.[4]

In July of 1933, the month this meeting took place, Leach had no awareness of these Indiana ex-cons. Had he known of their intentions, he would have balked at the knowledge that they had met in East Chicago. Leach had no control over what happened there, and he knew it.

Not far from East Chicago sat the Indiana State Penitentiary. The state prison was the McNutt administration's next big reform. New guards would be installed to replace experienced officers. It was a decades-old system of job placement, and it caused no reaction when it was announced. Nothing was said of the residents of the prison, the inmates themselves. The population was an afterthought.

Known informally as Michigan City, the state prison was a cauldron of those enemies of society one would rather forget. In this world teenagers comingled with men who were wizened from the criminal life. The prison in its physical layout was unobtrusive. A passing bystander might not notice the sprawling complex of roads, low-lying brick edifices and steel tracks holding cargo bins, all of it existing in the shadow of the walls. The face of this complex was the administration building. This structure was the façade to the outlying community. The building housed the usual staff of nine-to-five office workers. It was the hub for the business machine operators, stenographers and typists that kept the prison running smoothly. The industries were situated behind the administration building. The administration building acted as a viaduct that connected to the prison through a series of doors. This construction leant access from the prison yards to the street.[5]

Working in the yards and shops were inmates fueled by hope of eventual parole. Perhaps they'd studied a law book or two, or had friends inside who could write appeals to the parole board. Then there were others, with dreams of brutal-force freedom. Their talk of insurgency mirrored the political changes taking place outside. As McNutt planned to replace sixty-nine guards with green recruits, an inmate clique formed a conspiracy.

As a demographic, this group was composed of men in their twenties, thirties and forties. At the core of the conspiracy sat the hardened ones, enthroned as imperial leaders. Convicted during the 1920s of bank robbery, auto banditry and first-degree murder, their terms averaged out to twenty-to-life.

Clamoring for inclusion in the escape was a lesser, auxiliary group. Its members had the same conviction and sentencing profiles, but lacked the alpha qualities of the leaders. The nascent escape plan was a duplex structure of planners and workers.

Far removed from these conspirators sat a governing body, wearing not prison khakis but fine woolen suits. Its board members embarked on the task of releasing the current staff of corrections officers, their jobs to be taken by friends of the new order. McNutt's secretary Pleas Greenlee was in charge of staffing. His only experience with Michigan City had been his stint as part owner of the Michigan City *Dispatch*. The ramifications of the prison personnel turnover went unnoticed. At the same time, a public clamor erupted over the firings of librarians at the Indiana State Library. Yet in the din, not one suggestion was heard that the hiring of green guards posed a security breach that could possibly result in a prison break.

The convicts planning their escape had a broad network. One liaison, Mary Kinder, was an Indianapolis woman whose brother was part of the lesser group of escapees. With an estranged husband, brother and brother-in-law in Michigan City, Mary knew the visitors' section well. Mary's connections stretched to Kokomo, Indiana. There, madam Pearl Elliott ran the Paramount Hotel, a Kokomo brothel, with help from Tillie Clevenger and Sylvia Clevenger Williams. Pearl, an old friend of escape conspirator Harry Pierpont, was prepared to launder money and rally for assistance.

Within this outreach circle sat a cache of parolees. They were on standby, ready to fund the escape with a spate of robberies. The buck would stop at the unshackled feet of an ex-inmate named John Herbert Dillinger. Facing release, he would launch a crime wave throughout three states in order to raise money. In the firm belief that his real friends remained behind the walls, he would be the glue connecting them to their network outside. His value system stayed in Michigan City, with all thought directed toward helping in the planned escape.

Dillinger never believed that his parole was a springboard to a respectable life. Once back in his community, he shunned the Mooresville, Indiana, neighbors of the hometown that had set the stage for the 1924 armed rob-

Pearl Elliott's brothel was a hangout and money-laundering location for Dillinger. Photograph ca. 1918 (Frankfurt Community Public Library).

bery resulting in his prison sentence. His sentencing nine years before was harsh and unfair by all standards. In 1933, the parole board became the recipient of letters from neighbors who took umbrage at his sentence, even while remembering little more than his hangdog expression.

In 1924 Dillinger had been involved in the holdup of Frank Morgan, a grocer in his neighborhood. While some accounts of the crime claim that Dillinger was drunk at the time of the crime, his intake card in Pendleton Reformatory listed his crime as "not attributed to the use of liquor." With his older accomplice, Dillinger struck Morgan in the head with a large bolt as the victim struggled. Dillinger was quickly caught. He appeared without counsel before Judge Joseph W. Williams, who sentenced the young man to concurrent sentences at Pendleton Reformatory of 10–20 and 2–14 years for assault and battery with intent to rob and conspiracy to commit a felony.[6] His accomplice, Edgar Singleton, received a lenient sentence and walked out of prison two years later.

Dillinger's family home in Mooresville, Indiana. As a youth, Dillinger preferred the fast lane. Photograph taken in 1989.

Dillinger's experience with the criminal justice system was a catastrophe that over time destroyed his personality. He entered prison in a state of denial and promised to escape. The threat never materialized.

He entered Pendleton Reformatory on September 16th, 1924. There he suffered the degraded situation of a convict. Yet he had a loving family, whose members visited him constantly during the first few years. That family included his wife, Beryl Hovius. Her visits ultimately ended with the service of a divorce summons. Five years into his stretch, Dillinger received a transfer to the state penitentiary at Michigan City.

The effort put in by his family went beyond what was expected of its members. Visits occurred regularly, as did letters.[7] Yet Dillinger withdrew further and further into the prison brotherhood. His life changed its direction during this period of transference. The one grip he maintained on the outside world was his obsessive letter writing. Dillinger always expressed his depressive personality through letters. Much later, he would show his creative writing flair on postcards addressed to Matt Leach.

Dillinger entered Michigan City and became removed from the outside world. One of his friends was Pendleton inmate Homer Van Meter. The two young men were individually transferred to Michigan City and later were paroled within a month of each other.[8]

By 1933, this prison bonding had a disastrous effect. Dillinger began to live on two levels simultaneously. By day he networked with the prison to get addresses of prospective jugs—banks and stores to rob—in the event of a parole. At the same time, he knew his family members were getting him out. Dillinger had years of parole strategy locked in his head, no doubt garnered through the prison bar review, that tutelage of jailhouse lawyers. Through desperate and lengthy letters, Dillinger listed the names of the Mooresville officials who were in the best position to sign his long-awaited petition.

When McNutt's new parole board opened Dillinger's case file, its members observed a wealth of signatories. There were the prestigious names, among them Judge Joseph Williams, who had put Dillinger away all those years ago. The surprise was the name of Frank Morgan, the poor old grocer and crime victim. Sheriffs, attorneys, clergy—they unanimously declared that John Dillinger was deserving of mercy. As such, the petition went before the board. The governor simply presided over the paperwork in his official capacity. He granted the release order on May 10th, 1933.

McNutt signed off on this prisoner with the speed and agility of a bureaucrat. Had he been able to predict the future, he would have stuffed the petition into the wastebasket with a lit match.

Then the system delayed Dillinger's release for no good reason, even though it was clear that Dillinger's stepmother was dying. A prisoner was a number consigned to a worksheet, no matter who signed his parole petition. Dillinger's life behind bars was extended for a few more days. It seemed as though he was completing time in Purgatory. With the timing of Greek tragedy, Dillinger arrived back at the farmhouse in Mooresville hours after his stepmother's death. Lizzie Fields Dillinger had married John's father after the death of John's mother, Mollie, when John was three years old. It was a close family, blessed with children from both Mollie and Lizzie.

The house, with its tidy upstairs bedrooms and cozy kitchen, was an inferno of grief when Dillinger arrived. He faced his father's grief,

John Dillinger's parole and release took place on the day his stepmother died.

as the tears of his young half-sisters joined with the stoic sadness of Audrey "Sis" Hancock and his half-brother, Hubert. Dillinger knew then that he was a doomed man, a condemned man, a remnant beyond repair.[9]

The horror of the funeral passed and Dillinger went straight to the underworld. It was the path he'd chosen before he'd crossed the River Styx out of Michigan City. With nothing on his mind except the friends he'd left back in prison, he joined a gang of lowlife thieves outside of Indianapolis. Introductions were made through Noble Claycombe, also on parole. William Shaw and Paul "Lefty" Parker were not anxious to take on the new guy who called himself Dan. Reluctantly, they brought him on. These talent scouts became known as the White Cap Gang. The source of this strange name is a mystery.

Stragglers out for petty cash, they ushered Dillinger into the world of stickups. Using a firearm was a new experience for the ex-con. With this rowdy bunch he developed his heart—or courage—through supermarket, luncheonette and drugstore robberies.[10]

Dillinger was fueled with the ambition to stockpile as much cash as he could. With his kinetic energy, the activities of the White Cappers escalated. Dillinger as "Dan" and Claycombe as "Sam" took their crime spree in different directions. On June 4th, in a stolen DeSoto, Shaw and Claycombe robbed a City Foods, Inc., market at 4609 E. 10th Street. Dillinger had a 32-20 revolver. With his weapon, he held up store manager Walter J. Reeves. Reeves didn't seem to be cooperating. Perhaps he was too frightened to follow orders. Dillinger became frustrated and hit him in the mouth with the gun. This was his first physical attack of a crime victim since he'd bludgeoned Frank Morgan. It was also a sample of more violence to follow. From here it was a string of robberies of sandwich shops and markets. On one of these jobs, Dillinger fired his gun wildly after someone threw a bottle at him.

The intensity of the robberies increased with the arrival of Homer Van Meter. He joined Dillinger in East Chicago in June, one month after both were paroled. One can only imagine the emotional reunion of the two ex-cons, on the outside together for the first time since Van Meter's sentencing on March 15th, 1925, to 10–21 years for robbery. Van Meter's arrival turned Dillinger from stickups to bank robbery.[11]

The summer was hot and the land was flat. East Chicago was dull, a bedroom community with a bland local strip. They were thugs, bored and looking for the next big score. After Dillinger embraced his dear friend "Van," they joined with Shaw and two more parolees, Harry Copeland and Sam Goldstine. As these were experienced men, being seasoned robbers and Michigan City ex-cons, the visibility of the gang was growing to dangerous levels. The stakes were raised, with bad consequences. In an attempted robbery of the Marshall Field's Thread Mill in Monticello, Indiana, Dillinger shot manager Fred Fisher. This marked Dillinger's first shooting and made his transition from bludgeoner to gunman. It also demonstrated how cool he was with the prospect of shooting anyone who stood in his way.

Among the nameless pit stops that the White Cappers targeted, some stand out. One of note was a roadhouse called the Bide-A-Wee Inn, located in Muncie. This Indiana town set the stage for the arrests of Shaw and Parker. While here, they were picked up by a team of Muncie police officers. In that kinetic summer, Shaw and Lefty Parker wouldn't see any more action. Muncie officers, led by Sheriff Puckett, arrested Parker and Shaw on July 15th. This police action took place two days before Dillinger's big score, the Commercial Bank of Daleville.[12] Copeland and Dillinger were within blocks of Shaw's hideout when the last members of the small-time White Cap Gang were apprehended. Upon seeing the police activity, Dillinger gunned the car and drove backwards to escape notice of the police.

Shaw later told a different tale when he accused Copeland of cowardice. Shaw believed that Copeland had turned and run away from him on the day he was arrested.[13]

The short-lived era of the White Cap Gang was coming to an end. The arresting officer, Sheriff Pucket, helped to elicit Shaw's clues as to the possible identity of his flamboyant partner in crime. Shaw proved to be a rapper, or one who would give information. He implicated Dillinger and Copeland, naming Dillinger as having shot and wounded Fred Fischer, the manager of the Monticello Thread Mill.

Shaw would live to regret he'd ever known Dillinger. Shaw had only called him Dan and occasionally, John Donovan. Shaw's liaison with the mysterious Dan resulted in a ten-year prison term for the nineteen-year-old stickup guy. Shaw admitted to the Bide-A-Wee job as well as twenty other holdups in Indianapolis.

With Noble Claycombe arrested, Dillinger worked more with Copeland. Shaw may have been correct when he called him yellow in the face of bank robbery. Copeland had been sentenced back in 1926 to 2–14 years for a grocery burglary. With that small-time background, he went back to the streets unprepared for Dillinger's ambitions.[14]

Unknown to Dillinger, Shaw had named him to the cops after being told he was being charged with twenty-one robberies in Indianapolis. Because he didn't have his friend's name right, he called him by the name of Dellinger—with an e—or Donovan. Had Dillinger known that his friend was talking to police, he might have kept a lower profile. But he couldn't avoid showing off. He had started jumping over bank railings like the movie actor of the day, Errol Flynn, as the legendary Captain Blood. In his misguided show of bravado, Dillinger distinguished himself to the police.

Shaw, meanwhile, was linked to the botched Monticello thread factory stickup. The young man, who had lost his wife along with his freedom, was in despair. His black mood deepened upon realizing that

Dillinger still enjoyed the thrill of a summer night. It was a moment experienced by Dillinger himself nine years before, when he was committed to Pendleton Reformatory while his partner, Ed Singleton, got off with two years.

After Shaw's arrest, Dillinger started doing jobs with Sam Goldstine. The career criminal was another in Dillinger's clique of springtime parolees, having been hatched from Michigan City on May 25th after serving 2–14 for assault and battery with intent to commit a felony.[15] At forty-one, Goldstine had spent most of his adult life behind bars. He was that type of criminal who never got far from the prison gates. His lifelong pattern was to get arrested, go to court, then to jail.

Dillinger was joining the get-out-of-jail club with gusto. He again jumped the guardrail of a national bank. On August 4th, Dillinger, Copeland and Goldstine robbed the National Bank of Montpelier. Dillinger's gymnastics were startling. His landing was precarious in more ways than one.

After Montpelier, the bank's carrier, the American Surety Company, began a probe into the robbery. They hired former Pinkerton detective Forrest Huntington. He was the right man for the job, having been one of the original members of the Indiana Crime Bureau, forerunner of the detective division of the Indiana State Police.

An old school cop, Huntington held the largest list of criminals available at the time. He was about to add a few more to his files. He entered the walls of Pendleton Reformatory and visited with Shaw. The young man told Huntington about his robberies, which numbered around fourteen. Huntington wanted to know about the accomplice, the one named Dan. Referring to Dillinger as "J. H. Donovan," Shaw implicated him in the New Carlisle bank job of June 21st without knowing for sure if he was there. Shaw also named Dillinger in the Daleville bank robbery, which had been in the planning stage on the day Shaw was arrested.

Then Leach arrived unannounced. That aggravated Huntington. Leach wedged himself into the interrogation without Huntington's okay, while Shaw did the talking. He expanded the gang's turf by exposing their activities in Lebanon, Kentucky. For Leach, who had not yet stepped outside the boundaries of Indiana, this seemed out of reach.

If the outskirts of Indianapolis had provided the topography for

Dillinger and the defunct White Cap Gang, then Kentucky was a satellite. Dillinger, with lookups Frank and George Whitehouse, robbed the People's Bank of Gravel Switch in Lebanon, Kentucky. Here was a new spinoff, the next generation after the White Cap Gang went under. Van Meter, Kentucky-based James Kirkland, and a new associate named Clifford "Whitey" Mohler robed the Lebanon bank using Dillinger's stolen DeSoto sedan. Dillinger made use of this vehicle in pleasure trips to the Chicago 1933 Century of Progress in the company of the Whitehouse brothers.[16] It was an offbeat take on Matt Leach's declaration that World's Fair traffic would present challenges to the police.

Called "A Century of Progress," the Chicago World's Fair opened its gates in the area that now houses Soldier Field on May 27th. Dillinger went wild with delight and went several times. He'd lived in a cage yet now had the world around him. There was the Chinese temple, Streets of Paris, Belgian and Oriental villages, as well as the South Pole shop.

He saw the Italian, Czechoslovakian, Polish and Egyptian pavilions, the Moroccan village and Maya temple. He brought his friends. In addition to the Whitehouse brothers, he hosted his new girlfriend Mary Longnaker and her friend Mary Ann Bucholz. He could afford it, at one dollar per person for admission.[17]

Dillinger wanted to live well, and he became more particular about his companions. The latest import, Clifford Mohler, came with a strange pedigree. Dillinger liked him because he was a sharp character with a new angle.

Dillinger was arrested in Dayton, Ohio, through police surveillance on Mary Longnaker. The two are shown here in 1933.

Mohler had been released from Michigan City in 1933 after he drank shellac to bring on tubercular symptoms that would land him in a sanatorium. It was an era when self-mutilation and the consequences were better than prison. Upon reviewing Mohler's symptoms, prison doctors recommended a sixty-day parole on June 20th, 1933. The state parole board granted him a two-month furlough from prison to regain his health. In a sanatorium in Illinois, he gained back the weight he'd lost during his feigned tuberculosis. Shortly thereafter, he was released on temporary parole.

Mohler was handsome, with all-American looks that could have aided him had his life gone a different way. A native of Fort Wayne, Mohler had been convicted and sentenced in 1926 to life imprisonment for the murder of a Fort Wayne policeman that occurred on the night of a robbery.

On March 10th, 1926, Clifford and his brother Bert had gone out drinking. Patrolman Matthew Gebhardt attempted to arrest them for disorderly conduct at the intersection of Wallace and Barr in Fort Wayne. A fight followed, with shots fired. Officer Gebhardt and Bert Mohler were shot. After Gebhardt fell, mortally wounded, either Clifford, his brother, or both kicked and beat the fallen officer. Then Clifford fled the area. In the altercation, Gebhardt was beaten and shot three times. A thirty-six-year-old veteran of the force since 1924, he died soon after his arrival at the Methodist Hospital. Bert Mohler, forty-two years old, died from one gunshot wound. For his night of serious drinking, Clifford was later arrested. While evidence indicated that Bert had died by Clifford's gun, Clifford denied having shot his brother. From that point on, he had a heavy burden to carry.

Seven years later, Mohler wasted no time with his medically induced walking papers in hand. He robbed the People's Bank of Gravel Switch, Kentucky, for $1,380, along with accomplices James Kirkland, Homer Van Meter, and others later identified by Shaw.[18] These included Maurice Lanhan, who was arrested for this job although he did not participate.[19]

In the company of his accomplice James Kirkland, Mohler moved into East Chicago. During the month of June, Dillinger and his gang hung out along the street in front of Art's Army Store near the Inland Hotel, both located in the Indiana Harbor section. At this point, Dillinger was surrounded by a sizable gang of ex-cons, all with bank robbing experience. In a short time, he had moved up in skill and association to a level where he could make money.

Back in the 1920s, the town's worst element hung out in Indiana Harbor. It was the underworld's prime location due to its close proximity to Long Beach, Indiana. This beach town on the shores of Lake Michigan could properly be called the gangster belt. Underworld members met in Indiana Harbor before driving up to Long Beach to vacation. The Harbor boasted a flea market of services from shops selling backroom items to landlords who harbored tenants wanted by the police.

Dillinger, Copeland, Van Meter and Mohler met Baby Face Nelson in July, during a timeframe that corresponded with Copeland's parole that same month. To Nelson's underworld connections—and he had no other ties save his wife, children and immediate family members—Nelson called himself "Jimmie." Meeting Dillinger's gang for the first time, Nelson found the group to be a bunch of rubes compared with the class of criminal he usually worked with. He was accompanied by munitions and bank robbery accessory dealer Art Stoss, along with a fence named Fred Berman aka Breman, and his brother. To Nelson, a Near West Chicago native who knew West Side organized crime figures, Dillinger's boys were typical Michigan City ex-cons, nothing more or less than that. Nelson was looking for people to go in on the planned robbery of the People's Savings Bank in Grand Haven, Michigan. Nelson shrewdly assessed this crowd and decided he couldn't bring any of them along on the planned job.[20]

Clifford Mohler and his associate James Kirkland had more moxie than Nelson gave them credit for. The job at Gravel Switch, Kentucky, had garnered some headlines. Before the end of that wild summer, on August 24th, Maurice Lanham as well as Mohler and Kirkland were picked up by police. Yet for a short time it seemed as though they had gotten away with it. Maurice Lanham, actually innocent of the Gravel Switch robbery, was arrested around August 16th when eyewitnesses picked his photo out from available mug shots. He was held in Kentucky, where he talked to police and named some names. Oblivious to all of this, Mohler remained in East Chicago.

At headquarters in the Indiana Statehouse, Leach struggled to stay involved in the investigation. Like all police campaigns of the era, it was managed by detectives and private investigators such as Forrest

Huntington. They kept things out of reach. In Leach's ascension, he was more of a figurehead than a detective. In all fairness to the ISP captain, his appointment required him to act in the public capacity of today's big-city police commissioners—yet he was still expected to chase down tips and lead raids and ambushes. It was pressure he'd put upon himself by endlessly accounting to the press. It didn't help that the McNutt administration issued constant press releases and made daily calls for action.

Making the situation worse was the built-in jealousy and lack of cooperation that the era's policemen exhibited towards each other. Often their paperwork reflected a minimal effort to share their leads. Sergeants, lieutenants and detectives showed little regard for those outside their own county lines. Fueled by Huntington, word got around that Matt Leach went to the press. This was rat poison for Leach's reputation among his fellow officers.

Then Huntington cracked the golden egg. Maurice Lanham, one of the Lebanon, Kentucky, associates, gave him Clifford Mohler's address on Guthrie Street in East Chicago. Huntington passed the address to the East Chicago police, who arrested both Mohler and Kirkland at the Traveler's Inn on August 17th. Of the East Chicago arresting officers, at least four later attended the fatal Dillinger ambush at the Biograph Theater. They were Chief Nicholas Makar, Sergeant Martin Zarkovich, Officer Peter Sopsic and Captain Timothy O'Neill.[21]

When Mohler was arrested, he gave his name as Clifford Martin or Joseph Martin, depending on whose questions he answered. Detective Huntington identified Mohler through a tattoo, his appearance, and fingerprints on file in Washington. The Washington connection, the involvement of a D.C. law enforcement bureau in the identification of two-bit cop-killer Mohler, was surprising for the place and time. Yet Huntington's vast network stretched as far as the Justice Department. This was a testament to the investigator's skill, amazing in light of the fact that before 1934, bank robbery was not considered the purview of the Justice Department's Division of Investigation.

Mohler confessed that he was "one of three" bandits who held up and robbed the Gravel Switch bank on August 8th. He linked the Dillinger/Donovan Indiana robberies with the Gravel Switch job in Lebanon. Mohler gave Huntington enough to connect the elusive

East Chicago, Indiana, police officers, 1934. *Left to right*: **Capt. Timothy O'Neill, Peter Sopsic, E. J. Conroy, and Glen Stretch.**

Donovan to one John Dillinger, through the transfer of the stolen, repainted DeSoto sedan to Frank and George Whitehouse in Lebanon. Huntington then named Dillinger, Copeland, Goldstine and Van Meter in the unsolved August 14th robbery of the Citizens National Bank of Bluffton, Ohio.[22]

Huntington then profiled Dillinger:

> [Dillinger] has stated he will never be taken alive.... Dillinger lived at the home of his father, Mooresville, Ind., most of the time but occasionally had a room somewhere north, usually around 1200 North in Indianapolis, and he was a hard man to keep a line on, as he had friends at Lebanon, Ky., named Whitehouse, and often visited them and some friends in Louisville, Ky.
>
> Dillinger does not fool around with any women—while Shaw was with him—and used to "lash" him for playing around with so many women. Dillinger, however, spends his funds fast for foolishness and as soon as his funds are low, he will start out again on other holdups. [In the Massachusetts

Avenue bank holdup] Dillinger is the one who jumps over the cage and is very mild mannered, and [Hilton] Crouch is very nervous.[23]

This mild-mannered outlaw had been living with Van Meter in an East Chicago apartment building at the corner of West 144th and Baring Avenue. Low-lying and unobtrusive, nestled on a quiet street, the building provided a perfect cover for them.

The steamy afternoon of August 14th was also the date of the Bluffton job. Captain Leach and a raiding party of his men broke down the door. They caused a noisy disruption over the sprawling apartment house on the tree-lined grid. When they arrived, the apartment was empty.[24]

Now Leach had two marks against him. East Chicago police had left him in the dark with the Mohler arrest. Then, there was this latest, frustrating Baring Street raid. The glory days of his first months in office had ended.

The department had one armored car. Its patrolmen were furnished with a gun and a badge. The manpower had to cover seven counties. While some Midwestern cities had radio cars, most notably Detroit, Feeney's radios were a fable, an election promise. Leach was stuck with pie on his face as he absorbed the blame for the no-show radios.[25]

Leach had conducted his dead-end raid just three days prior to Mohler's arrest. All his information thus far had been because the young men from Kentucky were willing to talk. Fortunately for Leach, these young men did not possess the steel-bar resolve of Sam Goldstine. The next suspect was James Kirkland. Before his arrest, he had gone broke and through his brother, Charles, tried to contact Dillinger for help. Charles Kirkland, for reasons that are not clear, did not contact Dillinger but went the other way. He gave two letters to Sheriff Spauding in Kentucky, who passed the information on August 14th to Leach and Huntington. Leach, conceding that the venue was again the "Region," a police nickname for East Chicago, sent one of his men there. Detective Gene Ryan arrived to join forces with captains Edward Knight and Timothy O'Neill.

Huntington now revealed that, between August 23rd and August 25th, he had learned of the "woman John Dillinger is hanging around with" from Fred Breman[26]:

> Dillinger has a female friend at Dayton, Ohio, whose given name is unknown, but her maiden name is Jenkins. She has a brother, James Jenkins, serving a life sentence at Michigan City, Ind. State Prison for murder....

[Dillinger] is driving a new Essex Terraplane 8 Sedan, black color, and probably is using Ind. License 418–673...

All guns were rented from "Shorty" George, a negro [*sic*] dope and whiskey peddler, who lives on Muskegon St. between Capitol Ave. and Illinois Street. Noble Claycombe introduced him to this negro and after holdups had been completed, they would give this negro a "saw-buck" ($5) or sometimes less, depending on what they got out of the holdup for the use of the guns. This negro had a good arsenal, which included revolvers, sawed off shotguns and two submachine guns which he would rent to anyone that was O.K.[27]

At this point, Matt Leach still benefited from department courtesy and a cordial relationship with both Huntington and the East Chicago police. Indeed, Mohler's arresting officers turned Mohler over to Leach on August 23rd. Mohler admitted to the one job at Gravel Switch. East Chicago captain Edward Knight said that Mohler was the most stubborn prisoner he had ever questioned.

There was a jurisdictional issue of whether Mohler would go to Kentucky to face charges in the bank robbery or be returned to Michigan City as a parole violator. For a time Mohler was kept in Indiana under the custody of Matt Leach. Without proper authorization, Leach glibly offered Mohler a deal for information. He then shot off a letter to Mohler's mother, Della, in Fort Wayne. The offer was to send Mohler to Kentucky to answer for the Gravel Switch robbery rather than returning him to Indiana to serve out his life sentence for the 1926 cop killing.

During the interrogations Mohler revealed a name that didn't resonate with the Hoosier simplicity of a "Parker" or "Shaw." The name was "Homer Van Meter." Shaw had denied knowing Van Meter. Mohler was helping to piece together the puzzle that included Van Meter, Dillinger, Copeland and Goldstine.

Once Leach received Indiana jurisdiction over Mohler on or about August 22nd, he got the young man to admit to several more bank robberies. If one is to believe a newspaper article that appeared shortly after Leach began his interrogation, Mohler participated in five bank jobs, including Bluffton and New Carlisle. In spite of the cooperation he gave to the law, Mohler's deal didn't materialize quite as promised. He went into Michigan City that September and spent the next nine years in prison. That didn't stop his mother from trying to get a deal. Communication continued for two years between Leach and Della, who met in his office as late as 1935. In one letter, Della Mohlar wrote,

Dear Sir, I am writing you a letter concerning my son, Clifford Mohler.

He wants me to come and see you and I thought it best to write and make an appointment with you. He said it would be best for me ... or you would be gone away and I would not get to see you.

I hope you will ans. [sic] my letter and let me know when it will be convenient to see you. I can come any time if you will be in your office.

Please let me know when I can see you. I was thinking some about coming Saturday the 29 if I can see you that day. Please write me as soon as you get this letter.

My address.... Mrs. Della Mohler, Clifford Mother.

Captain Leach was curt in his reply:

Mrs. Della Mohler, 723 Locust Street, Fort Wayne.

It will be convenient for me to see you on the morning of Saturday, June 29th, in my office at the State House. The room number is 126. See you at that time.[28]

It seems as though Mohler and his mother continued to believe that Leach held some power of clemency. In desperation, Mohler gave Leach information that should have turned the Dillinger case around. He revealed that Donovan was living with Sam Goldstine in Gary. Elated, Leach pulled together a team from state police and some Gary detectives. With such short notice, there was no time to cordon off a wide area. He had no men to watch the adjacent garage. Leach yelled at a garage employee, "Call the police if someone appears." Then Leach drove the eighteen miles to a nearby state police barracks, going at the highest speed, sixty miles per hour. After picking up a few more officers, he drove back to Gary. There they learned that the Gary police had arrested Goldstine.

The garage employee claimed he phoned the Gary police, that men had come to the garage, but nobody on the line listened to him. According to the garage man, the three men had left word for Goldstine to meet them at a roadhouse located nine miles out of town. Leach and his state police team went to this roadhouse but came up empty.[29]

Under interrogation, Goldstine did not crack like the young men who were implicated in the Gravel Switch job. His history dated back to 1919 when he'd escaped from jail, been recaptured and then went on to serve twenty years. He was old for this type of life and wasn't about to help Matt Leach. A standup guy while in the Dillinger gang, he provided no information once he was in custody.

The Indiana State Police cars of the early 1930s lacked a two-way radio system. It was a failed campaign promise (courtesy Sandy Jones).

After Goldstine's apprehension at the Beverly Apartment Hotel at 8th and Madison in Gary, Leach never again shared department courtesy with Huntington. Yet the Gary raid, even without Dillinger in custody, restored Leach's good reputation with the press. He'd known the benefit of publicity since the days of managing his brother's boxing career. With the Goldstine arrest, Leach's name was now everywhere. He became the new spokesman for all arrests relating to this incorporated gang of bank robbers. They were "a desperate gang believed responsible for twenty-three bank robberies in Indiana, Illinois, Ohio and Michigan," according to one newspaper which no doubt got its information from Leach. In the collective articles that appeared in the Gary vicinity after the arrest, all relied on him as the sole source of information.

Within weeks, Dillinger read the newspapers and found himself mentioned by Leach. The robber developed a grudge against the captain, whom he blamed for keeping his name in the papers.[30]

For different reasons than those pronounced by Dillinger, fellow police officers were also starting to dislike Matt Leach. Sometime after handing Mohler over to Leach, Huntington closed the iron door and refused to work with him again. It was a sentiment he gladly articulated through letters to other police agencies. It was not simple lack of department courtesy. Huntington had a right to feel mistrust and resentment. After all, he was the first lawman to identify Dillinger after questioning Shaw.

Huntington had been the officer who first entered Pendleton Reformatory while Shaw was in custody. Shaw, fresh from the streets and hoping to make a deal, had revealed to Huntington the facts regarding both Harry Copeland and John Donovan/Dillinger. It was Huntington who connected the name "Dillinger" to the bank-jumping antics, Huntington who first brought the names "Donovan" and "Dillinger" together. Huntington also provided Matt Leach with the lead that resulted in the Gary raid and the arrest of Sam Goldstine. The private investigator was just doing his job. In the course of these arrests, however, Huntington noticed a disturbing pattern.

Rather than defer to the fellow officers who had assisted him, Leach trumped both Huntington and the Gary police to become the lawman most identified with Indiana's developing crime wave. It is easy to understand that there would be anger, even by a lawman as reticent as Huntington. He wrote,

> I would like to explain that I have tried to work with Captain Leach and confided information to him two months ago that, had it been handled properly, would have resulted in the arrest of John Dillinger, Harry Copeland, Homer Van Meter and Sam Goldstine [sic], in Gary, Indiana and in East Chicago.... Leach, by his indiscreet methods of sensationalizing criminal information to the press, by his domineering attitude toward city and county officers and by other irrational and erratic acts, has antagonized the majority of police officials of the state and they will not cooperate with him. To disclose confidential information to him is to jeopardize the success of any important investigation. This condition has reached a state where I feel that it is dangerous to my client's interests and the public welfare to confide confidential criminal information to Leach or officers subject to his orders.[31]

On the surface it appeared that Leach was cooperating with other police departments. Two days after the August 22nd arrest of Sam Goldstine, in response to a request from the Toledo police department, Matt Leach wrote to Toledo police chief Daniel T. Wolfe:

I have asked the Bureau of Criminal Identification to forward to you at their earliest convenience, the photographs, fingerprints and description of Clifford Mohler, Fred Berman, Sam Goldstine, Homer Van Meter, John Dillinger and Harry Copeland.

We are not sure as to the number and exactly who participated in the bank stickup at Elida or Bluffton, Ohio.

However, we do know that it was this gang that were the perpetrators of the job.

Two weeks later Leach wrote to the chief of detectives at Terre Haute, Sam Burk. By now, several of the bandits were in custody. In addition to Mohler and Goldstine, Fred Berman, a peripheral member who had attended the Indiana Harbor meeting with Baby Face Nelson, had been caught. Leach wrote,

Please find enclosed the photographs of John Dillinger, Harry Copeland and Homer Van Meter. These men are wanted for bank banditry in this state and several holdups. If, by any chance, they are identified on any jobs in your locality, we will be glad to have you notify this department.[32]

The number of arrested bandits as summer ended was growing. Dillinger, who over his career regrouped constantly, joined up with two more parolees, Hilton "Tillie" Crouch and his brother-in-law, John Vinson. Dillinger's companions were, as usual, like-minded. Vinson had been an eighteen-year-old thug on June 20th, 1923, when he was arrested for the holdup of the Mohawk State Bank at Mohawk, Indiana, just outside of Indianapolis. Released from the state prison in April of 1930, Vinson ran to Haines City, Florida, while he was wanted for an Indianapolis robbery. He was arrested in Florida but released after Indiana declined to extradite him for trial.

Hilton Crouch was a dirt racecar driver. It was a job description that made him desirable on bank robberies. On September 6th, with Dillinger and Copeland, Crouch robbed the Massachusetts Avenue State Bank in Indianapolis. Dillinger's dream of helping his friends escape was getting closer to realization. After the Massachusetts Avenue bank job, Dillinger delivered $24,900 to Kokomo madam Pearl Elliott. They left their weapons for safekeeping with the trusted madam, who gleefully showed her stable of girls the money less $400, her share in silver half-dollars. Pearl then equipped a hideout in Terre Haute. Its future occupants were still imprisoned, but that was about to change.

As summer became September, there were men at Michigan City

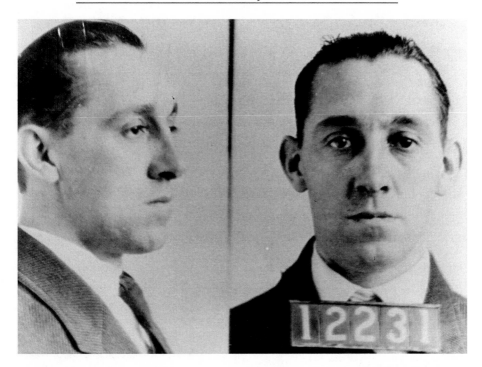

Harry Copeland, shown here in 1925, was a race driver, ex-con and early Dillinger associate.

for whom seasons had come to mean nothing. This was a heightened time, the advent of the planned escape. For the convicts behind the walls it was a period fraught with controlled hysteria while Dillinger continued on his methodical plan for his friends' escape.

The leader of the alpha group was Harry "Pete" Pierpont, sentenced in 1925 to 10–21 years for bank robbery. In the weeks before the planned escape, Pierpont asked his mother, Lena Pierpont, to pay a visit to Captain Leach at the Indiana Statehouse. It seems likely that Pierpont got word that Mohler's mother had also visited headquarters.

Mothers were considered vital to a wayward son's reformation in that era, a belief that Lena Pierpont tried to work. Although she didn't get past the receptionist, Lena delivered a letter that was eventually given to the captain.

The first time that Captain Leach heard of Harry Pierpont was through the convict's mother. If the adage can be applied, Leach did not kill the messenger as she delivered a letter to the Statehouse. Leach did decide to keep the woman in his radar as he read the missive. Her son, Harry, made an offer to turn in some companions who were plotting to deliver him from prison. Pierpont wanted one guard to take him out of the prison to meet the plotters. Leach declined the offer on the grounds that it seemed too much like a lone-wolf escape plan. The fact that Leach ignored Pierpont's letter was the first bit of official bungling in the mess that came to be known as the Michigan City escape. In the aftermath, Leach's role in ignoring the letter escaped scrutiny.[33]

Harry Pierpont was dubbed the "Trigger Man" and leader of Dillinger's gang. Photograph dated 1934.

Lena's trip to the Statehouse coincided with final arrangements for the escape. Dillinger had been hiding out in Pearl Elliott's Kokomo hideout with Harry Copeland while making deposits with Elliott's associate, a businessman named Omar Brown. Brown was arranging the delivery of guns to be targeted to the escape conspirators working in the prison shirt factory.[34]

No doubt Mohler had been privy to the escape plan in his weeks of running with Dillinger. Yet throughout his interviews with Leach, Mohler never mentioned Dillinger nor any talk of an impending prison escape. Likewise, Shaw had revealed that Dillinger had been putting together a nest egg for some friends still in prison. Hearing that, Huntington never connected it and did not tell Leach. Without that crucial piece of information, the ascending ladder of Leach's policing fell one rung short of reaching the top.

CHAPTER 4

Shirttails to the Wind

Threads, buttons and piece goods were sent down to me and on this particular day I was there when the box came and grabbed it as quickly as I could. I knew it was our box.—Walter Detrich, police interview

Envisioned within the walls by convicts, constructed by others on the outside, the Michigan City escape started with the unauthorized arrival of several revolvers. Dillinger purchased the guns, which he then tossed over the prison walls. A trustee or inmate outside the escape plan picked up a package on September 13th. It lay in the yard, wrapped to resemble cinderblock. The package, with a label indicating it was from N. Clark Street, contained three weapons and ammunition. This inmate, who was not a party to the escape, hastily turned his discovery over to officials. Deputy Warden Harry D. Claudy, either intentionally or through error, failed to acknowledge that there was an escape plan in the works. The intended recipient was Harry "Pete" Pierpont, the foreman of the inmate crew working in the Gordon East Coast Shirt factory, an industry operating within the prison.

Harry Pierpont was the convict who had tried to make a deal with Matt Leach by using his mother as the messenger. He was a hardened "incorrigible," serving time for bank robbery, and a friend of the recently paroled Dillinger. Claudy overlooked Pierpont, the inmate for whom the package had been intended. By ignoring the possibility of Pierpont's involvement, Claudy failed to connect the crucial dots that would identify the true ringleader of the planned escape. He placed inmates Danny McGeoghegan, Jack Gray and Edward Murphy in solitary confinement. These three, coincidentally, were part of the escape party. Matt Leach later stated that McGeoghegan played a key role in the escape due to his connections in Chicago along with five paroled convicts. Later, Matt correctly surmised that the inmates had bought their way out.[1]

Dillinger had paid forty-eight dollars apiece for the revolvers. He had amassed a nest egg out of the thousands of dollars stolen from banks over the past two months with Harry Copeland, Hilton Crouch, Homer Van Meter and the other ex-cons who were now in custody. Yet a larger quantity of revenue would have to come into play for a prison escape. It was more complicated than merely tossing a few guns over a wall. There had to be bribes, locations for hideouts, and most importantly, the weapons.

There were many roles, and John Dillinger played a small part by generating the funds. It was a sizable conspiracy, which included participants who smuggled in weapons and ensured the hiding place.

Less overt assistance came from unwitting guards who were negligent because they ignored the inmates congregating before the breakout. The state-sponsored assistance arose out of the new prison administration's creation of an atmosphere where an escape might be established, commonly known as the political "spoils" system.[2]

True to his mission of forming a new prison administration, in June of 1933 Governor McNutt replaced Warden Walter H. Daly with Louis E. Kunkel, a Michigan City attorney and old acquaintance of the governor. With no experience in corrections or law enforcement, Kunkel's appointment as the new warden was determined by patronage. Kunkel himself was political, so he dismissed the older guards and hired inexperienced men.

His new deputy warden was Harry Claudy, a holdover from the previous Daly administration. Claudy would have the misfortune to become the scapegoat for the escape. Inmates later stated that Claudy had meted out cruel punishments for infractions. On his watch, a punitive guard was free to beat an inmate into unconsciousness.

After the escape, Claudy took a defensive stance. As he found himself accused of aiding the escape through negligence and alleged complicity, Claudy made many accusations of his own. He declared that new warden Kunkel was rarely at the prison. He accused Kunkel of placing the inexperienced guards in the shops, such as the shirt factory where the escaped prisoners worked. He said that Kunkel was too busy talking to party followers to hear penitentiary reports. Claudy also pointed a

finger at McNutt for sacrificing personal efficiency for political obliga-
tions. In this way, older guards were fired to make way for political
plums to be given, such as the position of superintendent of prison
industries to Mutch Lawrence, who arrived at work an hour and half
late each morning.[3]

Three inmates later implicated Claudy in an escape conspiracy tale.
Their testimony, given after the escape, sounded like a rehearsed attempt
to discredit the despised deputy warden. In hindsight, it did appear suspicious that Claudy admitted to having heard rumors about an impending escape, but declined to tell Kunkel. Claudy later rebutted that he
was waiting until he had more proof. On another occasion, Claudy
claimed that he had thought the escape was planned for October, which
would have allowed him more time to investigate.[4]

William Behrens and Charles Northern were two inmates who
shared a family relationship to Pierpont's moll, Mary Kinder. They were
also long-time friends of Pierpont. They related an incredible tale to an
inquiry board. They testified that prior to the escape, Pierpont had
informed them that everything was fixed for the breakout, that Claudy
would be opening the gates. Behrens stated that Pierpont sensed the
deputy warden would try to double-cross him and be waiting with a
machine gun to shoot them down, and that Pierpont then moved the
breakout date ahead of schedule to avoid Claudy's possible betrayal.
Martin O'Leary, an associate of escapee Joe Fox, stated he had the opportunity to go along but refused, making the same statements against
Claudy as Northern and Behrens.[5]

Dillinger's former prison friends were a combination of types.
Harry Pierpont appears to be the one he most trusted and respected.
The thirty-year-old bank robber from Indianapolis, also known as
"Handsome" Harry, physically imposing at 6'1" with piercing blue eyes,
was considered dangerous. He had assaulted a guard and attempted
escape on numerous occasions.

Sentenced in 1925 for a Kokomo bank robbery, Pierpont had served
the initial phases of that sentence alongside Dillinger at the Pendleton
Reformatory before transfer to Michigan City. Dillinger later transferred
there in 1929. As the supervisor of the Gordon shirt factory, he had certain
liberties to move about in the shops. This is curious in light of his inside
record, which should have precluded him from serving as a trustee.

Charles Makley was another convict included in the breakout. The forty-four-year-old Ohio native, sentenced in 1928 for bank robberies committed in March of 1928 in Indiana, was not the dangerous type and committed only minor offenses in the prison. Considered amusing and with a long criminal record, Charley was both liked and respected among his fellow inmates.

Prison authorities also considered the tall, dark Russell Clark from Terre Haute, Indiana, to be dangerous. The thirty-four-year-old Clark was sentenced in 1927 for a Huntertown, Indiana, bank robbery. He had tried to kill his guards on a return trip from New Castle, where he had testified in another robbery. His inside record consisted of escape attempts, refusing to work and revolts.

The Canadian-born, red-haired John Hamilton was also included. Missing the index and middle fingers of his right hand, thirty-four with a stocky build, he also bore the stamp of being dangerous even though he appeared to get along with everyone. "Red" worked in the basement

"Terror Gang" principals, ca. 1920s. *Top left to right,* Harry Pierpont and Charles Makley; *bottom left to right,* John Dillinger and Russell Clark.

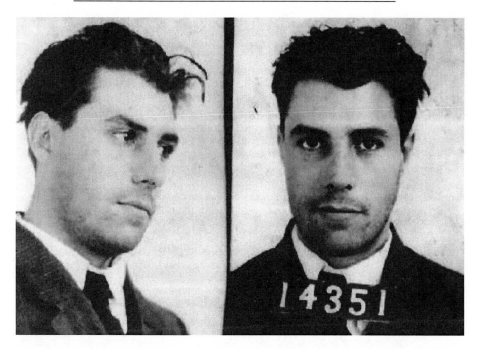

Walter Detrich helped engineer the notorious Michigan City escape. Mugshot from 1931.

of the shirt factory and unpacked shipments that arrived. His prison offenses were minor: skipping rope and being "noisy." This was not the portfolio of a desperate man.

One important participant was Walter Detrich, who worked with Hamilton in the basement shirt factory. Detrich assumed a key role in various aspects of the Michigan City episode without ever joining the gang after the escape. Instead of following Pierpont's clique, Detrich joined forces with a highly notorious gang that rivaled Dillinger's in relevance to the time and place.

Detrich had the blue blood of crime. He was a long-time criminal who, in the days before his prison commitment for bank robbery in 1931, had worked with the likes of Jack "Handsome Jack" Klutas and Thomas Bell aka Baron K. "The Baron" Lamm—the latter an ex–German army officer and father of modernized bank robbery, using timing and written plans. Detrich, not one to sit idle in jail, taught the Lamm system to the others in the dormant years before the escape plan materialized.

In his instinctive way, Matt later grasped that Detrich was important to the escape. Acting on his belief that Detrich held a higher post
than other peripheral members of the plan, Matt later elicited his startling confession. After his capture, Detrich confessed in a statement to
Leach that he himself had secured the guns once they arrived, hiding
them while Pierpont handled all incoming negotiations from outside.[6]
The escape appears to be Walter's only association with Dillinger. He
rejoined Jack Klutas after the breakout.

Another convict in the lineup was Joseph Burns. He was a mysterious character whose real name, John Heaps,[7] did not become known
for decades. He was added to the escape plan but had no plans of forging
ties with Dillinger afterward. Serving time for murder committed during
a bank robbery, he had been working in the can shop, where his duties
consisted of repairing the machinery throughout the shirt factory.
Another prisoner later claimed that, several hours prior to the escape,
he had seen Burns standing in the shirt shop basement with a set of
keys.[8]

There were others. Edward Shouse, a minor robber, most likely
joined the escape party after the first three inmates went into solitary
at the time the guns were discovered in the yard. The rest of the inmates
joining the escape plan would not forge any great notoriety on their
own.

James Clark, no relation to Russell Clark and also known as "Oklahoma Jack," had been another partner of Jack Klutas and Baron Lamm.
He went along with the escape due to urging from Detrich to seek med-
ical care outside the prison for ulcers.

Joseph Fox, a murderer serving life, seized the opportunity to join
the mavericks. He was the last of the inmates to be captured. Fox went
his own way after the escape and avoided Dillinger and the others completely.

Also joining the junket was convicted murderer James Jenkins,
who was a close friend of Dillinger's while both were in prison. Dillinger
wanted him included in the escape. Jenkins had introduced his sister,
Mary Longnaker, to Dillinger.

The last inmate, one who didn't make it, was Earl "The Kid" Northern. The brother of Harry's girlfriend, Mary Kinder, Earl had been Pierpont's co-defendant. Earl was in the infirmary with tuberculosis on the

day of the escape and too ill to escape. He was fated to die of the disease shortly thereafter while still incarcerated within the walls of Michigan City.

Aside from Earl Northern's untimely placement in the prison hospital ward, the group was all in place. The prison administration had grouped the inmates into a neat escape hatch months before, when they'd assigned nine of the ten prisoners to work in the shirt factory. Superintendent G. H. Stevens and Assistant Warden Albert Evans had assigned Walter Detrich and John Hamilton to the factory basement, with Claudy's approval.

Prison officials threw a scare into Detrich when they placed him in solitary for an infraction shortly before the escape. After several days, he returned to his basement position, bypassing the argument made by guard H. D. Burns, a floor man in shops 8 and 8A, who complained to Stevens and Claudy that the inmate should not be allowed to return there. Both Claudy and Stevens dismissed Burns's concerns. Even though appearing to be a cautious guard, Burns allowed the inmates to leave his area without permission. They did this on numerous occasions, including on the day of the escape. Burns was also fully aware that Detrich had manufactured a shower in the basement and that the inmates enjoyed the luxury of brewing their own coffee.[9]

The protocol used in receiving outside shipments for the prison factory suggested that only small or express packages were to be opened under a guard's supervision. The procedure for large freight, truck or carloads was boldly deferential to the inmates. These deliveries went directly to the factory basement, where Detrich and Hamilton opened them unsupervised. To add to the irony, the inmates kept the front door of the basement locked at all times from the inside. If a guard wished to enter, he had to knock, and one of the prisoners would allow him in. The only other entrance was a back elevator that connected the factories and basement, used by inmates going to retrieve material, as well as by guards. Detrich and Hamilton also controlled this, which necessitated that a bell ring to summon the elevator up. A tunnel adjoined the basement. The guards kept this locked, with the powerhouse holding the one lone key. Inmate Floyd Black later claimed he saw a key being manufactured for the tunnel several days prior to the escape by a plumber.[10] No guards were in the basement nor was anyone instructed to check it. The guard who served as the floor man, Burns, would verify that the door was usually locked throughout the day. He testified that it was locked at 1:30 the afternoon of the escape, even though the basement was never checked.

The escape plan was set in motion on September 26th, 1933. An inmate known as "Thomas, Inmate #12453" came across a mysterious man dressed in tan coveralls with a white shirt and tie on underneath, who was loitering outside the basement around 7:00 in the morning. The unidentified man asked Thomas where Detrich was. Thomas told him that Detrich wasn't there yet. The unknown man pulled out a watch to check the time. The inmate did not recognize him as a guard and his identity was never established. Thomas returned to the basement around 10:00 a.m. and discovered Pierpont, Russell Clark, Joe Burns, Detrich, Jenkins and several others congregating in a storeroom doorway. Thomas was forced to walk between them after retrieving the materials he had been sent for.[11] Detrich later admitted to Matt Leach that the original five in the plot had been in the basement that morning.[12]

At 2 p.m., John Cunningham, a floor man, was talking to Superintendent Stevens in the middle of the shops when Detrich approached and told Stevens, "Mr. Stevens, you're wanted in the basement. There's trouble in the basement over shirts and they want you to straighten it out." Since it was common for the superintendent to sell shirts, neither Stevens nor Cunningham was suspicious.[13] Stevens said that it was all right, and followed along with Detrich. This was the signal for any of the crash-out party remaining on the shop floor to head for the basement. Once in the basement, Stevens was confronted with an armed John Hamilton as the other inmates assembled. Detrich rushed back up to locate Assistant Warden Albert Evans out in the yard. Told that Stevens was having troubles in the basement, the prison official quickly followed along. Evans fell into the same trap Stevens had. Pierpont said, "You're going to take a walk or die right here." Told to do as they said and no one would get hurt, neither Stevens nor Evans resisted. Several prisoners who came to the basement to get shop materials were placed in the now unlocked tunnel and tied up. Floyd Black, who had seen a key made several days before, came down and was told by Russell Clark, "Come on Black, you're being tied up."

With only three possible revolvers, which Detrich later testified Pierpont, Hamilton and Russell Clark carried, they picked up boxes of shirts with Detrich and James Clark, who had steel bars to wield as clubs or possibly handmade guns concealed in the shirts. As a precaution, the rest picked up a large steel shaft, approximately five feet long and weighing several hundred pounds, to use as a battering ram on the prison gates. With Stevens also carrying shirts in the lead, Evans, who complained about his leg hurting from being hit by a foul ball during a ballgame, fell behind. Shouse ordered him to move up front. When Evans said he could not walk any faster, Shouse or another inmate responded, "You'd better move up or we'll knock your damn head off."

While listening to Evans complain about his leg pain, which sounded to the inmates like whining, Pierpont spoke to Russell Clark, telling him that they would now kill that "bald headed son of a bitch." Evans, who realized they meant the deputy warden, said, "If you mean Mr. Claudy, he's not here." Pierpont told him he was lying. Evans retorted, "All right, if that's the way you feel about it. I can't tell you no different." Pierpont then added, "Let's hurry along; we got something else to do."[14]

Frank Swanson was the turnkey at the first gate, called the Guard Hall. At his vantage point, all the guard could see was the superintendent with Detrich and Clark, whose arms were loaded with shirts. On seeing Stevens, Swanson immediately unlocked the gate out of habit without being asked. He was still unaware there was an escape occurring. Swanson later admitted during an inquiry that if Pierpont or Burns had been behind Stevens he would have known something was suspicious. After unlocking the gate, Swanson unwillingly joined the group.

Guy Burklow, obviously thinking the same as the first turnkey, unlocked his gate on seeing the superintendent. Then he discovered that there was a breakout in progress. Evans, now at least twenty feet behind Stevens, tried to signal the guard not to open the gate. But Burklow's view was obstructed by Stevens. Forced to march along, the group came to Fred Wellnitz at the administration gate. Fred, however, became alarmed and hesitated. He was promptly slugged unconscious and his keys taken. Evans, told he was going with them, was shoved through the gate, where he slipped and fell. Unlocking the door of the administration building, the convicts hurried in. Seeing Lawrence Mutch, the superintendent of prison industries, one of them shouted, "Let's get Mutch." They demanded that he open the arsenal. Mutch bravely refused and was beaten to the floor.

Several of the other convicts then vaulted over the counter that separated the offices from the lobby to herd the eight clerks into the vault. One elderly clerk, Finley Carson, was shot when a gun went off. This was either an accidental misfire or an intentional shot to prod Carson into moving more quickly. Evans, when asked where the warden could be found, told the convicts he didn't see him. They wanted to take "the warden and his secretary for a ride." Warden Kunkel was in the building at the time, but fortunately was not recognized. He was also forced into the vault with his secretary, who was spared the ordeal of "the ride."[15]

Sheriff Charles Neel of Harrison County had just dropped off a prisoner when he heard the commotion from the gate and witnessed the ten inmates rushing into the building. At first thinking a guard was bringing in prisoners, he quickly realized that was not the case. As the ten men ran out, Detrich—with Burns, Fox and James Clark—grabbed the sheriff and removed his gun. Detrich demanded the keys to Neel's car. Neel told him that his driving companion, Dr. Lee Wolf, had the keys outside, waiting in the auto. Detrich said, "Okay let's go get Wolf." By now, it was raining hard. Undaunted, the inmates took Neel outside to his car and relieved Wolf of his keys. They forced the sheriff into the auto with the four convicts. After asking nonchalantly if his friend could go with them, Neel received an abrupt "hell, no" for an answer. The car headed west on St. Rd. 12 toward Chicago.

The other six inmates, filing out of the prison main gate at the same time, ran across the street to the Standard Oil filling station. The attendant, when told to hand over the keys to his car, panicked and took off running. One of the escapees fired a couple of rounds at him, but all missed. The convicts quickly commandeered a passing vehicle driven by Herbert Van Valkenburg of Oswego, forcing him, his wife and Minnie Schultz, an eighty-nine-year-old relative, out of the car. Once they had control of their vehicle, the chase was on. They headed in the same direction as Detrich and the others.

Within thirty minutes after the escape, Lieutenant Fischer, Sergeant DeMont and a squad of eight members of the state police were speeding for Michigan City from the Tremont barracks. The state police headquarters in Indianapolis requested additional assistance once they picked up the trail near Valparaiso.

Then the farce began. A local radio station, WIND, hindered operations when it broadcast a so-called live shootout between the escaping convicts and police. It was five years before Orsen Welles' 1938 "War of the Worlds" radio hoax. The bogus gun battle bore the stamp of irresponsibility masking as playfulness. It is not clear whether the Indiana State Police heard it via a department radio call, given the fact that the ISP had not yet had their two-ways installed in all cars.

Perhaps Leach heard it on a radio along with the rest of the county. Leach and a handful of officers raced to the scene of the staged gun battle. There, he and his men discovered it was a fake. He let loose with a string of profanities before getting back into his patrol car and speeding off. Later on, the administration brought charges against the broadcasting service. Officials at WIND countered that several members of the Indiana State Police had assisted in the broadcast, a charge that Leach passionately denied. Eventually, the charges and countercharges were dropped.[16]

While this drama was occurring, an actual lawman was in peril. Sheriff Neel, a hostage of Detrich, Burns, Fox and James Clark, was being given up for lost. The convicts had been outside of the city when their hijacked car veered off south onto a side road. Realizing they were on a dead end, they performed a maneuver to turn around. While backing up, they mired the car in the mud. Two of the inmates walked to a nearby farm. They cajoled the owner, Carl Spanier, into getting his team of horses out of his stable in order to pull their car out of the quagmire. Not surprisingly, the farmer refused to accommodate his suspicious-looking callers. They reacted by taking Spanier's car and forcing him along on the ride back to the stalled car. After picking up the other two with Neel, they told Spanier to drive them south by staying on country roads and avoiding any cities. The auto was running low on gas and the farmer, seeing this as an opportunity, managed to escape when stopping to refuel.

With the car abandoned once it ran out of gas, the four inmates and Sheriff Neel cut across a field southwest of Michigan City and spent the night in thick underbrush. Still in prison blues, they went undetected due to the heavily wooded area. It rained most of the night.

On the following day, a Wednesday, they set out in the direction of Gary. They were a ragged crew, lost and disoriented, and soon

Radio station WIND, Indiana (shown here ca. 1933), broadcast a "live" gun fight in the hours after the Michigan City escape. The production was a hoax.

retreated to the woods. This situation continued until the next evening. Their collective condition was deteriorating as hunger and thirst set in.

By Thursday evening, they decided to tie Sheriff Neel to the underbrush near the road and go alone. James Clark argued that leaving the elderly man tied in the rain might kill him. The other inmates agreed, but issued Clark an ultimatum: if he was worried about the sheriff, he could stay with him. The five separated near Hobart at around 3:00 a.m. James Clark remained with Neel.

After walking for several hours, the unlikely team of convict and cop came to Highway 6 and managed to hitch a ride into Hobart. There Neel bought them both something to eat. This generosity continued as Neel gave Clark his coat. The convict caught an interurban for Gary, which signaled their separation. Neel went to a bus station in Hammond to call his deputy in Corydon. He relayed the good news: he was alive and well, released, and he needed someone to come pick him up.

The deputy taking Neel's message then called Al Feeney and notified him of Neel's status. Feeney relayed the information to Matt, who had already prematurely predicted the sheriff's demise in a statement to the press. "We fear Sheriff Neel has been slain," he'd just announced. "The convicts were through with him after they got away in his car and abandoned it. They probably shot him shortly after commandeering the second automobile."

After learning that the sheriff was alive, Leach rushed to the bus station to meet him. After much fanfare and picture taking, with the press called in to bear witness to the reunion, Leach went off the record. He treated Neel like a conspirator. He ushered the sheriff to Gary headquarters for questioning.

Neel had incurred Leach's suspicions by trying to protect the ailing Clark. Neel told Leach he had slept most of the day in underbrush after his release, and when he arrived in Hammond, had eaten and gotten his shoes shined before calling his deputy. This version sufficed until later in the day when Clark was arrested. Then the sheriff realized he'd made a mistake by protecting the convict. With some chagrin, Neel changed his story.

The escaped convict had made it as far as Gary when, after being traced through a hired taxi, he was captured that afternoon. Neel greeted his former captor like an old friend when Clark was brought to headquarters. Neel gave Clark five dollars before officials returned him to Michigan City.[17]

The other six convicts managed to make it to the home of Valley Werner, located near highways 6 and 43 within an hour after the break. They remained there for several hours, forcing the farmer, his wife and his daughter to remain inside with four of them, while two of the convicts remained in the barn. It was an active farm and not the isolated outback the convicts would have preferred. William Werner, a relative, called on the family while the convicts inhabited the farmhouse. They decided to hold him captive and looked over his car. When asked about the speed of the car, William replied, "Can do sixty but it shakes awful." This was enough to stave off the escapees, who decided not to take it. Then, a poultry dealer pulled up to the farm. One of the convicts pitched the next obvious question. Did the dealer have any money, he asked. The dealer admitted that he was carrying money. For some reason, the convict had a change of mind and retorted, "Keep it—we've got plenty."

The convicts took some of Valley Werner's clothing to change out of prison garb. This did not upset the farmer. He later stated, "They left some pretty good shoes and other things and they didn't act bad at all."

After dark, the six inmates left the family in the Dodge they stole in the outskirts of Michigan City and headed east on Highway 6. The Werners were unable to identify any of the escaped convicts from mug shots, and the police were not positive which set of fugitives had held the family hostage. This was a neat scenario with a tidy ending. It was all too happy for Leach's taste. He doubted the truth of the story but made a determination. Detrich's movements, as documented by Sheriff Neel, were now known to the police. That meant that the group holding the family hostage was most likely led by Pierpont.[18]

The six composing the other group were making a good getaway. They made it safely to Indianapolis early Wednesday morning to the apartment of Mary Kinder. They learned that John Dillinger had been arrested in Dayton, Ohio, four days prior to the escape. That prevented him from arranging a hideout as planned. It was then up to Mary Kinder. She would step into Dillinger's shoes and rent the hideout.[19]

By September of 1933, Huntington had soured in his relationship with Matt Leach. The two were at odds by now, in spite of their perceived commonalities. About the same age as Matt Leach, Huntington had been an original member of the Indiana Crime Bureau, which was the predecessor of the Indiana State Police detective division. Both Huntington and Leach were crime fighters, possessed the same drive, hunted Dillinger with the same determination, but most definitely did not have a great respect for each other.

The Michigan City crashout heralded a crime wave for Indiana (Bill Helmer Collection).

Huntington's views were not his exclusively. They were also shared by police officers in Ohio. Huntington solidified his dislike of sharing information with Leach when he professed that Leach revealed too much to the press. Leach, at this point, was livid with the bank investigator for not allowing him access to his informers. It was not a win-win situation.[20]

After discovering that Dillinger had a girlfriend in Dayton, Ohio, and that she was the sister of James Jenkins, Huntington relayed his information to the Pinkerton agency, which informed Inspector C. E. Yendes of the police department there. The information could have come from the Mohlar interrogations or from Huntington's informant, Michigan City ex-con Arthur McGinnis. Regardless of the source, the information was a tip that Huntington had garnered. He believed that Dillinger could be located through this woman. Yendes quickly assigned detective sergeants Charles Gross and Russell Pfauhl to investigate. After finding Mary's last name in the Michigan City visitor records, the two detectives moved into a ground floor apartment on 324 West First Street, where she lived, and waited for Dillinger to arrive.[21] After several weeks, the two police officers decided to spend the night at their own homes on the evening of September 21st. Late that night they received a call from the proprietor relaying that Dillinger had finally arrived. With a large group of police officers stationed outside and one downstairs, the two detectives quietly went upstairs to Mary's room with the landlady. Knocking on the door, she quickly stepped aside when Mary opened it. Gross and Pfauhl, armed with a sawed-off shotgun and machine gun, forced their way in. Dillinger was in his undershirt, holding photos taken while he and Mary had visited the Chicago World's Fair earlier that summer.

Told he was under arrest, Dillinger dropped the photos and raised his hands, then slowly began to lower them. Ordered by Pfauhl to keep his hands up or he would be killed, the Indiana outlaw obliged. Mary, obviously trying to aid John, suddenly fainted. The detectives ordered her to crawl out of the way so not to be between them and Dillinger.

A search of Dillinger's effects revealed five revolvers and $2,604 in cash, along with roofing nails and extra ammunition, found in his 1933 Terraplane.[22] The Dayton police discovered a diagram. They soon responded to news of the Michigan City breakout that they had thought all along that the map could have been a diagram of the state penal facility.

When news of Dillinger's arrest reached Matt Leach, he assembled a team composed of his trusted aides Claude Dozier and Harvey Hire and made haste to go to Dayton. Ostensibly it was for the purpose of presenting the outlaw to the victims of the Massachusetts Avenue bank—who claimed they could identify him. On a larger scale, it marked the start of a new phase in Leach's custom and practice. It was a new trend and one that would mark

John Dillinger in Dayton, September 1933: cool, calm and collected.

the Dillinger chase—the captain's leaving his own jurisdiction to cross state lines and go wherever Dillinger was contained.

Sergeant Pfauhl showed the gentlemen from Indiana all of Dillinger's effects, including his letters and the suspicious diagram. He later claimed that he tried to tell Leach, on that occasion, of the possibility of a planned escape from the prison. With Sergeant Gross and Inspector Yendes, who backed him up, he later stated that Leach had found it amusing that Dayton thought Dillinger was that big—and they had "been reading too many detective magazines."[23] The burden of proving the truth was on Matt Leach after Indiana investigator Forrest Huntington stood with the Dayton police in this disputed version of events. After the escape, Leach charged that the Dayton authorities had refused him permission to view the diagram. This created a heated topic, with Dayton declaring that Leach had been free to copy anything that he wanted but declined.[24]

While Indiana fought for the extradition of Dillinger to Indiana, the outlaw had his own ideas. Instead of returning to his native state of Indiana, he followed the advice of an attorney and pled guilty to a Bluffton, Ohio, bank robbery. That prevented his return to Michigan City. Then a technicality prevented him from going to a secure Ohio facility, the Montgomery County Jail in Dayton. He went instead to the Allen County Jail in Lima, Ohio.

With Detrich, Fox and Burns completely disappearing after the escape, Pierpont and the others hid out in the home of Ralph Saffel, who had had a few dates with Mary Kinder and now was forced to give the fugitives refuge. Early the next day, Pearl Elliott from Kokomo arrived with money that Dillinger had given her. By evening Harry Copeland, an associate of Dillinger's, had arrived, and they all left with him, warning Saffel to keep his mouth shut.

Police found an abandoned Oldsmobile between Brownstown and Seymour on September 29th on Road 50 near a schoolhouse containing prison garb belonging to Makley and Shouse. Witnesses stated that the men had headed east on Route 31 in a second car at around 7:00 p.m. This propelled Leach to notify Lt. Ray Hinkle and detail eighteen state policemen from his district to that vicinity. They combed the surrounding area for the convicts throughout the night.

Several hours later, Terre Haute police notified the state police that Frank Ratcliffe of 221 Paris Avenue was flagged down by the fugitives and forced to drive them east of town in his Franklin sedan, where he was told to get out. The group continued east on St. Rd. 40 in the Franklin and another car. Later that evening, Clifford Frazier of Greencastle was driving to the Midway Restaurant on the corner of

MARY KINDER'S RETURN AWAITED

Pierpont's Girl Friend Scheduled to Arrive in Indianapolis From Tucson.

Matt Leach leaked Mary's name to the papers, as this undated headline from February 1934 shows. Pierpont would never forgive Leach (Bill Helmer Collection).

St. Rds. 40 and 43 to visit his friend Gerald Keller, a diner employee. Frazier noticed a Franklin parked alongside the road, about 100 yards from the intersection. Remaining at the restaurant until closing time at 4:00 a.m., they headed home to Greencastle. They saw the Franklin was still sitting along the road. Growing suspicious, they reported the car to Sheriff Bryan, who had the car towed.

Abandoning the Franklin after a police pursuit near Brazil, Pierpont and the others continued on 40 in another large sedan, possibly an Oldsmobile with Illinois license plates, until they came to Plainfield. There a state police squad car sat, stationed to be on the lookout for the stolen Franklin from Terre Haute. As the car sped past with six men, Sergeant Bert Davis decided to give chase, even though it was not the stolen car. Following the car at a high speed, pushing his Ford speedometer to 80, he started to gain on the Pierpont car at Ben Davis, a small town near Indianapolis. Suddenly the fugitives' car screeched to a halt. One of the men inside broke out the back window and trained a submachine gun on bystanders at the intersection. They turned south onto High School Road, causing the police officer to veer around them, narrowly avoiding a collision. Pierpont's auto turned so sharply it hit a pole, throwing James Jenkins from the car. Jenkins fled on foot as a local jeweler, Edward Watts, got one shot off at him. The Pierpont car, not waiting, continued south. By the time the state police car was able to get turned around and came back, both the fugitives' car and Jenkins were gone.[25]

Jenkins ran until he came across Victor Lyle, who was getting into his car after dropping a date off in Ben Davis on Fruitdale Street. Jenkins approached and asked for a ride. He told Lyle he had been in a fight with some fellows and asked him not to take Washington Street (St. Rt. 40.) Instead they went east onto Lyndy Street. When told that Jenkins had a car waiting for him on Martinsville Road, Lyle obliged and headed in that direction. On arriving, the fugitive pulled a gun and told his hostage that he was in a jam and that Lyle would have to help him out. With Lyle almost out of gas, Jenkins ordered him to drive until the gas ran out. They travelled through Martinsville, on the outskirts of Bloomington. There, Jenkins ordered Lyle out of the car and relieved him of his money, a paltry seven dollars. With a sudden change of mind, Jenkins told Lyle to get back in the car and they headed for Nashville, arriving around 2:30 in the morning. At a filling station, a woman came to the door telling them that they were closed. She suggested going to another one, two blocks down, where they could get gas. Finding this station closed also, Jenkins went to the door to arouse the proprietor. Lyle quickly drove off, heading back to Bloomington at a high speed, where he notified the police there. After calling Brown County authorities, Sheriff Lester Bender, with two police officers and Lyle, headed back to Nashville where he met up with Sheriff Fremont Weddel. Lyle brought the officers back to the place where he had left Jenkins. The woman there stated that the man had just walked away after Lyle drove off.

Sheriff Weddel notified Lt. Ray Hinkle at Jeffersonville, and he sent in 12 state police officers to comb the woods in the Nashville area. By then, a posse formed consisting of farmers and CCC workers, along with the police, searching for the fugitive. The hapless Jenkins managed to reach Bean Blossom and asked a resident, Will Altop, if he knew where he could get parts for his car. Altop, suspicious, walked away and gathered three of his friends. Ben Kanter, Herbert McDonald and Ivan Bond armed themselves and went in search of the man. Finding Jenkins along on the main road, they told him they would help if he was unarmed. As McDonald alighted from the car, Jenkins hollered, "Don't get out!" Pulling a revolver, Jenkins shot him in the right shoulder. Kanter, nearby with a double-barrel shotgun, fired as Jenkins shot again. With the first barrel missing, the second discharge caught Jenkins in the side of the head and he fell into the weeds along the road.

Sheriff Weddel took him to the office of Dr. L. R. Crabtree in Nashville, where he died. The fugitive's father, the Reverend George Jenkins, stated he was glad it was like this rather than having his son kill someone else.[26]

With Jenkins dead, Pierpont and the others, who now consisted of Russell Clark, Makley, Hamilton, Shouse, Copeland and Mary Kinder, hid out in Ohio at the Pierpont farm near Leipsic. Copeland had also arranged for a hideout in Hamilton, Ohio. While Makley suggested robbing his hometown bank of St. Mary's, Ohio, Pierpont's priority was to get Dillinger out of the Lima jail.[27]

CHAPTER 5

Big Men

Here's my credentials.—Harry Pierpont to Sheriff Jess Sarber

With John Dillinger detained at Dayton, Ohio, Captain Leach along with Harvey Hire and Claude Dozier visited him. Although they questioned him extensively, they got little out of Dillinger except a rueful remark that "someone" had done a lot of talking.[1]

Leach asserted that Dillinger was the leader of the gang that had committed numerous bank robberies in Indiana and Ohio. Every attempt was made to connect him to several Indiana robberies so that Leach could have him extradited back home.[2] However, Dillinger had other plans and confessed to a Bluffton, Ohio, bank robbery, thwarting Leach's idea of dragging him back to his home state.

On September 28th, two days after the sensational Michigan City escape, Sheriff Jess Sarber arrived to transfer Dillinger to the Allen County Jail at Lima to stand trial for the robbery. Sarber having brought only four deputies, Dayton officials argued that the force was too small because the Indiana prison escapees might be plotting to liberate their benefactor. Dayton transferred Dillinger to the county line in an armored car, where five additional officers from Lima met Sarber at Piqua. Dayton warned Sarber to safeguard against a possible jailbreak, but the Sheriff dismissed Dillinger as "just another punk.[3]

Shuffling back and forth between his parent's farm at Leipsic, Ohio, and a hideout at 1052 S. 2nd Avenue in Hamilton, Harry Pierpont's main objective was to free Dillinger from Lima—but the gang needed funds. They robbed the First National Bank of St. Mary's, Ohio, on October 3rd, presumably because it was Charles Makley's hometown and he knew the area.

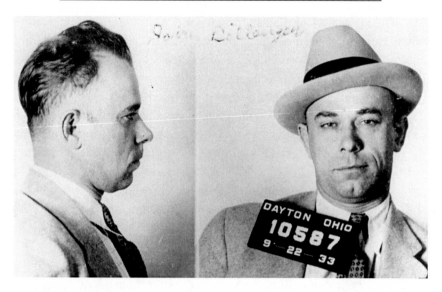

John Dillinger's arrest in Dayton on September 22, 1933, resulted in the death of Sheriff Jess Sarber.

On the eleventh, the gang spent the night at Harry Pierpont's brother Fred's farm near Leipsic. Omar Brown, an old family acquaintance, arrived from Lima after visiting Dillinger. Brown was later suspected of furnishing Pierpont with the layout of the jail.[4] Fred Pierpont later stated his brother left around 4:00 p.m. on the twelfth in an Essex Terraplane[5] with another gang member. The other three men left in a Chrysler, one group heading toward Lima and the other in the opposite direction. Fred also stated the group consisted of his brother Harry, Harry Copeland, Russell Clark, Charles Makley and Ed Shouse.[6]

Jess L. Sarber was a popular law enforcement officer who treated his prisoners well. A self-made man, he had started out running a livery stable, then moved on to operating a used-car dealership before going into politics. Winning with one of the largest votes in the Democratic Party for sheriff in 1929, he was reelected in 1931.

At around 5:30 that evening, the twelfth, two strangers called on local attorney Chester Cable to discuss Dillinger's sister (Mary Kinder) visiting the outlaw. Cable told the men he would discuss the subject with the sheriff the following day. After the men left, Cable called Sarber to warn him about the visit. From all accounts, the sheriff was unconcerned about the warning.[7]

The attorney had disrupted Pierpont's plan. After leaving Cable's office, Pierpont, Charles Makley and Russell Clark (or Harry Copeland)[8] entered the jail, liberated Dillinger and killed Jess Sarber in the process. From testimony at the subsequent trial, the events began with Sarber at his desk reading an evening newspaper while his wife sat nearby with a crossword puzzle. Deputy Wilbur Sharp, not in uniform, sat on a couch on the south wall. Pierpont approached the desk and told Sarber that they were from Michigan City and wanted to speak to Dillinger. Sarber politely asked to see their credentials, at which Pierpont whipped out a .38 Colt revolver and told him, "Here's our credentials." Sarber either shifted or reached for a gun in his desk. Pierpont fired twice, hitting Sarber with the first shot in the lower abdomen and sending him backwards to the floor. The second shot went into the wall.

Pierpont leaped at the sheriff and hit him across the head with the butt of his gun, demanding the keys to the cells. Sharp had leapt to his feet but Clark or Makley pulled a gun and told him to get the keys. The gunmen, unaware that Sharp was a deputy, believed him when he said he didn't know where they were located.

Sarber tried to rise, but Makley lifted a pistol and hit him on the head. The force of the blow caused his scalp to open to the bone. Mrs. Sarber screamed for them to leave him alone. Ignoring her, Pierpont hit the dying sheriff once or twice more, demanding the keys to the cellblock. Conceding, Lucy Sarber told him she would get them, and Pierpont followed her into a hallway where the keys hung. Pierpont went for the cellblock door, but thought twice and went back to remove the gun from the sheriff's desk drawer. Quickly unlocking the first door, Pierpont struggled with the final lock, and told Sharp to try to open it. At one point, Pierpont must have realized that Sharp was a deputy.

Dillinger had been playing cards. Upon hearing the first shots, he grabbed his coat; then stepped out as soon as the cellblock opened. Pierpont, fearing a mass exodus, fired a single shot down the corridor and told the other prisoners to get back, that he only wanted John. Dillinger had invited Art Miller, a prisoner awaiting trial for murder, along on the escape, but Miller refused.

Sharp later said that Dillinger appeared upset upon seeing Sarber. "Why did you have to do that?" he asked Pierpont. Pierpont ignored Dillinger's anguished question and forced Sharp and Mrs. Sarber into the cellblock. The hysterical woman begged to remain with her husband. Dillinger and Pierpont left through the kitchen, with the other two gunmen leaving through different doors. Dillinger, Pierpont and Clark joined Copeland in the Terraplane and drove it to a parked Chrysler. Copeland got out and joined Makley and Shouse. The two groups left town and headed for the Hamilton hideout.[9]

Sheriff Sarber died at 8:05 that evening at the Memorial Hospital. He had told his son Don that his killers were all big men. Six posse groups searched throughout the night for Dillinger and the gang. A raid descended on the Pierpont farm near midnight. Although the gang was not located, Fred Pierpont was taken in for questioning when the Oldsmobile was found in his barn. The murder sent Lima and the surrounding counties into a frenzy.

PART II

The Gadfly

CHAPTER 6

Denials

Leach threatened tonight that unless Copeland "comes through" with the real story of the break, he will be turned over to Lima authorities and prosecuted for the sheriff's murder.—*Indianapolis Star*, Feb. 8, 1934

During the month of Dillinger's parole, eleven inmates of the Kansas State Penitentiary in Lansing, Kansas, escaped during a Memorial Day baseball game. It was an era when Memorial Day was celebrated on May 30th, before the modern era of barbecues and department store sales that now define the holiday. The administration planned the baseball game, which ended with a walk-off grand slam when several dangerous men escaped. It was bloody and violent, using the threat of having explosives and with the help of smuggled guns and making a hostage of the warden. Two leaders were Wilbur Underhill, the "Tri-State Killer," and veteran bank robber Harvey Bailey, who stole over one million dollars during the 1920s. During Dillinger's first month of freedom, Bailey earned the title of Public Enemy No. 1 in the Midwestern big city dailies.[1]

Bailey was a man's man. His rugged persona and thick, wavy hair made him attractive in photos. He would soon be arrested, tried and convicted on circumstantial evidence in the kidnapping of oil millionaire Charles Urschel.

The Memorial Day escape from the Kansas State Penitentiary was a symbolic start to that lawless summer. Bailey and Underhill were immediately tagged as perpetuating a trail of crime in four states. That was before the epic bloodletting of the Kansas City Massacre.

On June 17th, in Kansas City, Missouri, the attempted rescue of recaptured bandit Frank "Jelly" Nash at Union Station, allegedly by Charles Arthur "Pretty Boy" Floyd, his alleged associate Adam Richetti, and the confirmed gunman Verne Miller, resulted in the shooting deaths of a federal agent along with municipal police officers.

Otto Reed, police chief of McAlester, Oklahoma; Raymond J. Caffrey, a federal agent; William Grooms and Frank Hermanson, Kansas City detectives; and the recaptured outlaw Frank Nash were all killed in the shootout.[2]

The event was christened the "Kansas City Massacre" by the director of the FBI, who did everything but break a bottle of champagne over Union Station. John Edgar Hoover exploited the shootout by releasing powerful suggestions to the public through mass media: The nation was a lawless frontier mismanaged by local police agencies; the United States needed a federal police agency whose officers would not be subject to corruption or graft.

The FBI did not see the Terror Gang as being under its jurisdiction. Sometime after the Union Station tragedy, the Attorney General Homer Cummings asked the FBI to offer Indiana help with their bank robbing problems. The response was simple: the FBI would not interfere with Indiana. As an entity it was standing by, ready to give any help sanctioned by the "Laws of Congress." This was a veiled reference to the fact that before June of 1934, the Division of Investigation was limited by restrictive guidelines that forced them to defer to local police agencies.

The press release was issued to deflect public attention from federal intervention. In secrecy, the federal agents from the Cincinnati field office had entered the case in the two-week period after the Lima breakout. From their budget they printed 35,000 Wanted posters and delivered them to Ernest Bodkin, the prosecuting attorney. Huntington was one insider who knew of the entry of the federal government. He wrote in an internal memo, "Only three people know of his agreement with the Agency. They are the County Auditor, Common Pleas Judge, E. E. Everett, and [Bodkin], and he does not want any information given out that might get in a newspaper."[3] This again was an allusion to Leach and his habit of taking everything to the press.

Hoover had not yet developed the Dillinger gang into a story to build his reputation. In late 1933, the director didn't need a Dillinger or a Terror Gang to act as an antithesis to law and order. He already had the myriad of crime stories popping into the headlines every day across the Midwest. There was prison escapee Harvey Bailey, who was an

This early FBI publicity photograph (from around 1935) suggested that members of the general public might visit the bureau headquarters for a sight-seeing tour.

innocent bystander picked up in the sweep of suspects in the Oklahoma City kidnapping of oilman Charles Urschel. Bailey was tried and convicted in the first of two federal trials that would result in his conviction along with the actual conspirators: Albert Bates; George "Machine Gun" Kelly and his wife, Kathryn; her parents, Ora and Boss Shannon; and their son, Arvid. Throughout the trial, Bailey remained the celebrated Public Enemy of the front pages. This was mostly owing to his handsome face and the sophisticated, graying curls that framed his intelligent eyes. The newspapers highlighted him until his conviction and commitment to Alcatraz Island, along with Bates and Kelly. After this conviction, Bailey lost his crown as Public Enemy No. 1 as he faded into the obscurity of Alcatraz.

Famous "snatch cases" had occurred with regularity since the sensational kidnapping of the baby of famed aviator Charles Lindbergh and his wife, Anne Morrow Lindbergh. Peculiar to the Midwest was the phenomenon of underworld characters snatching other mobsters. One such case carried a lot of contradictions. It was the story of the kidnapped Jake "The Barber" Factor and his accused, the members of Roger Touhy's gang. The papers called them the "Terrible Touhys," as though being "terrible" was a unique quality among this ilk. Touhy was also briefly implicated in the kidnapping of St. Paul millionaire William Hamm in St. Paul, before the real kidnappers, the members of the Barker-Karpis gang, became known to police. Touhy was involved in wars with the new Capone gang in Chicago, which, by 1933, operated under Chicago Outfit boss Frank Nitti.

The job of "Public Enemy No. 1" saw a lot of turnover. When one designated public enemy died violently or went into prison upon conviction, another quickly stepped up to fill the vacancy.

The first of two kidnappings of wealthy businessmen who were not officially associated with organized crime, perpetuated by the Barker-Karpis gang members, kicked off that June of 1933 with the snatching of St. Paul millionaire William Hamm, a brewer. He was held for $100,000 ransom. The crime brought underworld characters such as Verne Sankey into a general sweep of mobsters accused of the Hamm kidnapping, along with the beleaguered Touhys. The Touhy gang members also fell into the purview of the usual suspects, if not the correct suspects.[4]

With the arrests of Harvey Bailey and the Urschel kidnappers, the diminishment of the Holding/Keating/Nash gangs and the banishment of the Touhys, the first wave of the snatchers, bank robbers and prison escapees went meekly to their private incarcerated hell. The flagrant kidnappings, the unholy Kansas City Massacre, the Lansing Memorial Day and Michigan City escapes—these abominations created the crime wave that made 1933 shrivel like a grim reaper. Enter the Class of 1934.

Led by John Dillinger, who first appeared in the papers after the Dayton arrest, the new gangsters were called John Dillinger's Terror

Gang. The first Dillinger gang had blossomed and withered with the speed of a daylily. Although two members were still at large in the persons of Harry Copeland and Homer Van Meter, the latter was never a part of the Terror Gang and the former was soon to be arrested.

The Terror Gang assumed its place in history as the "First Dillinger Gang," as the White Cappers went silently into the good night of prison. The difference between the obscurity of the White Cappers and the international notoriety of the Terror Gang could be summed up in the name Matt Leach.

Around the time that Dillinger's image first appeared in the Indianapolis dailies, after the Dayton arrest, Matt Leach became a pundit. His insights came out like the weather report—with predictions and forecasts. Through the escalating hype, Dillinger went from a two-time loser to rising mastermind of the astounding $24,800 Massachusetts Avenue bank job.

At the same time, the public persona of Matt Leach rose from that of an easily ignored political appointee to that of distinguished professor of crime in Indiana. While virtually ignoring similar prison escapes and bank robberies, Leach latched onto Dillinger. In doing so, Leach became the most quoted source on the Terror Gang.

Leach didn't have a choice in his positioning as front man for the law enforcement segment of the new administration. It was a job that Al Feeney should have filled, but the safety director didn't have the same charisma as Leach, whose affinity with the newsmen of the *Indianapolis Times, News* and *Star* made him the likely press secretary. Leach could improvise on the question of progress, and in that stifling summer, there was precious little to report. McNutt's enemies as well as innocuous state factions were blaming the Terror Gang on mistakes attributed to Governor McNutt. Leach's behind-the-scenes police work could not be reported to the press, and that was where he was doing the most good. At that point he began to put his men in plainclothes and utilized Detective Art Keller's expertise as he built his team.

Publicly, they generated hot air. Feeney organized former servicemen into squads to put up roadblocks, mobilized the American Legion to set up shotgun volunteer armies, and vowed to set up machine-gunning sandbag blockades and tactical airplanes on loan from the National Guard. He asked the Indiana Bankers Association to form a

Matt Leach at his desk in the Indianapolis Statehouse, 1934 (courtesy James Emerson).

board of inquiry. Its purpose would be to raise funds for the statewide police radio hookup, the big campaign promise that had not materialized. He presented this straw committee as a sign that help was on the way.[5]

Feeney then assigned blame to the phony gun battle that had been broadcast from Gary after the escape. He charged Sergeant DeMont of the Tremont barracks for allowing some of his officers to participate in the stupid affair. Leach went against his own administra-

Al Feeney, ca. 1930s (courtesy Indiana State Library).

tion when he jumped in and defended the sergeant: "On the strength of any evidence presented against Sergeant DeMont, in command of the barracks at Tremont, there would be nothing to justify his dismissal," declared Leach. The matter was then dropped. He believed in assigning blame correctly and had telegraphed his ire to the federal radio commission. He raged against the staged "pitched battle between escaped convicts and forces of the law," in Station WIND, Gary. He loudly demanded the arrest of Steve Trumbull, whose connections with the Columbia Broadcasting System stretched back to New York. Trumbull's show gave a vivid account of a supposed battle going on in the woods eight miles south of Chesterton. CBS then fired "the man responsible," without naming him.

Leach had gone to the Federal Radio Commission. He demanded an investigation but later withdrew the request pending a further inquiry. His complaint had initially been sent to Eugene O. Sykes, a member of the commission.

> I desire to file formal complaint in regard to the almost entirely false and fake broadcast by the Columbia Broadcasting Company's News Service over station WIND and other stations ... this broadcast seriously interfered with the work of the 65 state police under my command and a considerable number of other law enforcement officers who were stationed in the neighborhood of where we thought some escaped convicts might be in hiding. We wasted several hours of what at that time seemed to be precious time in, first, determining there was no truth to substantiate the broadcast and, second, in making an inquiry into the hoax.[6]

Overall, the criticism aimed at McNutt started with the basic fact that he had paroled Dillinger. As a backlash, the parole board held a moratorium on paroles from the Indiana State Farm. Some enterprising investigators even resurrected Dillinger's parole papers, which were found to have contained a few clerical errors, a fact that McNutt jumped all over in explaining his signature on Dillinger's release. Then H. D. Claudy, the deputy warden fired because of the escape, declared that he had written two letters opposing Dillinger's parole and decrying the inmate's character, to no avail.

The paroles were reinstated almost immediately, but the moratorium further eroded the governor's popularity.[7] To counteract the damage, McNutt promised a full investigation into the escape, with the appointment of an impartial commission. The prison board of trustees had already made their report, which resulted in the dismissal of Deputy Warden Claudy.[8] McNutt's new investigation was conducted by Leach, along with two other appointees. Once again, McNutt charged insiders with a job that should have been handled by an impartial panel.[9]

At the behest of McNutt, Leach was running around like a windup toy. As hard as he performed, he heard the criticism of his handling of Dillinger in Ohio when he'd failed to bring Dillinger back to Indiana. That was considered a lapse of jurisdictional expertise, and it earned Leach yet another vocal enemy in law enforcement.

Indianapolis police chief Mike Morrissey was facing rumors that he was going to be fired. Amid his own insecurity about his job, he publicly admonished the captain for letting Dillinger stay in Ohio rather than face justice in Indiana. Leach had complained to the press after the Massachusetts Avenue bank job that Morrissey had failed to notify him that the robbery had occurred. Morrissey countered with a critique that Leach's unprofessional handling of the Dayton extradition attempt was the true cause of Dillinger's failure to return to Indiana to face charges for that job.[10]

Like kids in a schoolyard, McNutt, Feeney and Greenlee hid behind Leach, who defended them against the Republicans who attacked the spoils policies of firing and hiring. The buck finally stopped at the feet of Claudy. The deputy warden had made the first mistake, attributing the weapons shipment to the three inmates whom he had thrown into solitary.

Leach had also made a bad call in the dramatic hours after the escape from Michigan City. He had publicly condemned inmate Daniel McGeoghegan, whom he had charged with being a member of the escape party due to his "Chicago connections." That was an overstatement not befitting a practiced speaker like Leach. McGeoghegan was a notorious Chicago beer runner and gunman. He hadn't been in Michigan City that long, having only been imprisoned since his May 31st, 1933, arrest in South Bend, after being identified as a bandit who held up the State Exchange Bank of Culver, Indiana. No one up to now had looked at the long relationships that some of the escapees had with each other. That would have suggested that McGeoghegan, a high-profile prisoner, was not trusted enough to join the conspiracy.[11]

Claudy also admitted that he, as deputy warden, had ignored evidence of a conspiracy in the making. McNutt kept throwing blame in the direction of Claudy's former administrator, the former governor Harry Leslie, who had been casually overheard telling some friends that the inexperienced guards could "cause a big prison break or rioting."[12] Leach seized on this and hinted that Leslie knew more about the escape than he did. They all started to sound like vindictive playmates when Leslie countered that if he'd ever tried to contact McNutt, Pleas Greenlee would never let him through the door.

Governor Harold Leslie, whose Michigan City employees were fired by McNutt, ca. 1930s (courtesy Indiana State Library).

Leach's position was to act as a filter. Like a scapegoat, his own position faltered while he protected everyone else. The effect on him was the loss of respect of other officers. Most cops of that time saw things in black and white. Because Leach blurred the lines, bleeding police secrets into the hands of hungry press writers, most cops mistrusted him. Word went out to keep confidences out of his reach.

Leach also had to contend with a firestorm over the Dayton police who had arrested Dillinger. Leach had made the mistake of publicly blaming the arresting officers and their brass for not giving him Dillinger's possessions.

Dayton Inspector Yendes countered with his own version of the quest for the map. Both officers earnestly made their respective cases through their own newspaper people.[13] The problem was, the writers then scrambled the story like eggs in a frying pan. Some reports claimed that Dillinger only had letters. Other papers said that the maps detailed the environs of the Michigan City penitentiary as though to describe getaway roads. Some diehard reporters stuck to the story that the paper found in Dillinger's pocket was a map of Michigan City, with the suggestion of tunnels and escape routes clearly marked. Like a Hardy Boys mystery story, the question remained: Did it hold the clue to the escape? The answer was never made clear. The only given was that the two police jurisdictions were bitterly fighting and making it a public spectacle. The departments strove to appear credible and, with such believability, absolve themselves from blame in the escape.

It was impossible to ascertain the truth about the actual contents of the map—if it was indeed a map, because without being entered as evidence, it could not retain its value. Some letters written by Dillinger to Mary Longnaker came to light, their contents a dribble of puppy love.

Transferring a prisoner's possessions over state lines was unorthodox, yet Leach believed he was entitled to the items. Harder to figure out is why Leach accused the Dayton police of withholding Dillinger's possessions in the first place. Yendes, with Huntington colluding, later denied obstructing Leach's access to Dillinger's things and said that the captain had been given permission to copy anything he wanted.[14] The argument could have been made that Leach had no way to copy papers. It was an era before Xerox machines and scanners; the closest thing to a copier was carbon paper.

Believed to be the Rosetta Stone of the Michigan City escape, this group of items haunted Leach. An article published years later stated that Leach did receive the materials eventually. If this version is to be believed, on September 30th, Dayton finally relented and sent Leach the requested materials, including the map. This ended the deadlock between the states of Indiana and Ohio.[15]

There were other things to worry about. Leach as well as the Pinkerton agency had tried to warn Sheriff Jesse Sarber of the imminent danger of an attempted prison break. In a letter that was clearly worded, the Pinkerton Detective Agency wrote:

Dear Sheriff:
Re: Citizens National Bank, Bluffton, O. Holdup.
An informant advises us that a Cincinnati Attorney has been employed to represent John Dillinger. They have already paid his fee. The informant further states there will be an effort made to have Dillinger delivered from jail before the trial date is set. The ten men who recently escaped from the Michigan City, Ind. prison last week are all personal friends of Dillinger and they may seek his release. You may have this information but in case

you do not, it probably will be news to you. Yours very truly, Pinkerton's Natl. Detective Agency, Inc., E. S. Clark, Division Manager.[16]

After his Dayton arrest, Dillinger was identified as the robber of the S. J. Gully bank in Farrell, Pennsylvania, by employees of the bank who witnessed the robbery held on September 12th. As soon as this story got off the ground, the police captain there denied that any bank employees had gone to Dayton. This occurred in the days before it was decided to place Dillinger in Lima, while he was still under tight security in the Montgomery County Jail in Dayton. That was about to end. Under the counsel of attorney Jack Egan, Dillinger made a request to go to Ohio and come up on charges in the Bluffton robbery, which would consign him to the minimum-security county jail in Lima.

Dillinger, considered a rube with a blue-collar knowledge of bank robbery and cars, was suddenly represented by a lawyer with some experience on the bargaining table. This proved that Dillinger was not an unconnected country boy. Huntington believed that Pearl Elliott, whom Harry Copeland visited around that time, had steered Dillinger toward the backroom lawyer Egan.[17] As the officers made this connection, Leach wanted to raid Pearl Elliott's place. Huntington balked and said to hold off, because he needed to protect an important informant, and advised discretion. It was something Leach couldn't conceptualize. Huntington held out, believing privately without telling Leach that a raid would lead the gang to suspect his informant.

With the Dillinger gang leaving Indiana, Leach boldly moved into the town of Hamilton, Ohio. The gang either was tipped off by Huntington's informant or was ready to move on before the troopers arrived. Officer George Daugherty later said that the troopers, who had one armored car, learned that the convicts were supposedly traveling in a 1933 Hudson, which later turned out to be a 1934 Oldsmobile that had passed them on the road. The troopers rushed to a farmhouse. "We just missed them. A cigarette was burning in an ashtray," Daugherty later wrote.[18]

Leach was implementing his own agenda in someone else's jurisdiction. Somewhere along the path toward interstate policing, he lost his perspective. Along with running across state lines to question the Pierpont family, Leach started raiding the homes of those suspected of harboring the gang. He clung to the idea of crashing Pearl Elliott's place in Kokomo, but Huntington refused to expose his informant, Arthur McGinnis.[19] Relenting, Leach raided the home that Mary Kinder shared with her mother, sisters and brothers in Indianapolis. The Northern family would soon recognize the doorbell, late at night, bringing cops without search warrants.[20]

Pierpont believed that Leach had arrested his beloved mother, Lena, in Terre Haute. A more accurate account of Lena's Terre Haute ordeal was that the police of that jurisdiction acted on their own, with no interjection by Leach. Harry's parents and brother, much like Harry's girlfriend, Mary Kinder, were cultivating a deep hatred for Leach and his tactics, which to them amounted to harassment of the more innocent members of their families. Mary Kinder was a woman whom Leach had on his radar. She was his suspect in the Michigan City escape.

The raids on Kinder's mother, Mrs. Shirley Patterson, took place at the woman's home at 930 Daly Street. The first police intrusion occurred on October 6th. It was the night after Ralph Saffel's admission that he was Mary's boyfriend or casual acquaintance—whatever one wanted to believe—who had been forced to host the gang after the escape. After one of these searches, Leach made an unsubstantiated claim that raiders had found her diary and that it contained entries about Dillinger and photos of the escapees.[21]

After the gang escaped from Hamilton, they entered a period of relative domesticity that, in the underworld, translated into taking apartments with close female companions. Russell Clark lived with Opal Long, who had an undocumented past reputation as his moll. She claimed to be his wife but had no marriage certificate.[22] She was more likely an old girlfriend. Her sister, Patricia Cherrington, nested first with Copeland, then went over to John Hamilton as his girlfriend.

Ed Shouse, who stayed with the gang after the escape, didn't have a regular moll and angered the other men by flirting with Dillinger's girlfriend, Evelyn Frechette—whose name was first given incorrectly as Evelyn Frechetti.

Matt Leach, as captain of the Indiana State Police, signed the text for wanted bulletins, which described the exotic Frechette as "foreign" and "Jewish" in appearance. It is odd that he would sign off on these racially charged descriptions, with his own mother being of foreign origin and his wife a second-generation Serbian. The Frechette description was a bit kinder than the bulletin he wrote on Clark's partner, Opal Long. Leach described her as an unattractive "sloppy dresser." Later he would have more to say:

Evelyn "Billie" Frechette, shown here with unidentified male, ca. 1936 (John Binder Collection).

> Dillinger had two or three girls in all his life of crime. One was a Dayton, Ohio, woman whose brother was in prison and who had two children. He went with Evelyn Frechetti, the half-breed Indian girl, who was more attractive than the Ohio woman.[23]

Around the time that Leach began issuing police bulletins describing the Terror Gang's women companions, he issued a photo bulletin of Pearl Elliott and Mary Kinder. Elliott was incensed. Then Pierpont joined the "kill Leach" brigade. It was all very personal, all about the Terre Haute affair involving his mother.

On November 13th, the Terre Haute police arrested Lena Pierpont. Somehow local police had found Harry's father, who went into a local hospital after a minor car accident. Lena was hiding in an apartment under a false name. She was arrested along with her son Fred, and his wife and baby. Lena was held for questioning and released.

Pierpont linked the arrest to Leach. In his vow to kill the captain, he began taking trips into Indianapolis alongside Dillinger and Mary Kinder, in the hope of shooting the "rat" down in the street. Pierpont had his chance at one point, but either Dillinger or Mary Kinder told him to forget it. Pierpont spared the life of the gang's mortal enemy.

Dillinger's anger took a more benign form. He did not vow to kill Leach—that goal would come later in his criminal career. Instead, Dillinger started mailing postcards to Leach's basement office in the Statehouse. Addressed "Hey Captain," the cards were signed, "John Dillinger." On July 1st, Leach received a booklet in the mail entitled "How to Be a Detective." Dillinger later took credit for mailing the silly

BULLETIN
INDIANA STATE POLICE

AL. G. FEENEY   STATE HOUSE,   INDIANAPOLIS, IND.   MATT LEACH
Superintendent   Captain in Charge

PEARL ELLIOTT
Associate of Dillinger and Pierpont Mob

MARY KINDER
Associate of Dillinger and Pierpont Mob

Pearl Elliott and Mary Kinder's 1933 "Wanted" poster was broadcast across the Midwest.

pamphlet to the captain. The truth was that an International News Service reporter, Jack Cejnar, had jokingly mailed the ten-cent booklet from a secondhand store to Leach. Yet Dillinger would always claim he was responsible for the ruse.[24]

Cards and letters aside, the gang had become more brazen. On October 20th, they held up a police station in Peru, carrying away with them a large arsenal of weapons and bullet-proof vests. The take included a Thompson submachine gun, two .38s, a .30-caliber rifle, a semiautomatic rifle, a shotgun, a .45 Colt automatic, a Smith & Wesson .44 revolver, a .25-caliber automatic pistol, a 9mm German Luger, three bulletproof vests and ammunition. This subversive act was soon repeated in a police station raid in Auburn.

Unable to counteract these raids, Leach told his friends in the press corps to headline them as "The Dillinger Gang." Despite this new identity, individual members of the gang stood out. Charles Makley was positively identified as one of the robbers of the First National Bank in St. Mary's, Ohio, of $12,050. The notoriety of the Pierpont name was such that the Pierpont family members were living under an alias. Despite Leach's insistence that the press identify Dillinger as the leader, the reality was that this group was egalitarian, with the dominant force being Pierpont. He reigned as the alpha male of the Terror Gang through the sheer force of his personality.

One gang member still not widely recognized was Mary Kinder, who was being identified as a random "girl" in most news articles. Mary always claimed to love Pierpont. With his tendency toward murderous rages, he was nevertheless praised and adored by Mary and her sister, the loyal "Silent Margaret." In contrast to the love she had for Pierpont, Mary hated Leach. She and her cohorts routinely blamed their notoriety on the captain. It was as though they assumed no culpability for their actions.

The gang would next rob the Central National Bank in Greencastle, on October 23rd. An inflated amount of $75,000—in "cash and bonds" in order to justify the substantial number—was initially listed as the take. The Greencastle robbers were the nucleus of the Terror Gang, with Pierpont, Makley, Clark and Dillinger all in on the bank job.[25]

Sometime after the break and around the time that the gang went into hiding in Hamilton, an ex-con from Michigan City named Arthur McGinnis had become an informant for Huntington. McGinnis had contacted Huntington, the story goes, as the investigator was traveling to Dayton. The two men were related, so it was inevitable that the two would join forces. McGinnis told Huntington that he had information concerning the Massachusetts Avenue job. Since McGinnis had served time with Dillinger, McGinnis told Huntington he felt confident he could turn him in. He asked for a percentage of anything that was recovered from the Massachusetts Avenue job. He named Dillinger, Crouch and Vinson as the perpetuators of the bank job. It was then that Huntington decided to take this underworld character seriously. He introduced him to Inspector Simon in Indianapolis. The informant's identity was circulated around the police, with all agreeing not to tell Leach about the stool pigeon working against the Dillinger gang. When somebody realized that this informant was an Indiana ex-con, Huntington reluctantly told Leach about McGinnis as a required part of the protocol.[26]

McGinnis immediately earned his royalties on the Massachusetts

Avenue bank job. The informant revealed that Dillinger and the Terror Gang were in Chicago. Leach forged a successful merger with the Chicago police. He partnered with Captain John Stege and Sergeant Frank Reynolds. The two had publicly formed a forty-man command, known by insiders as the Secret Squad but publicly as the Dillinger Squad. Its purpose was to round up the Dillinger gang and "other desperadoes." Here was the key phrase that allowed the squad to randomly go after other wanted men. In late December Captain Stege led a raid into a North Side apartment at 1424 Farwell Avenue. There police killed Louis Katzewitz, Charles Tattlebaum and Sam Ginsburg, all wanted for the robbery of the Farmers' State Bank in Minnesota during which the teller, Carlton White, was killed. The police gave an official story about the three being mistaken for members of the Dillinger gang, specifically Dillinger, Pierpont and Hamilton. Mayor Kelly then announced, "This shows what the Chicago police can do."[27]

Chicago was a hospitable place for a policeman with an aggressive agenda. Leach, who had forged a good relationship with Stege, took three of his plainclothes troopers to the Windy City.[28] For department courtesy, Chicago proved to be more hospitable than Ohio. Detectives Art Keller and Gene Ryan, along with Lieutenant Chester Butler, began working at the Sheffield Avenue station. Captain Stege agreed that they belonged there.

Events unfolded in Chicago after that. Art McGinnis infiltrated the gang and became friendly with Hubert Dillinger, who was Dillinger's half-brother and, some said, a peripheral gang member. Hubert and McGinnis had visited Dillinger in the Dayton jail.

With information coming forth from McGinnis, the Massachusetts Avenue robber Hilton Crouch was soon arrested. McGinnis also told Huntington that Copeland was an envoy who traveled between Kokomo and Hamilton and back to Chicago.

McGinnis's presence in the police circle caused friction between Leach and Huntington. In answer to Leach's request to bring McGinnis to the state police headquarters, Huntington refused but agreed to call McGinnis to question him about the escape.

Showing how unsure Huntington was of Leach, he brought McGinnis not to state police headquarters but to Indianapolis police headquarters to meet with Inspector Simon and Chief of Police Mike

Chicago Sergeant Frank Reynolds (*right*), killer of a dozen felons and head of the newly established "Dillinger Squad," with fellow officers, ca. 1930s (John Binder Collection).

Morrissey. This clique formed an axis of Leach opponents. There McGinnis admitted to meeting up with Copeland at Pearl's place in Kokomo. This solidified the trio's decision to exclude Leach, who was dangerously close to raiding the Kokomo brothel. Huntington violently opposed a raid on Pearl's Kokomo hideout. If cops broke down that door, he knew the gang would link McGinnis to the raid.

The relationship between McGinnis, Dillinger and the police came to a crescendo when Dillinger, suffering from a scalp infection, went to an underworld physician, Dr. Eye, to have it treated.

Before that, on November 12th, Huntington had gone to Chicago with Lieutenant Chester Butler and Detective Gene Ryan of the state police to meet with Lieutenant John Howe of the Dillinger Squad. Howe, in pre-empting an encounter with Matt Leach, said of himself that he "only answers to Chicago." Howe told the Indiana cops about a branch of the Chicago police known as Scotland Yard, which only did phone taps. These secretive cops knew all about McGinnis and had found out that he was living with an ex-con named Fred "Happy" Meyers.

While he was in Chicago, Huntington met with McGinnis. The informant told the investigator that Dillinger had showed him some of the Greencastle bonds. McGinnis led Huntington and Howe to a place where they would be able to observe Dillinger in a meeting at a Chicago street corner. That ended with Huntington able to see and identify Dillinger, but with no arrest. At this point Huntington was in a camp with Howe.

Huntington had wanted this to be a stakeout, with Dillinger tailed to catch the rest of the gang. This was based on the promise that McGinnis had given him, that the entire gang was just waiting to be caught. McGinnis then told Huntington about the planned trip to Dr. Eye's office by Dillinger. When the next move was made to catch Dillinger, it became obvious that the Indiana State Police who were stationed in Chicago, Butler and Ryan, were acting as Leach's spies. When they heard that the Chicago police and Huntington were setting a trap for Dillinger, they phoned in the information to their own superior, Captain Leach. Upon hearing this, Leach called Huntington in an excited state, yelling that he wanted Dillinger taken or killed and not merely shadowed. Huntington was worried about his informant, realizing that if Dillinger got away, McGinnis would live under a death sentence as a stool pigeon.

The camp in favor of a shooting ambush was augmented by Inspector Rooney of the Lima police. Howe relented and called for reinforcements. Assistant Chief of Detectives William Blaul sent three cars.

The outlaw did in fact keep his appointment, and went inside the building at 4176 Irving Park Boulevard, on the corner of Irving Park and Keeler Avenue. He had left his girlfriend, Evelyn Frechette, sitting in his fast and sporty Essex Terraplane. Three squads from Chief Blaul's Chicago detective bureau had staked themselves out on Keeler Avenue. The sergeants from Indianapolis, Eugene Ryan and John Jenkins, were there as backup. Dillinger was outnumbered on all points of manpower, automobiles and weaponry.

Dillinger came out of the office, spotted the police, shifted into reverse and sped into a five-point intersection on Irving Park Boulevard. Sergeants Ryan and Jenkins fired as Dillinger's Terraplane headed east. The cars followed, and the uniformed drivers later said they'd avoided firing directly at Dillinger to avoid a chaotic car accident in the busy intersection. The Terror Gang later made statements that the police fired through their own windshield. The event prompted the newspapers to print wild stories about Capone-like autos with bulletproof windshields and turrets that opened for machine guns. After the Irving Park Boulevard escapade, McGinnis retreated from the police circle. His role in the ambush was quickly deduced by the gang, who vowed to kill him for putting Dillinger "on the spot."[29]

At 11:12 a.m., the day after Dillinger was ambushed while leaving the office of Dr. Eye on Irving Park Boulevard, the phone rang at the hideout of Fred "Happy" Meyers and the absconded Art McGinnis.

HAPPY (answer): Hello.
BOB (unidentified caller) CALLING: Happy?
HAPPY: Yes.
BOB: Bob.
HAPPY: Have you seen the paper this morning?
BOB: No.
HAPPY: Well, by all means get one.
BOB: Anything wrong?
HAPPY: Plenty.
BOB: Well for Christ's sake, let's have it. Don't keep me in suspense this way.
HAPPY: McGinnis put Johnny (Dillinger) on the spot.
BOB: For Christ's sake.
HAPPY: They didn't get Johnny though.

BOB: Anything in the papers?

HAPPY: Yes, but it don't mention "Mac" (McGinnis).

BOB: Was Johnny's name mentioned?

HAPPY: Yeah, I didn't want Mac to know, but I knew Johnny was going to the doctors.

BOB: Jesus…. If Johnny comes in treat him good; treat him nice.

HAPPY: I saw him (Johnny) Monday, and I told him about Mac and he said he thought Mac was OK.

BOB: Do you suppose Bill at Warren Avenue or Jack could have told him I was trying to find Mac so I could kill him?

HAPPY: Yes.

BOB: I believe Mac is a good friend of Matt Leach.

HAPPY: Well I'll tell you, he's (Mac) got a cousin by the name of Forrest Huntington, who is an investigator for the Indiana Banker's Association and he's got two pictures of a guy we will call Tillie (Crouch)—know who I mean?

BOB: Yeah.[30]

These excerpts from a Chicago police wiretap of actual conversation taken on November 15th, 16th and 17th, 1933, of Dillinger, Makley, Pierpont, Copeland, Happy Meyers and Mary Kinder talking never identify "Bob." But the wiretaps of a few minutes later indicated the gang's new nickname for John Dillinger—they called him "newspaper." The conversation is the first mention of the fact that Pearl Elliott, "Tootie," was dying of cancer. Her friend, Ruby aka Sylvia Clevinger, is talking on the phone to Mary Kinder (Mrs. Meyers).

WOMAN ANS.: Hello.

RUBY: Mrs. Meyers?

MRS. MEYERS: Yes.

RUBY: This is Ruby. How are you?

MRS. MEYERS: Pretty good.

RUBY: How's Tootie?

MRS. MEYERS: Well, she's still got dizzy spells. But the doctor says that's to be expected. Gosh, she only weighs about 80 pounds. She's awful skinny. She was unconscious for four days and she had hemorrhages.

RUBY: I guess she'll be all right.

MRS. MEYERS: Yes, I guess so. Say, did you see the paper?

RUBY: Yes, that's terrible.

MRS. MEYERS: Mac (McGinnis) did the spotting.

RUBY: He did, eh.

MRS. MEYERS: Yeah, and gosh. He just called up here.

RUBY: Who? Mac?

MRS. MEYERS: No.

RUBY: Who?

MRS. MEYERS: The newspaper (John Dillinger).[31]

The episode on Irving Park Boulevard illustrated how deeply Huntington was at odds with Leach. Huntington didn't want his informant compromised and had resisted the idea of an ambush in the hopes of honoring McGinnis's promise to bring in the whole Terror Gang rather than just Dillinger. Huntington was frustrated with Leach for insisting that the bandit be met with a full force of police activity rather than be shadowed to his hideout.

Huntington's low-grade frustration now turned to rage. Leach then told the press that he'd had a "November 15th prediction," an allusion to the episode on Irving Park Boulevard, which strongly hinted that the shootout was based on information he'd received earlier. He couldn't have outed McGinnis any more clearly if he had hoisted the informant's name on a flagpole.

Fed up, Huntington now went through formal channels. He had already written several letters to superiors in state government complaining about Leach. One of his complaints had said that Huntington had the backing of the police of East Chicago and Gary in opposing Leach.

> Leach, by his indiscreet methods of sensationalizing criminal information to the press, by his domineering attitude toward City and County officers and by other irrational and erratic acts, has antagonized the majority of police officials of the State and they will not cooperate with him. To disclose confidential information to him is to jeopardize the success of any important investigation. This condition has reached a state where I feel that it is dangerous to my client's interests and the public welfare to confide confidential criminal information to Leach or officers subject to his orders.

Huntington then moved the personal enmity into the realm of the political. On November 16th, he wrote:

> The root of our trouble throughout this investigation has been interference with the work of our informant by an overzealous and jealous State Police department under fire generally by the press of Indiana for inefficiency; and, in this case, they would do anything for some favorable publicity to alleviate the "heat" on the present administration for playing politics with the penal institutions and the State Police force.[32]

Within a few days of the Chicago ambush, the gang struck again. They robbed the American Bank and Trust Company in Racine, Wisconsin, on November 20th. This robbery bore all signs of a Terror Gang job. The principal bank robbers were Makley, Pierpont, Clark, Dillinger, and a fifth man named Leslie "Big" Homer. In the annals of Dillinger's bank jobs, Racine was a hallmark.

The $27,000 robbery was a sensation as well as a disaster. One of the robbers entered the bank ahead of his associates and walked directly to Grover C. Weyland, the bank president, and ordered him to open the vault. From the beginning, the gang was foiled by the collective spirit of the bank employees. An assistant cashier, L. C. Rowan, stepped on the bank alarm button. Harold Graham, an assistant cashier, was hit by a bullet. The other robbers came in and opened the money cages. During the commission of the robbery, they shot a police officer, William Hanson, when he rushed into the bank with a pistol drawn and was met by the robbers. At one point, they ordered the female employees, Ursula Patzke, Helen Crespkes, and Jane Williams, to lie down on the floor. Two of the robbers led Weyland, head cashier Loren Bowne and assistant cashier L. C. Rowan back to the vault while cleaning out the loose cages.

After Rowan stepped on the alarm button, unknown to the robbers, the police made haste to get to the scene. At the same time, a mob formed outside of the bank. Sergeant Wilbur Hansen, holding a submachine gun, and Officer Cyril Boyard entered the front door of the bank. "Let the cop with the machine gun have it," one of the robbers yelled. One of the robbers hit Hansen and he fell wounded to the floor. He would survive a shot to his arm and one that grazed his forehead.

By now, the Dillinger gang members were on their way out of the bank. To protect themselves, the robbers pulled a group of bank employees and formed a cordon of hostages as they exited the bank. They forced four hostages out the front door, but two of them fell back into the crowd that had assembled outside the bank.

Then they ordered hostages onto the running board of their getaway car. Among the hostages was the bank president, Grover Weyland; a police officer, Cyril Boyard; and the bank's bookkeeper, Ursula Patzke. They let Cyril Boyard off the speeding vehicle and made their escape with hostages Weyland and Patzke. They eventually let Weyland and Patzke out of the car, and tied them to a tree before leaving. The two were happy to be alive.[33]

Leach's gadflies, Gene Ryan and Detective Arthur Keller, went to Racine after the holdup. Unknown to the Leach camp, Huntington and

Lieutenant Howe were there conducting a deeper investigation. They arrested Michigan City parolee Leslie "Big" Homer in Chicago and charged him with the Racine robbery. Then they brought Homer into Indiana as a Michigan City parole violator.

Homer, knowing the gang would want to shoot him in the assumption that he had confessed, admitted that he was the fifth gang member at Racine. He furnished essential information on the Terror Gang, but more importantly, confirmed Huntington's worst fear: McGinnis was under a death sentence and would be killed by the gang at first opportunity. Huntington and Lieutenant Howe bought some time by withholding news of the arrest from Leach. Sensing the absence of the omnipresent Dillinger hunter, Big Homer then requested that Chief Morrissey join Huntington for a conference with the promise of a secret revelation. "Release me and I'll bring in the gang," he proposed, without much hope for fulfillment of that request. When that failed, he told a hallmark story that reflected poorly on Matt Leach:

The sister of Mary Kinder, he related, was Margaret Behrens, a woman married to an inmate from Michigan City. She had garnered the nickname "Silent Margaret" and, depending on which cop you spoke to, "Silent Sadie," because of her refusal to cooperate with police. As part of the raiding parties on Mary Kinder's household, police had arrested Margaret in Indianapolis. Dillinger was in touch with Leslie Homer at that time, and had sent Homer to hire an attorney named Jessie Levy. She would become, by all accounts, the trusted family retainer of Mary Kinder and the Pierponts, as well as counsel to Charles Makley and Russell Clark. Leslie Homer allegedly paid Jessie Levy the sum of fifty dollars and asked her to visit Matt Leach in the Statehouse. According to Homer, Leach then told the Northern family's attorney "everything he knew" about the details of the gang. The attorney then relayed the context of their conversation back to Dillinger through the emissary, Leslie Homer.

Shortly after Homer became comfortable enough with his arresting officers to share underworld gossip, the Racine officials arrived with plans to abscond with the prisoner. John Brown, Racine County district attorney, and Lyle L. George, Racine detective, planned to take Homer back to Racine to face charges there as a member of Dillinger's bank robbery gang. The jurisdictional move was a prescient warning that

Wisconsin would fight a protracted battle with Indiana over the gang. Leach followed them into Racine. There he came up against D. A. Brown and Detective George, along with the formidable police chief, Grover C. Lutter of the Racine police department. Without extending the usual department courtesies, Leach demanded Homer for Indiana as an ex-convict and parole violator. Leach tried some bargaining with the Racine officials to the effect that Homer had to answer as an Indiana parole violator before serving his time in Waupun Prison in Wisconsin.

Then the captain, characteristically, contacted the news agency United Press, and mapped out the plans for Homer. According to D. A. Brown, "That put us on the spot."[34]

The Homer incident left the Racine officials with a strong dislike for Captain Leach. The repercussions would play out in the town of Tucson, Arizona, within two months of the Racine robbery.

With the Chicago police now dominating the hunt for the gang, and the infighting between factions in Indiana, it seemed like an opportune time for the Justice Department's Division of Investigation to enter. On November 14th, the Cincinnati office, which had stood witness in a benign fashion up to now, contacted Matt Leach.

The captain was accustomed to letters back and forth between police departments. Despite the reputation he'd garnered for lack of cooperation, Leach was at his desk most days. There he would compose countless letters to police officials in neighboring cities. It didn't raise any eyebrows when the Acting SAC in Cincinnati, Agent Bliss Morton, wrote to him with a request: Would he please share

Leach compares notes with Captain Jake Ferrar, 1933.

information on Michigan City escapee Joseph Fox's relatives who were living in Reading, Ohio? Leach responded that he hoped the Cincinnati agents could help him by covering Reading, Ohio, an area Leach said was out of bounds due to his department's limitations of equipment and manpower.[35]

Shortly afterwards, the Cincinnati federal agents arrived in Indianapolis. Matt Leach met the agents. He gave them his files, calling the data he'd accumulated "all the information at the disposal of the state police department." The Division never thought to return the favor, and never extended the same courtesy to him.[36]

Huntington, in his report of November 15th, had put his disgust with Matt Leach's political machinations into writing. But this controversy came to a head within a few weeks of the Lima escape, when Leach was in control of official attempts to derail the search for one of the actual killers.

In the weeks after the Greencastle and Racine robberies and with the gang in Chicago, Harry Copeland was arrested in a pistol-waving episode. He had gotten drunk and started fighting with a woman on a Chicago street corner. In the office of Chicago captain Gilbert, Copeland gave his name as "John Stanton." A quick check of his fingerprints outed him as Terror Gang member Harry Copeland.

With Leach entrenched in Chicago, he had no problems getting to Copeland. He credited his own men, Gene Ryan and Arthur Keller, with aiding in the bandit's capture. Leach greeted Copeland as soon as he was brought in.

Copeland's post-arrest journey was convoluted. He went first to Michigan City. Then he was transferred to Indianapolis, where Feeney demanded he be locked up in the Statehouse under heavy guard.

Feeney and Copeland then began reminiscing about that bastion of male bonding, football; they discovered they had competed against each other years earlier as young men.[37] Small talk aside, important things were happening, and this looked like Copeland's lucky day, after all.

The earliest reports of Copeland's arrest placed him squarely in the Lima jail on the night of Sheriff Sarber's murder. On November 21st it was reported that witnesses to the Sarber death identified Copeland as one of three men who entered the jail, but that they believed he was not

Harry Copeland (*center*) was sent to the Indiana State Penitentiary after copping to a lesser plea of bank robbery to escape murder charges in the killing of Sheriff Jess Sarber. Photograph dated November 1933 (John Binder Collection).

the invader who had fired the shot at Sarber. This led to his indictment for first-degree murder on October 27th by the Allen County grand jury. Prosecutor Ernest M. Botkin had promised an early trial and arraignment before Judge E. E. Everett, a week or ten days after his arrest.

Suddenly, Ohio was derailed when Indiana authorities got Copeland delivered to Indiana's Michigan City prison. There, Feeney promised Botkin and Inspector Bernard J. Rosey that they would have their prisoner back soon. The consensus asserted that the men suspected of the attack were Pierpont, Makley and Copeland, and that they were three out of five men who went to deliver Dillinger.

Then, a big cop with a big mouth arrived to claim jurisdiction over Copeland. Indianapolis chief Mike Morrissey demanded that Copeland stand trial for the Dillinger holdup on Massachusetts Avenue. He wanted Copeland to stay in the Indianapolis City Jail and be charged in Marion County.

Along with the Dayton police and Huntington, Morrissey believed that Leach was unprofessional. The animosity that Morrissey felt for Matt Leach had started with Dillinger's arrest in Dayton, when the chief accused Leach of failing to bring about Dillinger's extradition to Indianapolis. He believed that Leach had failed to veto the power of Ohio in holding Dillinger there.[38]

Copeland's arrest occurred simultaneously with the release of a report that the escaped prisoners of Michigan City were aided by inside accomplices. McNutt's standing argument, echoed by Leach, had been, "They didn't shoot their way out. They bought their way out."[39]

The McNutt faction tried to use Copeland's position as a suspect in Sarber's murder to get him to reveal the inside story of the break at Michigan City. *The Indiana Star* reported, "Leach threatened tonight that unless Copeland 'comes through' with the real story of the break, he will be turned over to Lima authorities and prosecuted for the sheriff's murder."

Huntington's assertions of political chicanery were becoming self-fulfilling. Leach had taken over as the official leader of the management of Copeland. The unofficial leader was Huntington.

Six witnesses had failed to identify Copeland as being at the Greencastle robbery. While the witnesses to the Sarber murder did identify

Copeland as among the band of murderers, he stayed in Indiana. It was looking like the promised land, as Copeland saw it. As an aside, or to further reinforce Indiana as his resting place, witnesses to the Montpelier and Daleville robberies were also brought in to view Copeland.

An unidentified witness, most likely Deputy Sharp, as only he and Mrs. Sarber had witnessed the murder, identified Copeland as having been present at the time of Sarber's death. Leach was still at the helm, making announcements pertaining to the investigation.

Behind the scenes, Huntington was trying to get Copeland to inform on the Terror Gang suspects to avoid prosecution for the Lima capital crime. Copeland did not readily accept that as a deal. Huntington then asked Greencastle authorities to prosecute him for Greencastle. Even though Copeland was not identified at Greencastle, Huntington backed the plan to allow him to plead to bank robbery rather than face murder charges at Lima.

Copeland's attorney was Bess Robbins, who had experience in the Indiana State Legislature, a fact that hinted that this was a backroom bargain in the making. She met with Huntington and Leach and suggested that Copeland plead guilty to Greencastle and not be turned over to Lima for murder. The second half of the deal was prophetic: Copeland would stall until after the other defendants were caught and put on trial; he would then plead not guilty to Greencastle, but would be prosecuted as an associate of the Terror Gang.

With Huntington in the background, and angry at Leach for stalling and blocking his access to Copeland, Leach publicly oversaw the commitment of Harry Copeland to Indiana. He was remanded to Michigan City.

Harry Copeland, in a few hours with Leach at the helm, had agreed to be quoted as saying that Michigan City was an inside job. For that, he was rewarded with a lesser charge of bank robbery. In that moment, he escaped going to Ohio, escaped being charged with capital murder, and escaped the penalty of the electric chair.[40] For the next two months Copeland remained the prime suspect wanted by the Lima prosecuting attorney, Ernest Botkin. Upon consultation with McNutt, Botkin agreed to accept another Terror Gang member, Russell Clark, to stand trial by proxy.

It is said there is no honor among thieves. Yet the honor system seemed to have escaped both Huntington and Leach at this crucial juncture. Leach was an honest cop who was being pressured beyond endurance to save the reputation of McNutt. Even Huntington recognized that and had put it into print, charging that the state police department was "under fire generally by the press of Indiana for inefficiency." Yet Huntington was not above piggybacking off Leach's desperation. Their mutual goal was to get a lead on the Terror Gang by exploiting Copeland's position.

Copeland's information on the Michigan City escape had less value than a losing "Win Five" ticket stub. Yet his inference that the break had been an inside job was all McNutt needed to get out of the firestorm. Leach, with all the power of the governor's seat behind him, cut Copeland a handsome deal.

That same month, on December 15th, the first in a series of cop killings forged by members of the escaped convict group began. Sergeant William Shanley, a decorated Chicago police officer, tried to singlehandedly question John Hamilton about ownership of a car that the escapee had left for repairs in a garage at 5320 Broadway. The car had been traced to the Broadway garage, and Shanley was ordered to arrest its owner. A shift change occurred and Shanley told his partner, Detective Frank Hopkins, to take their car to a chauffeur to drive back to the stationhouse, and leave the car for the next shift. Hopkins was outside when Hamilton walked in with his unwitting girlfriend. Shanley tried to arrest the gangster, but Hamilton gunned down the sergeant and fled, leaving his dumbfounded girlfriend behind to face the consequences. Elaine Dent knew little to nothing about Hamilton and his status as a nefarious member of the Dillinger gang. Leach, who had installed state policeman Gene Ryan in the Sheffield stationhouse, asked the detective to question her in relation to the Dillinger gang.[41]

In the inner sanctum of the gang, there was trouble. Ed Shouse was violating the gangland code of flirting with another mobster's moll. He and Evelyn Frechette were getting too friendly, in the eyes of Dillinger and Pierpont. There were other reasons. Shouse wasn't an organic member of the brotherhood and their cliquish girlfriends. With a payoff and a sendoff, Pierpont threw money at Shouse. In this florid fashion, Pierpont disenfranchised him from further contact with the gang. Shouse then left in Russell Clark's car. It is believed that Clark took pity on Shouse and gave him the keys.

Shouse had connections that reached beyond his fellow escapees from Michigan City. On December 17th, the ousted gangster held up Atlas Gardens, a Fort Wayne, Indiana, nightclub, with three other men. One man remained anonymous and the second may have been someone named Carl Miller. The third accomplice played a key role in events that were about to unfold. He was named Breman or Brehman.

Within the next day or so, leading up to December 20th, Breman aka Brehman had an argument over a planned robbery with Shouse, who never thought about the possibility of an informant's revenge. His disgruntled partner, or someone nearby, called the Statehouse to inform Leach that Shouse's new gang was planning a bank robbery and a meeting in Terre Haute, culminating in the meeting at the La France Hotel in Paris, Illinois.

Indiana State Police officer Eugene Teague, ca. 1933. He was killed in a police shootout with Dillinger gangster Ed Shouse. He was the first ISP officer to be killed in the line of duty (courtesy Indiana State Police Museum).

Upon receiving the outlaw's itinerary, Matt Leach raced to the scene. He went first to Terre Haute, arriving with lieutenants Chester Butler and Ray Hinkle, and a young motorcycle trooper recovering from a motorbike accident named Eugene Teague.

They were in Terre Haute when they received a call from Paris that Shouse and some other people had checked into the LaFrance Hotel. They quickly drove to Paris, arriving on December 20th. By ten o'clock that morning they had an ambush set up outside the hotel.

Leach positioned his men outside the hotel in tandem with Paris police officers. Lieutenant Chester Butler was standing on the hotel porch at the front door. He stood next to another officer, with his riot gun ready.

Shouse drove up at 10:20 in a Terraplane with two women and two men. Officer Teague immediately drove his car up to the Terraplane on a slight angle, his right fender boxing the car in. Shouse put his car in reverse, but another squad car jammed into his bumper so that he was trapped.

The Paris officers and state troopers had a plan to shoot in relay fashion should Shouse fail to surrender. This relay system was described by Matt Leach: "The instructions were that no one was to shoot until the officer preceding him in the order of firing either had emptied his gun or killed the convicts. This was done to prevent a lot of wild shooting."

Shouse interfered with this offensive when he remained behind the steering wheel of his car. Leach later told the press that Shouse "cowered behind the steering wheel of the bandit car when he realized the odds were against him." What Leach didn't tell the press was that Shouse was only momentarily slouched behind the wheel, that he was planning the moment in which to spring from the car. During those tense moments, the second man jumped from the car and escaped.

Eugene Teague jumped out next, holding his gun. Butler fired on Shouse from the porch, just as Eugene Teague stepped up to the car. He went into the line of fire and was hit by buckshot slugs to the base of his brain. The wounds were fatal. According to Leach,

> Poor Teague was number one man. He was stationed directly in the rear of Shouse's car as it pulled up in front of the LaFrance hotel. The orders were "shoot to kill." His only error was that he became too anxious to immediately effect the arrest of the convict. He fired several shots at the car, which pierced the windshield, but miraculously missed Shouse.
> It was his turn to stop shooting and the turn of the next man, Lieutenant Chester Butler, to open fire. Butler followed his instructions and began shooting, but Teague, in overzealousness, ran around the side of the convict's car and attempted to open the door, no doubt intending to drag Shouse bodily from the car. He stepped directly into the fire of Butler's shotgun.

Paris officer Albert Stepp held a gun to Shouse after he'd thrown up his hands. The outcome was that Shouse and Carl Miller were caught, but the outlaw known as Bremen or Brehman unaccountably escaped— which added to the theory that the tipoff had come from him.

Eugene Teague was the son of a retired trooper, a twenty-four-year-old man still living at home with his parents. He became the first trooper to be killed in the line of duty in the new, reorganized Indiana State Police Department. As though to add gravity to the moment, Feeney came immediately to Paris. Leach's explanation seems hurried and impromptu: Teague moved too fast; Teague didn't see what was coming. This was all based on an immediate investigation, which disclosed that Teague had been killed by a bullet fired by Lieutenant Butler. During the horror of that afternoon, Leach appeared detached, almost uninterested as Lieutenant Butler cried piteously, "My God, he was my friend. I killed him."

In his cold demeanor that day, Leach did one crucial thing: he withheld Butler's name from the press. It was possibly the first time that Leach used true discretion in making public statements. It was part of his approach to his job, as Leach always protected his men from press coverage even as he put himself out there for the slings and arrows of public opinion. Nonetheless, Lieutenant Butler, in his hysteria, told reporters, "I'm the man."

A circus followed. The two molls picked up with Shouse made a display of themselves in the papers. One, who gave the name Ruth Spencer, offered to pose in a bathing suit, "if you'll bring the suit." The feature was a disgrace. The other woman called herself Francis Colins. Her real name seemed to be Frances Brehman. She was the wife, presumably, of the escaped associate Bremen aka Brehman.

Eugene Teague was buried for Christmas, the funeral paid for by the State of Indiana under orders of Governor McNutt. The trooper's untimely death caused a change in the atmosphere in the Statehouse. The outrage over Teague's death trumped the partisan wars.[42] Before putting these matters to an end, Matt Leach had one more chance to vindicate his political party.

On January 6th, 1934, Walter Detrich was captured in Chicago in a sensational shootout while hanging out with his new gang, run by Theodore "Handsome Jack" Klutas, at 619 South 24th Avenue in Bellwood, Illinois. Detrich had been the foreman of the Michigan City shirt shop and was a central figure in the escape. After the inmates' collective breakout, Detrich left them in favor of forging more anonymous inner-city connections. Jack Klutas was a former University of Illinois student who led a $500,000 gang of kidnappers, known as the "College Kidnappers," that snatched members of the underworld. The shootout with police resulted in Klutas's death and the arrest of Detrich. Two other mobsters were picked up in the raid, Earl McMahon and Adolph Anzone. Police suspected that the gang was planning to kidnap a gambler named James Hackett.

Upon hearing of Detrich's arrest, Matt Leach went straight to Chicago, where the Michigan City escape engineer was being held. Leach could be assured of department courtesy in Chicago; he knew he could avoid the jurisdictional cockfights reminiscent of Ohio. In confidence, Leach prepared to bring the latest of the Michigan City escapees to the Marion County Jail. Leach's mission was to groom Detrich to reveal the unknown aspects of the Michigan City escape in a way that would vindicate the McNutt administration.

On January 30th, Leach interviewed Detrich in the Statehouse. For the occasion, Leach invited news reporters and strongly suggested they take Detrich's statement. The mock interrogation was a stage for the many roles that Leach had to play. Leach established Detrich's key role as the man in charge of the Gordon East Coast Shirt Factory. Leach steered the interrogation. It was worded to cast blame away from McNutt and onto the previous warden, Walter Daly.

Detrich agreed to these revisions. In return, he got to broadcast some of the abuses that were, in his words, executed by Claudy. "We would wake up in the hole kicked and bruised with lumps over [our] body and usually a few ribs broken." That prompted Leach to say, "That verifies what I believe—that the state prison, under the old officials, who had got in a rut, was fifty years behind the times."

Detrich avoided naming McNutt's appointees in favor of concentrating of Claudy and Daly, and their mismanagement of the prison. "When I first went to work [in the shirt factory], I saw I could get anything I wanted to in there," stated Detrich.

"Then they could have shipped an elephant in there to you?" asked Leach.

"Yes, if they got a box big enough," Detrich said with smug compliance.

The escaped convict's confession detailed the elements of the escape. His version was accepted at face value without addressing the rumors that there were bribed officials behind the escape. In addition to casting blame on the "Deputy Warden," who was "responsible for the enforcement of rules and conduct inside the wall, and it is his duty to see in what manner merchandise and supplies are shipped in," Detrich got his shots:

> Had all such supplies been thoroughly unpacked and inspected by a guard or officer it would have been impossible for us to have secured the guns in this matter. There were three .38 automatic caliber pistols and three extra clips for each gun in this box. I could have had a ton of machine guns shipped in like manner had I have been so minded. The system is old and antiquated, and it is easily possible for the convicts to have many things in their possession, which is forbidden them by regulations.
>
> It was also the custom and practice of the Assistant Warden, while I was admitted to that institution, to brutally punish prisoners for infractions of various rules. They would be knocked unconscious, kicked and bruised and perhaps several ribs fractured and thrown into a dark hole for several days.
>
> Harry Pierpont handled all outside negotiations for this break. I am not sure but I believe that John Dillinger furnished the guns and had them shipped to us.[43]

Detrich provided cursory details and peripheral accents to what was already known about the Michigan City escape. There was a sense that to Detrich, this was personal. Despite the vengeful tone of the statement, Leach encouraged the news coverage to editorialize with a celebration over the "confession." Matt Leach wanted to spread the good tidings, the sense that Indiana had cleaned its own house without help from its nosy neighbors. In the Statehouse, there was gloating victory over Ohio and a belief that Chicago's Dillinger Squad was diminutive as compared to the cops from Indianapolis.

Soon Huntington would leave the Dillinger investigation. His role had come to an end and he would go on to gumshoe other cases. He had been a strong source of intelligence and information. The bitter truth was that Leach had depended from the start on Huntington's work.

The Pinkerton had a simple ethic in developing leads and nourishing informants. He even submitted his expense accounts in plain language, asking for seventy-five cents for "supper," rather than padding a bill with entitlements for a fancy "dinner."[44] Sadly, for law enforcement, the period between Teague's untimely death and the capture of Walter Detrich marked the last active involvement that Huntington had with

Dillinger. This was a blow to the investigation. Huntington, a taciturn man, knew more than he cared to admit. His motto seemed to be that if it wouldn't help the disposition of a case, don't bother bringing it up. This was part of Huntington's creed.

The common theme of the Dillinger campaign was that too often, crucial pieces of information were withheld while the wild and stupid leads went out to the press. The treatment handed to Walter Detrich after his arrest, and the scripted explanation of the Michigan City escape, left out a crucial meeting between Harry Pierpont, an underworld visitor, and Claudy. Huntington remained silent on it, even though the Pinkerton administrative offices had a copy of a telegram that Kokomo businessman Omar Brown had sent to Lena Pierpont that attested to the fact.

Brown was a fixer who worked closely with Pearl Elliott. Huntington had wanted to issue him a warrant but held back on going after the associates in Kokomo. Brown was known to masquerade as a legitimate businessman or sheriff, or whatever the occasion demanded, to make things work for the gang members. Brown had tried to secure a parole for Harry back in July of 1933. On one occasion, Brown met with Claudy privately. It was never revealed whether any gratuities were exchanged between the deputy warden and the fixer from Kokomo. But they had ample opportunity to exchange an envelope. That was a possibility that was hushed up in the investigations. The letters exchanged between Brown and Pierpont's mother, Lena, broadly hint of an exchange of something besides good will:

> Mrs. Pierpont.
>
> ...I visited Harry yesterday. I was permitted a private interview. Mr. Claudy was very fine to Harry and myself. You may know I will keep you informed.
>
> Sincerely, Omar F. Brown, Kokomo.

Subsequent letters to Mrs. Pierpont affirmed that Harry's parole application was a bust. Interestingly, Brown had asked a legionnaire, a Mr. Sexton, to speak to Governor McNutt about Pierpont and the possibility of a temporary parole. From this example and from others, it is obvious that the Pinkertons had had the back story on Dillinger and his gang since the immediate aftermath of the escape.[45]

The Detrich press conference was a public spectacle and a private joke. McNutt had from the beginning insisted, "They didn't shoot their way out. They bought their way out." Despite the superficiality of Detrich's remarks, the interview was a high point for Matt Leach. The cronies who were leeching off him expressed gratitude for this crucial goal point. In committing both Detrich and Copeland to Michigan City, Matt Leach had kept his home state in charge of the massive Dillinger hunt. This was the last time that Leach

Matt Leach, shown here ca. 1933, made it a habit to smile for photographs (courtesy James Stack).

won for Indiana. He couldn't have known that to the victor would go betrayal, duplicity and ruin.

CHAPTER 7

Double-Crossing Dirty Rat

When we got out of there, Matt Leach and all of his new organization started putting out stories—we were morons, rappers and everything else.—Harry Pierpont, conversation with Mary Kinder

It was quiet in the aftermath of the deaths of Sergeant William Shanley of Chicago and Indiana motorcycle trooper Eugene Teague. There was a period of relative inactivity for the members of the Terror Gang as they vacationed in Daytona, Florida. Huntington had known of the planned trip to the Sunshine State through admissions of an informant known to him as Heck Trimby. Despite law enforcement's prior knowledge of the Florida hiatus, nothing came through to pinpoint the gang's exact location, and they enjoyed themselves there without interruption. Dillinger lived in a large Daytona house in the company of his blood brothers, the insular members of the Terror Gang and their molls.

All of that changed on January 15th, 1934. From that day forward, Dillinger was a fugitive wanted for a cop killing in the commission of the theft of $20,000 from the First National Bank of East Chicago. The first reports stated that John Dillinger was positively identified, along with John Hamilton, a Michigan City escapee and Dillinger's old jailhouse friend. Hamilton was shot during the robbery. His substandard bulletproof vest failed to protect him.

While the controversy still rages over whether Dillinger actually shot and mortally wounded the officer, one thing is sure. The robbery bore Dillinger's trademark greeting, "This is a stickup." It also featured the marker of the Dillinger Gang's strategy of taking hostages out of the bank for protection from the bullets of police and armed citizens. During this bank job, the robbers exited the building with the vice president,

Walter Spencer, being dragged along as a hostage. East Chicago P.O. William Patrick O'Malley was the first policeman to answer the bank's burglar alarm. The robber identified as Dillinger shot at O'Malley while the officer rushed toward the building as Dillinger exited. Spencer, a hostage and future witness with the best view of the shooting, identified Dillinger as O'Malley's killer.

After the holdup, Matt Leach ordered eight state troopers who were stationed in the Tremont barracks to cover the roads in search of the killers. Tremont was the closest location—and it was sixteen miles away. As though in tandem, the East Chicago police sent officers out to follow the robbers' tracks.[1]

Dillinger, slipping away unseen, brought Hamilton to Chicago, where he was nursed in the home of a relative of Art "Fish" Johnson, a local fence. There, Hamilton clung to life as his cronies drove in separate cars out west.

Tucson was the end of the line for the fugitives of the Terror Gang. They were discovered there by a handful of police officers. It was a fantastic series of arrests, with newspapers nationwide covering the story with front-page verve and typeset. The arrests were called random and remarkable. The reality is that there was deep intelligence charting the gang's movements prior to arriving there.

The gang was tracked to Tucson by Federal Department of Justice agents who were on the case without public knowledge of their activities. The Department of Justice monitored mail that Russell Clark's extended family member Naomi Hooten was sending to the gang. Hooten was Clark's Hamilton, Ohio, connection and the woman who had arranged for the gang's hideout there after the Michigan City escape.

Naomi Hooten left Hamilton after Leach's failed raid on the house there. She moved to Phoenix, Arizona. In Hamilton, Chief of Police John C. Calhoun and Postmaster Walter Bruning arranged with federal officials to intercept mail postmarked Phoenix, Arizona, coming to the old Hamilton address. They found that Hooten was writing to Pierpont and Dillinger just as they were arriving in Tucson. That led federal agents to the conclusion that the Dillinger gang was hiding in Tucson. They notified Chief of Police C. A. Wollard of the Tucson police that the gang was going to be there. While firemen and salesmen were two factions bearing witness to the gang's presence, the police already had the information. Federal agents then went to Hamilton to compliment Calhoun and Bruning for their detective work.[2]

On January 21st, 1934, Clark, Makley and Opal Long stayed in the Hotel Congress, at 311 East Congress, while they waited for the availability of the place they'd rented at 927 North 2nd Avenue. They went out that night to Charlie Chase's Nightclub, where Clark, in violation of the gang's unwritten rule, talked to outsiders. A couple of salesmen were acting tough. To put them in their place, Clark offered to show them his machine guns and bulletproof vests.

The beginning of the end of the Terror Gang happened by chance the next morning, on January 22nd. A fire broke out in the building and the flames and smoke quickly spread to the third floor. An aerial ladder was placed on the third-story ledge for third-floor occupants to escape. Later, in the firehouse, the firemen, William Benedict and Kenneth Pender, recognized the fire victims in a copy of *True Detective* magazine. They told Deputy Sheriff Maurice Guiney, who relayed the information to the sheriff's office. There a whispered exchange told him that the Tucson police knew the gang was in Tucson.

Aside from the earlier intelligence garnered by Huntington that the gang was going to Tucson, a foot officer named Harry Hugh Lesley had received a tip from several salesmen that some "questionable characters" were in town.[3]

The arrests occurred almost simultaneously on the afternoon of January 25th, 1934. Charles Makley, traveling alone but spending the day with a singer in Tucson, was arrested by Chester W. Sherman, Mark L. Robbins, Frank Eyman, Kenneth A. Mullaney, Dallas S. Ford, and Captain Jay D. Smith while shopping for a radio in a small storefront called the Grabbe Electric Company, on Congress Street. His Studebaker sedan was parked outside with its Florida license plates. Makley, who was also staying in the house at 927 North 2nd Avenue, was charged as a "fugitive from justice." The entertainer whom Makley hoped to keep company with, who gave the name May or Marge Miller, was arrested for possession of a machine gun. Once the police determined that she was just a local with no affinity to the underworld or machine guns in general, she was released from custody and the charges against her were dropped.

John Dillinger and Evelyn Frechette were also peacefully arrested.

They had left an address at 1304 E. Fifth Avenue, rented for use by Dillinger, Evelyn, Pierpont and Mary, to see Russell Clark at a rented house at 927 North 2nd Avenue. The rooms on East Fifth Avenue would never be occupied. Dillinger and Frechette were only there for a few hours before being arrested.

After getting out of their car, as they walked toward their house, officers Milo "Swede" W. Walker, Kenneth Mullaney and Detective James C. Herron accosted them. Dillinger threw up his hands. It was his pattern to do so when arrest seemed imminent.

Dillinger later gave some of the officers some additional information on the contents of the house at 927 North Second Avenue: "You were awfully lucky. But you worked it right. Where you were smart was getting one of us at a time. If you had gone in that house when Clark and Makley were both there, it would have been too bad. There were guns in the back room. It would have been a fight. Some of us might have been shot, but some of you would have been shot, too."

Dillinger, the fabled Mr. Davies of 927 North Second Avenue, continued to give his name as "J. C. Davies." He would not admit his identity until fingerprinting revealed that he was Dillinger. Evelyn Frechette, who gave her name as "Ann Martin," was carrying significantly less money than her friend Mary Kinder; Evelyn carried $67.97 to Mary's $3,118.95. Evelyn was "held for the U.S. Government," an allusion to her status as an American Indian. Dillinger was charged as a "fugitive from justice." Captain Ben West later said, "I do not claim the glory of catching Dillinger, but I did search him when he was being booked and found about $6,500 in his pockets. He turned to me and said that I would be foolish if I turned in that money, but I did."

In their first days in Tucson, Dillinger, Pierpont, Kinder and Frechette had been staying in the Arizona Tourist Court located at 1749 S. 6th Avenue. They also are thought to have stayed at the Close Inn Motel at 1521 South 6th Avenue. It was in this vicinity that Pierpont and Mary Kinder were arrested, on that street, near the intersection of South 6th and 18th. Here Pierpont stopped Tucson officers Earl "Mickey" Nolan and Frank Eyman. Pierpont had a protocol for when he thought he was being followed by police: he would stop a police officer at a call box and say he was being followed. It was a strategy that usually broke up the police tail.

On this afternoon, Pierpont followed this procedure and told the officers that he was nervous, new in town, and afraid that someone was following him. He was driving his new 1934 Buick with Florida plates, with a radio. He gave his name as "J. C. Evans" and introduced Mary Kinder as his wife. Walker and Nolan recalled this after the arrests of Makley and Clark. They especially remembered the Florida plates, which were the same as Makley had. Now Captain Jay Smith accompanied Frank Eyman and Earl C. "Mickey" Nolan as they headed out to the location where Pierpont had told the officers he was staying. They spotted the car at the intersection of South 6th and 19th, while stopped for a light in their Buick sedan.

The officers stopped the Buick and suggested to Pierpont that he needed a visitor sticker to be driving in Tucson; that to avoid police harassment, they should make a quick trip to the police station. Frank Eyman got into Pierpont's car. Having figuratively dug his own grave the previous afternoon by making himself known to the officers, Pierpont now had to follow the officer's directions to the stationhouse. Eyman's ruse prevented him from reverting to a Dillinger-type escape. Pierpont later said, "I had my gun in my lap when [Eyman] got into the car and could have used it at any time. But [he] outsmarted me."

When Pierpont arrived at the police station, he saw the machine guns and bullet-proof vests of his friends. His reflexes went into action as he went for his .38 Super in his shoulder holster. Mickey Nolan, Frank Eyman and Jay Smith got the gun away from him. They then found a second gun in Pierpont's sock. It was the gun belonging to Sheriff Sarber. Officer Harry E. Foley noticed that Pierpont was trying to eat a piece of paper. Foley stuck his finger in Pierpont's mouth. Pierpont bit Officer Foley but the paper was retrieved.

The officers charged Pierpont with "resisting an officer." Although the trigger man did drive willingly to the stationhouse with officers Earl C. Nolen and Frank Eyman and Captain Jay Smith, he was later brought down in a scuffle when he realized he'd been led into a trap.

Clark and Opal Long also did not submit to arrest peacefully. They were accosted inside the apartment at 927 North 2nd by officers Chet Sherman, Eyman, Mullaney, Mark L. Robbins and Dallas S. Ford. Chet Sherman carried a letter up to the house, with the idea that he would act as a messenger. This plan failed immediately when Sherman, not knowing that Clark was using the alias "Art Long," asked for Russell Clark. Clark charged to the door, and Sherman pulled out his .45 automatic. Clark and Sherman began to fight. Clark was trying to get a gun, which was said to have been stashed under a mattress. Opal Long, meanwhile, began attacking Sherman, as his backup team, composed of Kenneth Mullaney, Frank Eyman and Dallas Ford, tried to enter the apartment. She broke Ford's finger while trying to slam the door on the officers. Ford hit Clark over his head with his own .38 revolver. That, and an iron claw that was also used on Clark's head, managed to bring him down. Clark's head injuries were apparent throughout the Tucson court proceedings and jailhouse interviews.

Milo Walker later said of Opal Long, "She was his moll, she's a redheaded gal, and boy, just as tough as a boot. I've heard a lot of profanity in my time, and in fact I have a pretty fair vocabulary of cuss words. But, man, she was something else."[4]

For the duration of their residency in Tucson within the Pima County Jail system, the Dillinger gang split into factions based on whose entertainment value was the highest. Dillinger played the role of a loner, Makley an innocent bystander, Clark the wounded warrior in head bandages and dried blood. Pierpont won the prize for being the scariest clown. A pure outlaw, his ire was directed at Matt Leach. The captain fell onto Pierpont's radar the moment he entered Tucson.

For the arriving Midwesterners, accustomed to bleak winter weather, Tucson was paradise in late January. The light skies and cactus dotting the landscape lent a vacation atmosphere to these grim proceedings. The weather was warm enough for spring coats. A relaxed attitude prevailed in this region of tropical plantings, terracotta houses and Westerners, some of whom wore large Stetson hats.

Matt Leach, who never relaxed, arrived in a caravan. The entourage included the ISP officers Gene Ryan, Vernon Shields, Donald Winn, Harvey Hire and Marie Grott, whom the press referred to as "Miss Grott." The policewoman was a clerk and fingerprint expert for the Indiana criminal bureau who would serve as Mary Kinder's de facto matron. Also on the junket was William "Tubby" Toms, a news reporter. Toms was a Leach supporter who bolstered the captain at every opportunity through the *Indianapolis News*. Leach arrived at the same time as his Chicago allies, Sergeant Reynolds and Captain Stege.[5]

Opal "Bernice Clark" Long, shown here under guard in June 1934, served a six-month term for harboring the Dillinger gang.

Leach soon learned that his position as a representative of Indiana and Ohio was compromised. Two of his Indiana-based enemies had gotten there before him. Determined and aggressive, they were Robert G. Estill, a Lake County prosecutor, and Nicholas Makar, the East Chicago chief of police. Flanking them were Carroll O. Holley, chief

Matt Leach and members of his entourage arrive in Tucson, Arizona, January 1934.
Left to right: State Police Officer Gene Ryan, unidentified, Captain Leach, Detective
Harvey Hire, fingerprint expert Marie Grott, Detective Vernon Shields and State
Police Officer Donald Winn.

deputy of Lake County and the nephew of Sheriff Lillian Holley, and
Hobart Wilgus, the East Chicago patrol officer who was a witness to the
killing of Officer O'Malley.

Robert Estill had travelled by plane.[6] He continued to use the air
age to his advantage when, within days of arrival, he departed from Tucson by air with Dillinger his prisoner. After going to the Pima County
court, Estill, along with Chief Makar, demanded that Dillinger be extradited to Indiana's Lake County. When Leach arrived, he became enraged
at the idea that Dillinger would go to a small county jail in Lake County
rather than a maximum-security prison to await trial. He got into a
shouting match with Makar. The two were nose-to-nose until somebody
pulled them apart. Barring the fact that it was all politics with each man
carrying out his orders, it was an omen. Maker had brought several of

his officers, barely more than thugs themselves, from the East Chicago and Indiana Harbor police force to Tucson, and it was going to get ugly.

Leach was an emissary of McNutt but his briefcase contained only warrants. In this chilling paper chase, Estill rushed Indiana Harbor captain Ed Knight to Indianapolis to get extradition papers. Knight found Wayne Coy, McNutt's secretary, and asked him to sign Estill's documents.

Coy knew that McNutt was backing Leach against Estill's strategy. Coy, a shrewd state official, knew who was boss, and that boss was the governor. He drafted a second set of extradition papers, which named Leach as the state's agent. Not to be put down so easily, Estill accused McNutt of preventing Lake County from getting Dillinger. His appeal was emotional in the wake of the murder of Officer O'Malley. Ultimately, Lake County won the battle of jurisdiction.

The victorious Estill submitted the required paperwork to prosecutor Clarence Houston. It was Dillinger's indictment for first-degree murder of Sergeant O'Malley "in perpetration of a robbery." The indictment named both John Dillinger and John Hamilton—the latter a Dillinger mob member generally ignored by Leach. Then Estill started making his own broad statements to the press. "We will make a fight all the way to bring Dillinger back to Indiana for trial. We are not so much interested in the others as we are in him, hence we waited only long enough to get the extradition papers for Dillinger."[7]

Leach's headaches escalated when he met with officers from Racine, Wisconsin. Because the Terror Gang had conducted their hall-

Dillinger, photographed in Tucson, January 1934.

mark bank robbery in Racine, they were candidates for extradition to Wisconsin.

Racine had been feuding with Leach since December of 1933, when Leslie "Big" Homer was arrested and held as a suspect. A fight had ensued when Leach tried to take Homer to Indiana as a parole violator and lost when Wisconsin got him.

Leach now had to face the same people from Wisconsin all over again. This time the issue was the remaining Racine robbers. Leach objected over Wisconsin's preemptive telegraph, which said they would pay a $2,000 reward for the Terror Gang. He predicted that the large amount would prejudice Tucson into handing the robbers over to the highest bidder.

It seemed for a time that everybody was in favor of Wisconsin— including Pierpont, Makley, Clark and Dillinger. During the preliminary hearing, defense attorney John Van Buskirk presented the waivers of extradition and demanded that the gang go to Wisconsin. Leach, deputized on behalf of Ohio as well as Indiana, wanted them for the death penalty. Capital punishment was nonexistent in Wisconsin. That was a moot point anyway, as no deaths had occurred during the Racine holdup.

The arresting officers were at first sympathetic to Wisconsin. The brave policemen, as well as Sheriff John Belton, stamped Leach with the mark of the double-crosser. The reasoning involved the reward. If the gang went to Wisconsin, their arresting officers would stand to split the $2,000. This was the Depression, and money was the secret word. Indiana was only offering $100 each. To prevent a cash prize from thwarting justice, Leach called McNutt. The Indiana governor called Arizona governor Benjamin Moeur, who ordered that Wisconsin be left out of the extradition proceedings.[8]

Despite the newspaper reports that money was the reason behind the arresting officers' hostility to Leach, their statements reflected that it was more a matter of Leach's attitude. "His conduct was ungentlemanly and undiplomatic," Sergeant Eyman said.

Stan Benjamin, a retired Tucson police officer who interviewed the arresting officers decades later, believed that money had never been important to the men who captured the gang members: "Not one officer mentioned anything about reward money. None of the officers I talked to ever indicated they were disappointed that they did not get any reward, or that they ever expected any reward money."[9]

Sergeant Eyman and Captain Sherman, whose angry feelings toward Leach were reported in the papers, later retracted and said their inflammatory statements had been distorted. What they said amounted to libel, with Eyman saying Leach was drunk. The story, accompanied by unpublished artists' caricatures of Leach, reported that Leach was intoxicated the "whole time he was in Tucson."

Sherman and Eyman later clarified their story, saying, "Although we did not see Leach drunk at any time, whenever we wanted him we found him in bed or in a

Leach generated negative press in Tucson. Here, a caricature of Leach was superimposed onto an anonymous photograph in January 1934.

saloon. In our county we use different methods. We do not think Indiana sent [in Leach] a fit representative to work in harmony with our people and our way of doing things. With Prosecutor Estill, however, everything was different. We gave him our fullest cooperation. Our only difficulty was in obtaining the aid of Leach."[10]

On another occasion Sherman said, "If Captain Leach said that we tried to make a deal with Wisconsin authorities to hand over the Dillinger gang for a larger reward than would be paid by Indiana, he is a liar. We intended all the time to send Dillinger to Indiana and Pierpont to Ohio."

Weeks later, while traveling to Indiana, Sherman and Eyman denied

Standing, left to right: Det. Dallas Ford, Chief of Police C. A. "Gus" Wollard, Sgt. Harry Foley, Officer Frank Eyman, Capt. Jay Smith, Officer Chet Sherman, Det. James Herron. *Kneeling, left to right*: Officer Milo "Swede" Walker, Kenneth Mullaney, and Officer Earl "Mickey" Nolan. The Tucson arresting officers had feelings of ill will against Leach for his actions in Tucson. Photograph dated January 1934.

these statements, claiming they had no allegiance to Estill. Eventually the state of Ohio paid a $3,000 reward, which was split between Chief Wollard and the arresting officers.[11]

The arresting officers were soft on Leach compared to Pierpont's reaction to the lawman. When Matt Leach first walked into the Pima County Jail and surveyed the outlaws, Pierpont went into hysterics: "You're the one who arrested my mother in Terre Haute.... I should have killed you when I had the chance."

Pierpont, for all his backstreet eloquence, wasn't straight on the facts regarding the arrest of his family members in October. As far back as October 23rd, the prosecuting attorney of Allan County, Ernest M. Bodkin, had secretly filed warrants against Dillinger, Pierpont, Copeland,

Makley, Shouse, Hamilton and Clark. On that day, Ohio police arrested Fred Pierpont, Harry's brother. They called in Huntington to interview Fred. Pierpont's brother had dropped useless tidbits such as the Hamilton hideout, which was by then defunct. Huntington wanted to keep Fred's conversation quiet, "due to the newspapers giving out every bit of information they get." So stated Huntington's report, with its implication that this information was to be kept out of the hands of Matt Leach.

One thing Fred Pierpont had revealed was that Omar Brown, the Kokomo businessman who had visited Claudy in Michigan City, had also visited Dillinger in the Allen County Jail. Brown had identified himself to Sheriff Sarber as a former sheriff of Howard County. On October 11th, the day before the escape, Brown visited Fred Pierpont's home. There Brown briefed the Terror Gang on the layout of Sarber's facility.[12]

While Pierpont railed against Leach for arresting his mother, he did not know that Matt had made personal revelations to the *Indianapolis Times* writer Basil Gallagher about his common-law wife, Mary Kinder, which were published right after the Tucson arrests. For the first time, Matt had revealed Mary Kinder's name to the papers. She was Mary Kinder, the "Queen of the Gun Molls," and "master strategist of terrorists." As though to underline his talking points, Gallagher published the fact that Mary was connected by family relation to several men who were imprisoned. Her husband, Dale Kinder; her brother, Earl "The Kid" Northern; her brother, Charles "Chuck" Northern, and her sister, Margaret Behren's husband, were serving time or had served time recently in state prison. For the press, Leach outlined Mary's career "from the time she joined the Dillinger mob, following the outbreak of ten convicts from the Indiana state prison, to her capture in Tucson, Arizona."[13]

It looked like the queen of the gun molls was becoming an honest woman and heading to the altar. For one torrid week in January, she tried to get married to Pierpont. The gunman had declared his love for Mary when he realized that his arrest marked the end of their relationship. He must have known that only a wife with civil papers would be allowed to visit him once he was held on capital murder charges. On January 29th Pierpont applied for a marriage license by "any regularly licensed or ordained minister, judge or justice of the peace." Justice Bud-long reviewed the request but blew Pierpont off, stating that Mary was already married to Dale Kinder. This was not true. Mary Kinder had been divorced seven months earlier in June of 1933. Pierpont was denied the chance to get married to his loyal sweetheart. Of course, the couple blamed Matt Leach for not allowing the marriage to take place. He most likely had nothing to do with it.[14]

Dillinger, never as melodramatic as Pierpont, needled the Tucson police and offered them money to help him get to Wisconsin. He told Sheriff John Belton that he had $100,000 hidden and could get his hands on it. Then he made an offer to pay the Tucson police $5,000 if they would get him to Wisconsin and away from the death penalty.

In spite of his best efforts, it began to look as though Ohio was going to get Pierpont, Makley and Clark. Botkin conferred with McNutt on extradition to Ohio for the three, as well as Shouse and Copeland. Leach told the papers that the Ohio prosecutors were confident of a murder conviction of the five and had eyewitnesses to the attack.[15]

Makley's mug shot had been sent in the days after the attack by the Pinkertons to Deputy Sheriff Don Sarber, the son of Jess Sarber, to be identified by Mrs. Sarber and the deputy who witnessed the attack. They positively identified Makley as having been inside the jail at the time of the murder of Sheriff Sarber.

The identification of Charles Makley as having been inside the jail, rather than Harry Copeland, matched up with a profile developed on Copeland by Forrest Huntington. The investigator remembered Shaw's feeling that Copeland was "yellow" and would do whatever he could to avoid being in the forefront of a robbery. Shaw believed that Copeland had turned and run away from him on the day he was arrested.[16]

Soon it was settled. Governor Moeur ruled that Ohio should get Pier-pont, Makley and Clark. Indiana should get Dillinger for the East Chicago bank job, which included capital murder in the death of Officer O'Malley.[17]

Al Feeney authorized Leach to take control of the Ohio defendants. Estill was given Dillinger, whom he removed from the Pima County Jail, bound for a regular American Airways plane to Chicago. Makar shared the plane with Dillinger, along with Deputy Sheriff Carroll O. Holley of Lake County. Caught by surprise and unwilling to return to East Chicago, Dillinger had put up a fight.

Sheriff John Belton (*right*) directs the guards around the Pima County Jail in Tucson after the arrest of the Dillinger Gang in January 1934. Capt. Ben West (*fourth from left, wearing glasses*) helped subdue Pierpont in the stationhouse. Sgt. Mark Robbins stands in the back, second from right, next to Belton. Capt. C. A. "Gus" Wollard stands third from right.

The outlaw wasn't the only one who was surprised by Estill's move. Leach had been visiting the local Elks club while the drama was taking place. Leach later accused Estill of getting Dillinger into an airplane and leaving Leach behind to chaperone the rest of the Dillinger gang.[18]

While all this was occurring, the arresting officers gave a statement through Mark Robbins, a fingerprint expert: "I can't understand [the] idea that the police department, the fellows who risked their lives to go out and get these fellows, should have no voice of any kind in the disposition of the men."[19]

Mary Kinder was taken to Indianapolis pending a grand jury investigation into her role in the Michigan City escape. Leach escorted Pierpont, Clark and Makley to the train depot. Evelyn Frechette, still going

John Dillinger (*wearing handcuffs*) was rushed out of Tucson to his Indiana extradiction on January 30, 1934. Lake County prosecutor Robert Estill (*left*) took charge of Dillinger. Carroll Holley (*2nd from left*) and E. Chicago Chief Nicholas Makar (*right, holding Dillinger's arm*) surround the outlaw (John Binder Collection).

as Ann Martin, and Opal Long as Mrs. Bernice Clark, both left town quietly by rail after being released.[20]

At the station, Leach handed the arresting officers a one-hundred-dollar bill each. That was the last indignity for them. Sherman and Eyman gave Leach a blue, off-color, go-f-yourself salute. Leach's recollection of the event was painful. "They called me such names as I almost pulled my gun on them. No man ever called me such things in all my life. It was more than any man could endure." Leach later whitewashed the exchange by saying, "Two Tucson police officers demanded to be brought back east with the prisoners." Leach claimed in hindsight that he assumed they would be asking the state of Indiana to pay their expenses, and refused.[21]

The three Terror Gang members were bound for Chicago's LaSalle Street station, where Captain John Stege would lead a convoy of police escorts. Mary Kinder was put on the train with the men. When told she could not ride with Pierpont, she lost her composure. "Why can't I ride with him?" she pleaded. "Captain Leach told me I could." But Leach had seated himself in a separate car with Attorney General Philip Lutz, Jr., and Deputy Attorney General Ed Barce. Both were Leach's allies and at this juncture, they all sat together. So Mary was forced away from Pierpont at a moment when neither expected to be separated. In deep sadness, Mary joined her matron, fingerprint expert Marie Grott. The officer somehow subverted her usual docile appearance for the job. Also sharing the train with Mary was Detective Harvey Hire.

Mary was taken from the train in Kansas City, where she was put into a separate train for Indianapolis. The Terror Gang went to Chicago. As they separated, the doomed couple raged at Leach. During a prison visit some time later, Pierpont reminded Mary of all that Leach had taken away from them: "He wouldn't let us be married in Tucson, would he honey? If it hadn't been for him, we would have been married."[22]

DILLINGER'S MEN IN PRISON AGAIN

Three Face Grilling by Ohio Authorities in Sheriff Murder Case.

PUT IN SOLITARY CELLS

Massed Guard Escorts Gang Members on Last Lap From Arizona.

BY WILLIAM L. TOMS,
The News Staff Correspondent.

MICHIGAN CITY, Ind., February 1.—Guarded relentlessly by the most formidable array of Chicago and Indiana state police ever assembled, Harry Pierpont, Charles Makley and Russell Clark, members of the notorious Dillinger gang, were back in the Indiana State Prison here this afternoon after a fast trip from Chicago.

On their arrival the three immediately were placed in solitary confinement in what is known as "the hole" of the prison from which they escaped September 26.

The prisoners, as well as the Indiana state police who had brought them back from Tucson, Ariz., scene of their sensational capture last week, were weary from the long ride.

Pierpont, Makley and Clark left Tucson for Michigan City. They stood trial in Lima, Ohio. Headline dated January 1934 (Bill Helmer Collection).

CHAPTER 8

East Chicago Rising

I am "on the spot" every minute of the day and night and it is not much fun knowing that any minute may be your last. If that's playing politics, Estill can make the most of it.—Matt Leach, statement to press

The feud between Estill and Leach, festering for months, had come to a head in Tucson. Leach would never again have an exclusive on Dillinger. The moment Indiana got extradition of him, the Lake County prosecutor took over. This was a departure from the fates of Shaw, Mohler, Goldstein and Copeland, all of whom were remanded to Michigan City. Even while his fellow gang members, Pierpont, Clark and Makley, were being thrown into the bowels of Michigan City, Dillinger's Indiana extradition took him to Lake County. He was sent to Crown Point, Indiana, under the order of Judge William J. Murray of the Circuit Court.

Leach took charge of the convoy that escorted the three defunct Terror Gang members from the train, where officers from the LaSalle street station, under Captain Stege, escorted them to Michigan City. Stege and Sergeant Reynolds of the Dillinger Squad accompanied the three Terror Gang outlaws to Michigan City. Reynolds, who had already killed thirteen outlaws, molded himself from a lawless prototype. As such, the lawman was a match for Pierpont, Makley and Clark. Driving along the Chicago South Side Boulevard, they left LaSalle Street, crossed the Indiana/Illinois line and went directly to Michigan City.

Once the disenfranchised Terror Gang members entered the dreaded penitentiary, they met with an interrogation. Leach, Stege, and Reynolds, as well as Warden Kunkel, each took turns questioning the prisoners.[1] "Get it while you can" should have been the motto of their questioning. The Dillinger Squad and Leach were about to be pushed out. Tucson had given the Leach haters a chance to organize. Between January and February of 1934, Lake County and East Chicago took control of Dillinger.

With jurisdiction established, Chief Makar escorted Dillinger by plane to Lake County, along with Deputy Sheriff Carroll Holley, a cousin of the sheriff of the Crown Point County Jail, Lillian Holley.

Leach would not be silent:

> In my opinion there was absolutely no need for Estill and his squad to rush to Tucson by airplane. Dillinger would have been returned to Lake County along with the other fugitives, who arrived yesterday morning. I don't know who gave Estill the idea of making his spectacular flight and I do not know who paid the expenses.
>
> I do know, however, they could have been spared the time, trouble and expense and that Dillinger now would be in the same jail if they had stayed at home and tried not to have assumed the duties of state policemen.[2]

As though a polar shift had occurred, a new cast of public officials was about to enter the Dillinger realm. Louis Piquett, a night-school criminal lawyer, arrived in Crown Point. Lew Baker, the jailor, trusted his gut and refused to allow the gruff-looking man into the jail. In his demeanor, Piquett bore little resemblance to the nondescript lawyers usually assigned to defend Dillinger. Yet Piquett had a strong bearing as a criminal attorney. He talked the talk and thought the thoughts— qualities that made him a natural counterpart to Dillinger. His first act of jurisprudence was to introduce the alibi witness, an underworld character named Meyer Bogue. It was a weak strategy of alleging that Dillinger had been in Florida at the time of the East Chicago bank robbery and O'Malley's death.

Arthur O'Leary was Piquett's assistant who called himself an investigator. His job description was that of the modern paralegal, with some wheeling and dealing thrown into the mix. He introduced Dillinger to Meyer Bogue, the alibi witness sent in by Piquett.[3] All the while, money was being negotiated for Dillinger's escape—a release that would not involve a courtroom strategy but a bribe.

The sheriff there, Lillian Holley, had taken over the term of her husband, Roy Holley, who had been killed by a crazed gunman during his tenure as sheriff. Appointed in January of 1933, Lillian Holley was deemed "entitled to the office by the laws of precedent, particular deserving the high honor under the circumstances, and fully capable to undertake its duties through her wide experience as jail matron and the close touch she kept on its affairs through her husband's two years of service." In short, she was a competent administrator. Her reputation was about to be destroyed by merciless reporters questioning the abilities of a "lady sheriff."[4]

Heading the new order was Robert Estill. The man who had obtained the indictment charging Dillinger with the murder of Officer O'Malley, Estill had worked to become an attorney by pulling himself up by his bootstraps. Some biographical accounts claimed he had been a preacher, a Spanish interpreter, and a law student. His highest achievement to date had been the conviction and sentencing to life imprisonment of James "Fur" Sammons, a Chicago gangster. His de-

PRINCIPALS IN JAIL BREAK

GUARD TIGHTENED AROUND LIMA JAIL

Extra National Guardsmen on Duty in Ohio Following Dillinger Escape.

LIMA, O., March 3 (A.P.)—Immediately after they were informed of the escape of John Dillinger from jail at Crown Point, Ind., Allen county officials ordered extra precautions to guard Harry Pierpont, Charles Makley and Russell Clark, Dillinger henchmen, awaiting trial for first-degree murder here.

General Harold Bush, of the Ohio national guard, assigned by the state to help guard the three mobsters, ordered extra men to duty at once, saying he feared an effort would be made to free the men held here.

Pierpont, alleged "trigger man" in the killing of Sheriff Jesse Sarber in October in a jail road that resulted in the liberation of Dillinger while the gang leader was held for bank robbery, is to go on trial Tuesday.

Pierpont's attorneys, Charles Long and W. M. Fogarty, left early today for Crown Point to take a deposition from Dillinger for use in establishing an alibi for Pierpont. They were accompanied by E. M. Botkin, prosecutor, who planned to cross-examine Dillinger, and were on the road between here and Crown Point when word was received of Dillinger's escape.

Above—Profile and front views John Dillinger, gangster, in sensational escape from the Lake County Jail. He was held on charges murder, bank robbery and bandit in connection with the robbery the East Chicago First Nation Bank and was accused of oth bank robberies and crimes.

Below—Mrs. Lillian Holley, La county sheriff, in charge of the j from which Dillinger escaped. S had previously announced the j was a safe place for keeping t prisoner and that there was danger of his escape.

Sheriff Lillian Holley (*lower right*) was held accountable for Dillinger's Crown Point "Wooden Gun" escape. Headline dated March 3, 1934, newspaper not identified (Bill Helmer Collection).

tractors leaked an insinuation to the press that Sammons' quick commitment to prison under Estill was a favor granted to the local syndicate in getting Sammons out of the Gary/East Chicago area.[5]

Loyal to Lake County, Estill took his fight with Leach to a new level when he ran with Tucson arresting officer Frank Eyman's statements that Leach had been intoxicated in Tucson.[6] Estill was stacking the cards against Leach. The intoxication story was potent in this post–Prohibition incubation period when individual states were still working out the taxation of newly legalized beers and hard liquors, when control of liquor on a state-by-state basis was still big news.[7]

Estill must have lost sleep thinking that Leach would pull rank under McNutt and claim Dillinger. So, he stood with the drunk accusations and claimed Leach was intoxicated, and thus useless, at the critical juncture when the Terror Mob was close to the Wisconsin extradition. Specifically, Estill accused Leach of wanting to be the "big shot" and of almost bungling the extradition proceedings for Indiana. Although Estill reiterated his accusation many times, he never went into detail. If anyone had asked him to clarify the charge that Leach almost caused the Dillinger gang to go to Wisconsin, Estill would have been at a loss to explain. For a fleeting time, it looked as though Estill had the press under his own control. That was soon to change.

The Lake County prosecutor, in another move to counteract Leach's power, aligned himself with the police from East Chicago. They were a bloodless crew who had closed the iron door on Matt Leach back in the steamy August of 1933 when Leach was staging raids in their precinct and getting no department courtesy from them. There was a history of corruption and actual convictions of police officials and politicians within the East Chicago and Indiana Harbor region. These conditions had stunted Leach's earliest attempts to track Dillinger. It was a frustrating situation. Leach had found the East Chicago police force to be impenetrable.

Although Leach knew that Dillinger cronies lurked within the East Chicago police force, he was unable to prove it. He was most likely told to keep quiet about it by someone in the administration. His silence, however, did not make him privy to the private club. Leach remained an outsider. It must have raised his temper to see East Chicago police officer E. J. "Stretch" Conroy standing guard over the Crown Point County Jail.

Estill vowed to have Dillinger tried for the murder of Patrick O'Malley in the court of Judge William J. Murray shortly after February 15th. While claiming that Dillinger would receive no undue sympathy, Estill allowed himself to be photographed arm-in-arm with Dillinger during what could be called the outlaw's reception. Dillinger posed with the Lake County officials for newsreel footage. In hindsight, Estill's act of affection toward the outlaw was a mistake that occurred out of the excitement of the moment. One look at the faces of the others in the photograph confirms that spirits were flying high.

The streets around Crown Point were patrolled by East Chicago police officers such as E. J. Conroy, pictured here ca. 1920s (courtesy East Chicago Public Library).

During Dillinger's Crown Point reception, reporters fired questions at the outlaw. Some of his remarks were calculated, such as his attempt to throw police off the trail of his partner, John Hamilton: "Hamilton was shot four times, once in the stomach. We got up a bunch of money—$7,000—for his kids. I had it in a sack. They took it away from me in Tucson."

During the press conference, Dillinger slipped into curious, stream-of-consciousness retorts about Art McGinnis, of all people. Dillinger's vengeful mindset included his other nemesis. He repeated the chronic lie that he, not a reporter, had mailed Leach the fabled booklet, "How to Be a Detective," back in January. Dillinger didn't mention to reporters that his obsession with Leach also manifested itself in weird stalker mailings. The outlaw's last postcard to Leach had been postmarked Chicago and said, "Hey Cap! From Chicago—Ha Ha."[8]

Perhaps to avoid the hostile nation of Crown Point, Leach took off by automobile in the direction of the state penitentiary just days after

THE INDIANAPOLIS NEWS, THURSDAY, FEBRUARY 1, 1934.

DILLINGER "SNOOZING" IN PLANE; GROUP AT JAIL

The infamous Crown Point photograph showed Dillinger (*right*) on friendly terms
with county prosecutor Robert Estill (*center*). Sheriff Lillian Holley (*left*) looks on.
Her nephew Carroll (back, facing front) would succeed her in the sheriff's post (Bill
Helmer Collection).

the gang left Tucson. After interviewing Mary Kinder in the Indianapolis
County Jail, Leach set his sights on Ed Shouse. Wayne Coy, McNutt's
secretary in charge of penal affairs, and Ohio prosecutor Ernest Botkin
learned that Shouse was ready to make a confession from his cell in Michigan City. Shouse, no doubt, learned through the prison grapevine that
Pierpont, Makley and Clark had returned to the prison on February 1st.

Mr. Coy sent for Matt Leach to witness the confession. As he made
his customary haste, Leach asked Marie Grott to take a ride with him.
Her mother lived near Michigan City and it was a convenient way for
her to visit. It was two days after the policewoman and fingerprint expert
had escorted Mary Kinder to Indianapolis as her matron.

Miss Grott came dangerously close to losing her life. Leach was
driving when the car skidded off the road on State Road 29 near Hamlet.
The car rolled down an embankment, turned over, and stopped short
of the Kankakee River. Grott suffered a concussion and injuries to her
chest, and remained in critical condition for weeks afterward. Matt, a

driver who was known to be reckless, especially when in a hurry, suffered less severe injuries. More bruised was probably his ego. Because of his injuries, Leach didn't get to Michigan City in time to take Shouse's confession. The ousted Terror Gang member gave his statement to Mr. Coy instead.

This accident, from the skidding down an embankment to the fact that Leach was behind the wheel with a female passenger, was a mirror to the accident that would kill Leach and his wife twenty-one years later.

Marie Grott eventually recovered from her wounds. The aftermath of the accident was quiet. While it was quite a breaking point for Leach to be deprived of his interview with Shouse, he didn't suffer any repercussions for traveling with an unmarried woman. Marie Grott, similarly, suffered no reprisal and avoided serving as newsprint fodder. Somehow the fingerprint expert was not mocked by the press. Grott, however, received recognition by 1935 as a "good looking blonde" who took over as head of the Indiana Police Bureau of Criminal Identification.[9]

Although his proximity to Indianapolis gave him a vantage point from which to watch the outcome of the Mary Kinder grand jury investigation, Leach did not contribute anything that would force an indictment to stick. After her separation from Harry Pierpont on the train from Tucson in Kansas City, during which she had screamed at Leach, Kinder was taken to the Marion County Jail. Prosecutors there tried to piece together enough evidence to indict her. She was arraigned in criminal court before Judge Frank P. Baker on a charge of aiding and abetting the escape of the terror mob from the prison in Michigan City, specifically on September 26th. The family retainer, Jesse Levy, an attorney at law, appeared in court with Mary. Levy brought a motion to quash the indictment, which was heard by Judge Baker.

The grand jury had indicted Mary specifically for aiding the escape of Harry Pierpont, her "admitted lover." On the motion of Deputy Prosecutor Oscar Hagemeier, the charges were dropped. The judge then ordered Kinder to be held under a $25,000 bond for a new grand jury action under a statute making it an offense to aid a person to evade arrest after committing a felony. Kinder was held on $25,000 bond. Levy protested that the bond was prohibitive.

"I think society is better off with Mary Kinder in jail than out," said the judge.

"Is your honor deciding this question on the merits of the case before it is tried?" Levy challenged. Mary sat with her mother and sister and smiled when the judge said, "I want this bond to be prohibitive. If Mrs. Kinder got out of jail, she is dumb enough to run around the country with a bunch of machine gunners."

Judge Baker's court dropped the charges against Mary Kinder on February 15th. There simply wasn't enough evidence to indict her.[10] The same day that Kinder was released from the Marion County Jail, Harry Copeland was brought to Greencastle to answer charges of bank robbery there. In an about-face, officials returned Copeland to Michigan City because they felt that his presence in Greencastle presented a security risk. They scheduled him for a February 10th trip to Lima, along with Ed Shouse, to stand trial for the murder of Sheriff Sarber. Copeland had asked for a hearing before the governor to be allowed to remain in Indiana and answer for Greencastle.

Matt Leach commented that Copeland might never be arraigned for the Central National Bank. Copeland, who was supposed to "make a statement" on Greencastle, refused to answer questions posed to him. Copeland felt sure of staying in Indiana.[11]

John Dillinger escaped from the Crown Point County Jail before 9:15 a.m. on March 3rd. The curtain opened on Dillinger holding a wooden gun on Deputy Sheriff Sam Cahoon, a trustee who worked as a handyman. Dillinger ordered Cahoon to call Warden Lou Baker. Cahoon, who had heard the prisoners say there was going to be an escape, said, "John, I can't go through with this." Dillinger then told Cahoon to call Deputy Sheriff Ernest Blunk.

Blunk arrived in seconds and without a gun. He helped lock Cahoon into a cell. Blunk, who was later the subject of a grand jury investigation into the escape, changed his story post-escape and said that Dillinger had pointed a real gun at him.

Dillinger then told Blunk to call Warden Baker. Blunk complied with the order. Blunk walked into the center of a corridor, 75 to 80 feet long, leading to the rear of the county jail, which was the new section. Blunk stood in the middle of the hall and called to Baker, then Deputy Kenneth Houk, Deputy Marshall Huntley and Matt Brown. When Baker came out, Blunk was standing in the center of the hall, yelling, "Come back here a minute." Baker went into the corridor, saw Blunk, and followed him. Dillinger appeared from the left tier of the cells, put the wooden gun to Baker's back, and placed the warden in the cell with five or six trustees who were on the first floor at the time. That left Blunk alone with Dillinger, until Dillinger's partner in the escape, an African-American inmate named Herbert Youngblood, joined forces with him. They took two Thompson submachine guns from the jail office. Baker related that Dillinger said to him, "This is what I did it with," and waved the wooden gun in his face.

Other prisoners went with Dillinger and Blunk into the jail kitchen. With customary loyalty to his fellow thugs, Dillinger issued an invitation to the cellblock: "I'm going out. Anybody who wants to go with me, leave now." It sounded like "Party's over here!" to inmates Fred Bever, James Posey and Lester Caron. They left with Dillinger, and accompanied him to the jail kitchen, but soon decided that it wouldn't be worth it, for whatever reason. They ran back to their cells. In the kitchen, Dillinger, Blunk and Youngblood found three deputies and two women. They locked the deputies into cells and escorted the women into the basement laundry area.

Now that all the jail employees were locked up, the trio walked out the kitchen door and walked along the exterior southern wall to South East Street. There they entered a garage whose doors opened onto South East Street with its entrance directly around the block from the sheriff's quarters. There they found two county Nash cars that had no keys—the term "county car" being synonymous with "sheriff's car." Now that Dillinger was in the realm of stealing government-issued automobiles, he walked confidently back into the jail to look for the keys. Not finding them, he returned to the Nashes and pulled the wires to disable the automobiles.

The three then walked in a northwest path for half a block, snaking into an alley, where they entered the Main Street Garage, which was some forty feet north of the jail, and whose entrance was on the same side of the street as the sheriff's quarters. There they encountered Edward Saager, a mechanic. Because Youngblood was a black male and therefore a target, he stayed out of sight while Dillinger and Blunk negotiated for the fastest car. Saager pointed to a 1933 Ford V-8. The trio, with Saagar now making it a quartet, left the garage. Blunk sat in the driver's seat; Dillinger took the front passenger seat. Saagar and Youngblood climbed into the rear.[12]

Back at Crown Point, with confusion and hysteria taking over, either Carroll Holley or Lou Baker sent out the wrong license plate number for this car. This, of course, gave Dillinger more time to get out of town. When the escapee noticed that he was in a police car, he made Saagar remove a red searchlight from the front. Then, in customary 1930s desperado fashion, the car went into a ditch. Saager and Youngblood did the work of pulling it out. After arriving in Lilly's Corner in Illinois, Dillinger released Blunk and Saager.

Dillinger and Youngblood drove through Illinois, an interracial act that would have raised some eyebrows in those Jim Crow days. Dillinger, confident and relaxed, did not realize that by driving across state lines with a stolen car, he had violated the Dyer Act, or National Motor Vehicle Theft Act, which made him a federal fugitive. Youngblood soon parted ways with Dillinger and went on to his own notoriety as a wanted man.

The aftermath of the escape so confounded the authorities that they could not immediately establish a blueprint of Dillinger's movements through the building. After the escape, Estill defended himself by saying that he had requested that Dillinger be transferred to Michigan City to prevent an escape—and that Judge Murray had vetoed the request. According to Estill, Murray had said with prescient arrogance, "A hundred men couldn't release the outlaw from such a jail."

A few days afterwards, with Dillinger hiding out in Chicago, a ward of the malfeasant Piquett, authorities found the escape car on the North Side. That prompted Captain Stege to reactivate his forty-man Dillinger Squad, which he had decommissioned after the arrests in Tucson. Stege then declared, "We'll find him if he's in Chicago, and when we do he'll never go back to Indiana—except maybe in a box." Stege couldn't have predicted that when Dillinger finally did go into a box—a black wicker basket, to be exact—the Chicago police would be kept in the dark.[13]

Three days after the escape, under orders from Indiana deputy attorney general J. Edward Barce, the ISP took Blunk and Cahoon into custody for aiding and abetting the escape after Estill filed affidavits before Judge Murray. Although the state police brought Blunk into custody, Matt Leach's name was absent from coverage of the arrest. Leach's rival, Chief Michael Morrissey, may have taken Blunk to Indianapolis. The cagey Morrissey denied knowing anything about Blunk's whereabouts.

Legendary Chicago police captain John Stege, ca. 1930s (John Binder Collection).

Months later, the investigations would narrow down and ISP police would arrest Baker and Blunk for questioning.[14]

The fabled wooden gun escape turned out to be a smokescreen for the fact that Dillinger bought his way out of Crown Point on a promise to pay several thousand dollars. The exact dollar amount is not established but is somewhere between $11,000 and $30,000, a fact revealed by Arthur O'Leary, Piquett's investigator. Captain John Stege was one of the officials who was privy to this information. Because Stege was not hostile to Leach, it is highly possible that Leach was on the inside with this story. By 1938 the *Chicago Tribune* was reporting that Dillinger had paid at least $11,000 for his release, a sum that was delivered in a saloon in either East Chicago or Crown Point. While the persons in power who received the payoffs have remained unnamed to this day, the bribe is taken as truth.

Throughout the mess, Leach blamed Estill's "petting party" on the escape. "That picture deprived the jail guards of fear of Dillinger," Leach said. "Their reaction was 'that fellow Dillinger can't be such a bad fellow after all, if our prosecutor is not afraid to be on such friendly terms with him' ... the laxity [of the guards] then permitted the escape," said Matt. "Lovemaking between prosecutors and notorious criminals was shockingly out of place."[15]

In the week following Dillinger's escape, Estill asked East Chicago sergeant Martin Zarkovich to help him investigate the escape from Crown Point. Estill officially brought him over to Crown Point by claiming that Officer O'Malley had been their police officer. The jurisdiction went automatically to them. Privately, it was about Leach and it was personal. Zarkovich was a cop that Matt Leach

East Chicago sergeant Martin Zarkovich, pictured here ca. 1920s. Leach tried to out him as a conspirator in the Dillinger ambush at the Biograph Theater (courtesy East Chicago Public Library).

never thought of tangling with. There was always the possibility that Leach would claim that bank executives had put the job out to the underworld to hide its own internal shortfall.

Because Leach kept himself well away from the action in East Chicago, Estill fortified himself with the very people that had some kind of hold over Leach. Coming into Crown Point with Zarkovich was James W. Regan. Regan and Zarkovich went back to the 1920s, when Mayor Raleigh P. Hale had brought Regan over from Chicago, where he had been a sergeant. Regan was appointed as a chief of the East Chicago police in spite of the fact that he'd never lived in East Chicago. By 1930 he'd been found guilty, along with Zarkovich and Mayor Hale, for conspiracy to violate the national prohibition act. They were sentenced to two years, but none of the three served time.

Once he was secure in Crown Point, Zarkovich requested that one East Chicago criminal court former prosecutor, Martin J. Smith, be appointed as one of the investigators. Barce and Estill stonewalled the actual reason for the four East Chicago investigators. Barce said it was "protection," while Estill said it was for the overall "investigation."[16]

Another reason for Estill's East Chicago fortification was the fact that the prosecutor was now on decidedly bad terms with Judge Murray by virtue of the fact that Estill had blamed the escape on Murray. In spite of the fact that police from East Chicago, Hammond, and Gary had been called to escort Dillinger to Michigan City, Murray had refused to release the prisoner. In this backdrop to a fight between two public officials, the new regime was self-evident; Lake County police were taking over the job previously performed by Leach and the ISP officers.

Estill and Judge Williams tossed accusations at each other as Williams cited prosecutor Martin J. Smith and a grand jury for contempt after they found that Dillinger should have been sent to Michigan City. Murray had the record expunged.[17]

Matt Leach said nothing during this time, possibly because McNutt wanted to fiddle while Crown Point burned. Later, after the "wooden gun" escape, Leach received a postcard, allegedly from Dillinger. Postmarked sometime in 1934, it said, "Ha Ha Captain. Come over and see me and my wooden gun. Don't be scared."

Dillinger had no way of knowing that his nemesis, Captain Leach, was a lame duck. Now that Dillinger had committed his first federal offense, he had a new opponent. The entry of the FBI into the case corresponded with an agreement entered into in early 1934, encompassing the states of Indiana, Illinois, Michigan, Ohio and Minnesota in offering a $5,000 reward for Dillinger. It was called the "Five-State Pact." This pact came into play after Leach had crossed state lines to conduct police work in Chicago, Illinois, and Dayton, Ohio.[18]

It is commonly held that the FBI did not enter the Dillinger hunt until after the Crown Point escape. That may have been the public event that brought them in, but the Cincinnati field office had been involved since Dillinger's arrest in Dayton, and weeks beforehand. Even in Tucson, that bastion of Western autonomy, the FBI's field office was active in the case.

The first steps that the FBI took to acquire Matt Leach's files occurred in the two-week period following the escape. During that time, the FBI compiled its own version of the steps that Dillinger had taken out of the Lake County Jail. Agents visited Tucson and spoke to the arresting officers. Chester "Chet" Sherman compiled a list of the makes and models of cars that the Terror Gang members used to drive into Tucson: Pierpont had a Buick sedan; Makley and Clark had a Studebaker sedan; Dillinger drove a 1934 Hudson sedan.[19]

During that period of stockpiling information, Agent Mullen visited the Tremont Barracks sometime before March 12th. He asked a staff sergeant if anyone there knew the whereabouts of Dillinger. In a respectful way, the sergeant answered the agent's awkward question: "The entire matter is being handled by the plainclothes division of the Indiana State Highway Police, with headquarters in Indianapolis, Indiana, under the direct supervision of Captain Matt Leach."

Within days of that incident, the FBI sent an agent from the Cincinnati field office to take Leach's Dillinger files from Michigan City. The agents wanted to view the list of Dillinger's visitors while he was incarcerated.[20]

When the Cincinnati field agents entered Leach's office in the Statehouse, they asked for, and got, all his files. This is further evidenced by the fact that the agents then backtracked over what Leach and Huntington had done months before. They went to the Lebanon connections, such as Maurice Lanham, Glenn Zoll, James Kirkland and George Whitehouse.

The agents also investigated Sam Goldstine, who was now incarcerated in Michigan City. They reported that they had found Goldstine tightlipped about Dillinger. The agents wrote memos concerning Hilton Crouch, another ex–Dillinger associate now serving time in Michigan City. They made plans to talk to Noble Claycombe and Paul "Lefty" Parker. They raked over Mary Longnaker and her sad existence. Initially, they gave Leach the credit, by signing off, "All of this information was in possession of Matt Leach, the head of the Indiana State Police at Indianapolis, Indiana."

These White Cap–like characters had long since dropped out of Dillinger's life. This happened because all the men were, by now, incarcerated. Mary Longnaker had put the notoriety behind her and was planning to get remarried; a new name to replace the one associated with Dillinger could give her a fresh start.

Dillinger's static connections, those still on the street, were Mary Kinder and the Pierponts. The agents piggybacked off Leach's longstanding habit of harassing Mary Kinder and her family. They used all his material on the Pierponts to set up surveillance on Harry's parents. The Cincinnati office compiled information about Fred "Happy" Meyers, who had been Art McGinnis's roommate back in December when the calls were coming in over his telephone line.

Then Special Agent J. S. Johnson contacted Leach to ask about the Dillinger family. Leach recommended that they put a cover on Hubert Dillinger, the outlaw's half-brother who remained in contact with him.[21]

The FBI began to dominate the investigation. At this juncture, McNutt and Feeney began distancing themselves from the captain. One probable reason for this was that McNutt, tiring of the political tug of war between his faction and that of Estill and East Chicago, may have suggested that they take Leach out of circulation. With Estill the latest political controversy, Leach had no further interest in publicly attacking him. His comments about Estill and Dillinger's "petting party" were duly noted at the same time that McNutt became less publicly associated with Leach. Feeney did not ask Leach to provide officers to cover the remaining Terror Gang members as they went on trial in Lima. Simultaneously, the assembled Crown Point investigators unanimously ignored the captain.

Leach slowly realized that the only recent duty he'd been given had been his last act in an official capacity towards the Dillinger gang on February 10th, when Feeney had authorized Leach to assemble the detail to escort Pierpont, Makley and Clark to Lima to stand trial for the murder of Sheriff Sarber.[22] Almost without noticing it, Leach found himself fading from the dailies that had once made him king.

While Leach did enjoy a brief honeymoon period with the FBI, it was fraught with trouble from the beginning. The agency early on pinned Captain Leach as "either extremely friendly or rather, unfriendly toward the Bureau."

Leach soon realized that the Division was a bigger opponent than Estill and the East Chicago contingent. Leach soon learned that his new rivals, the federal agents, were staking out at the Detroit address of Russell Clark's family home. The FBI agents were trying to find out if Red Hamilton was still alive and under the care of Pat Cherrington, who was rumored to have been nursing him back from his wounds suffered during the East Chicago bank robbery of January 15th.

Upon learning of the surveillance of Clark's family home, Matt traveled to Detroit. The FBI was waiting for him. They presented a hostile environment for Leach, accusing his assistant, Detective Ryan, of unprofessional conduct.[23] The Division of Investigation had no reason to court his favor once they had taken his files on Frechette, Long, Longnaker and the defunct White Cap Gang. Leach, in turn, realized that they had allowed no option for him to participate in the investigation. Federal agents even took over Leach's job of raiding Mary Kinder's home, something that had always been his purview.

It must have felt like things were crashing down on the captain when a letter arrived on his desk the second week of March. Penned by a citizen lawyer and arriving in a stack of mail to the Statehouse, it offered sage advice: "By giving the names to the public and press you are only aiding him in being at large. Call all persons X Y X, and let it go at that. Yours truly, Ernest Cummings."[24]

As he was unofficially demoted from the Dillinger campaign, Leach's last official act was to send Lieutenant Chester Butler out to supervise the investigation in Warsaw after the outlaw raided the state arsenal there in April.[25] Butler himself was showing the strain of the job. He is recalled as having been a right-hand man to Captain Leach. Butler's shooting of Trooper Eugene Teague, though accidental, heralded a serious decline for the lieutenant. Eventually Butler was moved down to patrol status. Lieutenant Butler, like Matt Leach, was now a living casualty of the Midwest crime wave.

CHAPTER 9

Unsung

If it hadn't been for Matt Leach, you never would've heard of me.—
Harry Pierpont, in *Indianapolis Star*, March 8, 1934

The final blow to the Terror Gang arrived with the murder trial in Lima, Ohio. While Pierpont, Makley and Clark were tried separately, Copeland was out. He would stay in Indiana. Don Sarber, the twenty-four-year-old son of the victim, Jess Sarber, had originally identified Copeland as the man who'd killed his father. "My father was lying on the floor," was his original statement, "and I went over and asked him what had happened. Mother was locked in the jail at the time. He was complaining about the pain in his back. I asked dad if one of the men was Harry Copeland and gave him a general description. He said, 'I did not know any of the men. They were all big men.'"

Under trial examination by prosecutor Ernest M. Botkin, Don Sarber rescinded his prior identification of Copeland. Reports of the trial testimony quote Don Sarber as denying that his father had ever said that Copeland was the trigger man.[1] His retraction confirmed that Copeland would never go on the docket in Lima. The deal he'd made with Leach and Huntington back in December was sealed.

Pierpont and Makley were convicted with no jury recommendation of mercy. This meant that the two would get the death penalty. The recommendation of mercy was the only way that a defendant convicted of first-degree murder could avoid capital punishment. Very often a convicted defendant had to depend on a jury's flawed understanding of this recommendation, due to the bench's lack of scholarship and inability to tutor the jury in its intricacies.[2] Perhaps this was the case in Lima, but more likely, the mood was for swift hanging justice.

Harry Pierpont (*center*), on trial for murder, flanked by attorney Jesse Levy (left) and his mother Lena Pierpont, March 1934 (John Binder Collection).

Matt Leach arrived in Lima on March 18th. His arrival prompted Pierpont to take one last verbal swipe. He told Prosecutor Botkin, "If it hadn't been for Matt Leach, you never would've heard of me."[3]

The most damaging witness was Ed Shouse. The expatriate of the Terror Gang had rehearsed his testimony by running it past Wayne Coy,

Russell Clark, on trial in Lima, Ohio, for murder in March 1934. Family members joined him for a brief recess (John Binder Collection).

McNutt's secretary in charge of penal affairs, and Ohio prosecutor Ernest Botkin during interrogations in Michigan City. Despite the democratic nature of the gang, Shouse asserted a basic untruth that Pierpont was the real leader of the gang. Shouse apparently remembered that Clark had been good to him, because he refused to testify against Clark. This dated back to the night the gang had kicked Shouse out of the gang; Clark gave Shouse his keys so that the ousted gangster would have a car. Shouse's refusal to testify saved Clark from the electric chair. He was given life in prison. Clark would serve thirty-four years before his release shortly before his death.[4]

While Leach lingered in Lima— some said loitered—another character from the Dillinger cast of characters arrived. Dillinger had asked Piquett to go to Lima to see if there was a way of helping the gang escape. But the National Guard as a presence answered that question. As soon as police noticed the toughened face of Louis Piquett, they arrested him on disorderly conduct charges. Because they didn't know much about the

Terror Gang expatriot Ed Shouse's 1930 mugshot.

Dillinger roster at that time, local reporters factored Leach into the Piquett story. Designed as light copy, it nonetheless lumped Leach in with the nefarious Piquett in the minds of the reading public.

"Capt. Leach refused to say what had brought him to Lima, but he has devoted himself almost exclusively to Dillinger and members of his gang for months. Whether the search for the jail-breaker was the cause of his sudden presence here, he declined to say." The remark cast Leach as a sketchy interloper whose Lima appearance was unnecessary.[5]

The shifting tide of departmental and public opinion regarding Leach was conspicuous in Lima. When he returned to Indianapolis, he noticed that he never seemed to appear in front page coverage of the Dillinger gang.

After he lost the Terror Gang, Dillinger located his Michigan City friend John Hamilton. Hamilton, the clay pigeon of the Midwest crime wave, was recovering from the gunshot wounds of the East Chicago bank robbery. Homer Van Meter also connected with Dillinger in St. Paul. "Van," Dillinger's close friend, was of little interest to Leach. Van Meter had contributed to the campaign of corrupt mayor Thomas "Big Tom" Brown in St. Paul. For his contribution, Van Meter stayed, for a brief time at least, in the protected St. Paul underworld.

The twin cities of Minneapolis and St. Paul, like East Chicago, were underworld safe cities. Their corrupt political and police system began between 1900 and 1920. At that time, Prohibition was the gold standard that made it pay. The St. Paul police chief, John J. O'Connor, had pioneered the system that allowed vice parlors and gangsters to operate openly.[6] The hallmark of the neighborhood was Dapper Dan's, later The Green Lantern, a speakeasy run by Dan Hogan, a crime boss who died in 1928 when his car mysteriously exploded.[7] His successor, Harry Sawyer, changed Dapper Dan's shingle to read "The Green Lantern." The sign changed but the corrupt system stayed intact.

Van Meter, working with jug marker and Green Lantern employee Pat Reilly, put Dillinger together with Baby Face Nelson's gang. They were about to rob the Security National Bank and Trust Company in Sioux Falls, South Dakota. Dillinger and Van Meter had reconnected with "Jimmie," their gun connection from their post-parole days in East Chicago. Jimmie, aka Baby Face Nelson, had brought in a low profile member of the St. Paul underworld named Eugene Green. Completing the sextet was Tommy Carroll, a St. Paul machine gunner and bank robber.[8]

The Sioux Falls robbery was run by Baby Face Nelson, who planned it while Dillinger was still in jail. Dillinger joined this heist within hours of escaping. This fact lends credence to the rumored "fix" that Nelson supposedly put in to help Dillinger escape from Crown Point. Nelson had planned a second robbery for March 13th at the First National Bank of Mason City, Iowa, using Carroll, Van Meter, Green, Dillinger and Hamilton.

Mason City, with Nelson at the helm, proved to be a venue where the gang met a tough defensive in the figure of bank guard Tom Walters, who stood at a vantage point in an overhanging cage, throwing down smoke bombs. Hamilton was shot alongside Dillinger, who was also injured. Large crowds of spectators also marked this robbery. The gang followed the Racine and Sioux Falls prototype by taking hostages, too many to comfortably fit on the running boards. The chaos made Racine, with the civility that the gang demonstrated toward Mrs. Patzke and Mr. Weyland, seem nostalgic.

In a retraction from his former pattern, Matt Leach did not go to Mason City or Sioux Falls. In fact, he publicly declared that Dillinger could never have been involved in Sioux Falls or Mason City, because the outlaw had only been out of jail a few days. Leach was not aware of Van Meter's arrangement that had brought Dillinger into Nelson's gang.[9]

These sensational robberies should have had his nose to the cat roads, but he had no positioning now. Leach had a tendency toward sidestepping towns and cities that were openly guarded by corrupt municipalities. The fact that the twin robberies of Sioux Falls and Mason City were plotted in St. Paul was not known to anyone until the FBI shot and killed bank robber Eddie Green and arrested his wife. Beth Green's revelations of the inner workings of Van Meter and John Dillinger in St Paul, garnered through a deal she'd made with the FBI, exposed the Dillinger connections within the St. Paul underworld and the fact that Dillinger had gone there during the period of the Sioux Falls and Mason City robberies.[10]

In the immediate aftermath of the twin robberies, an insider told Leach to stay away from the crime scenes, as well as the haunts behind these twin bank robberies. The word may have come to him through Captain Stege. His friendship with Stege couldn't help Leach beyond that. The FBI was under Special Agent in Charge Melvin Purvis's watch. The field office, schooled but not street smart, was not finding it easy to work with the Chicago police. The result was a blackout on both sides. With Huntington no longer working on the Dillinger case, Leach had no access to inside information. Huntington, upon whom he had relied so heavily, had left the hunt to pursue other cases.[11] The shortfall of Huntington's intelligence eroded Leach's status as a power broker. In addition, McNutt and Feeney had stopped assigning Leach responsibility. To cope with these subtle demerits, the tenacious captain changed his strategy. He began traveling to quiet locations that lent themselves to more covert investigations.

March 16th found Leach in Detroit, where he staked out the family home of Russell Clark. It must have been a crowded street corner. The FBI considered the house their purview, since they'd garnered the trust of informants living in the building. It didn't take long for the two factions to get into a confrontation. Gene Ryan, Leach's assistant, stood his ground with the agents. Their complaints about his deportment resulted in Ryan's suspension for an indefinite period of time. Leach should have taken heed that the FBI considered him and his crew to be obstructionist. He stubbornly stayed oblivious to the repercussions of tangling with FBI field agents.

Nearby, in Port Huron, Michigan, police officers acted on a tip and went to a Moak Avenue store. Herbert Youngblood, Dillinger's African-American partner in the Crown Point escape, was reported to be brandishing a gun and boasting of a recent jailbreak. Leach dropped everything in Detroit and rushed to Port Huron. There, four officers led by Sheriff William L. Van Antwerp went to the store. According to published accounts, Youngblood fired on the officers, hitting Undersheriff Charles Cavanaugh and Deputy Howard Lohr, as well as Van Antwerp. Youngblood fell mortally wounded from shots to his heart and abdomen. Before he died, he admitted who he really was. By that time, Leach had arrived. Leach confirmed Youngblood's identity as the "negro" who was facing a murder charge when he escaped with Dillinger.

Sadly, Leach now found himself being shadowed by the FBI wherever he went. John L. Murphy, an FBI agent, also showed up in Huron to conduct his own investigation.[12] From this point on, Leach unwillingly shared his lunch with the FBI on every tour of duty associated with Dillinger. As late as June of 1934, Leach traveled to Wichita, Kansas, to interview relatives of Dewey and Pearl Elliott, hoping for new information concerning the Elliotts. Leach, working directly with Captain D. J. Hayes of the Wichita Police Department, tried to work autonomously. The FBI got to the department first and approached Hayes for information about Leach. Taken off guard, Hayes revealed to them whatever information he had. In turn, the FBI monitored Leach's operatives in Wichita.[13]

Chicago's Special Agent in Charge Melvin Purvis was about to lose his professional stature. In some ways this mirrored the McNutt administration's attitude toward Leach. The event that resulted in Purvis's demotion was the battle of Little Bohemia Lodge. Part of the strategy that the Bureau employed was to avoid mingling with local law enforcement. For this reason, the FBI showed disdain to the local police when

Purvis rushed up to Manitowish Waters, Wisconsin, on a tip that the Dillinger gang was staying there. The fact that the FBI did not know the terrain resulted in the Dillinger gang's escaping. The gang members had backed onto a natural ridge behind the building. The FBI did not know that this ledge existed, and believed the building abutted the lake. The aftermath, the slaughter of an innocent civilian with two more severely injured, brought the FBI down in the eyes of the press and its readership. Rather than distribute the blame directly among the agents in charge, such as Hugh Clegg, who commanded; William Rorer, who arrived somewhat later in the offensive; and Werner Hanni, who testified at the inquest, Hoover aimed straight at one agent. Purvis became the scapegoat.[14]

The hostility between Leach and the FBI came to a head when Leach put a formal complaint in writing in the spring of 1934, addressed to the seemingly distant Governor McNutt. In his missive, Leach charged the FBI with endangering the lives of both the civilians and police of Indiana.

Leach knew his own home state and could recognize a potential tragedy in the works. In this case, federal agents were riding around Mooresville unidentified in cars bearing what he called "foreign" license plates—that of the states of Illinois, Wisconsin and Ohio. A concerned citizen called it in after seeing that men in these vehicles were brandishing guns. Then the caller identified an occupant of the gun-wielding auto as John Dillinger.

The captain got on it and ordered a patrol to the location. Then his assistants used common sense and said that Dillinger would not stop at a gas station where he was known. Although Dillinger sightings were everywhere in the spring of 1934, Leach had to take each one seriously. He sent his patrol out to investigate this car with its armed passengers. Sometime later, his patrolmen called the barracks and informed the operator that the men in question were federal agents.

Leach sat down and wrote the angry letter to McNutt. His report did not directly blame the agents; he blamed the "policies of the FBI which outright discouraged agents from informing local police of their actions and whereabouts." It might as well have been an open declaration of war. From then on, the FBI treated Leach as an avowed enemy.[15]

After his escape from the Little Bohemia Lodge, Dillinger's friend John Hamilton succumbed to his gunshot wounds. Hamilton died in agony while lying in the back seat of the gangsters' car. His death seemed cacophonous. He was shot by police in a car chase just outside of St. Paul in the days following the FBI ambush of the gang in Wisconsin's Little Bohemia Lodge.

Dillinger's most obscure period was about to begin. The mortalities were disturbing: Eugene Green and Tommy Carroll died weeks after John Hamilton. The gang had scattered to the wind after Little Bohemia. Baby Face Nelson's murder of FBI agent W. Carter Baum had forced the gang leader into hiding on the West Coast. There he kept his wife Helen Gillis at his side, along with John Paul Chase, Joseph "Fatso" Negri, and an assortment of California and Nevada organized crime figures.

Dillinger, who saw Nelson only at strategic meetings in Chicago during this period, depended upon the protection of the people that Piquett, through O'Leary, brought to him. This included an underworld plastic surgery team that changed the look of the outlaw's face, a rumored Gary prostitute who accompanied him through his last weeks in Chicago, and a vice madam who would deliver him to his death.

Anna Sage, née Cumpanas, was known by two equally flaming monikers. Locals knew her in the roaring twenties as "Katie from the Kostur Hotel." The Kostur, located in Gary at 1349 Washington Street, was the scene of a basement establishment called the "Bucket of Blood" because of the numerous stabbings and shootings occurring there. Ten years later she was world famous, the iconic emblem of the 1930s, known mythically as "The Woman in Red."

Anna Sage started out as a friend of East Chicago sergeant and Crown Point investigator Martin Zarkovich. She operated as a local madam in the years when Leach was climbing the ranks of the Gary Police Department.

Unless Leach had had his head buried in the sand pits of Gary, Sage would have been known to him. This conjecture was confirmed one week after Dillinger's death, when Leach told the press that he had known Anna Sage and her associates in Gary for many years. Had the captain been aware in July of 1934 that Dillinger was living with the notorious Katy from the Kostur Hotel, things would have turned out a bit differently: Dillinger would not have been killed in the fashion that he was; he would have been taken in a raid staged by the joint forces of the Chicago and Indiana police.

Sergeant Zarkovich, Sage's long-term friend, was among the Lake County Leach detractors. It meant that Leach, along with Stege and officers of Chicago's Sheffield and Maxwell Street stations, was left out of the plan to bring Dillinger in. Dillinger's death warrant appeared between the lines of the agreement forged between the federal government and the corrupt outback of East Chicago.

The Chicago field office operatives, SAC Melvin Purvis and Inspector Samuel Cowley, planned to take Dillinger into custody. Zarkovich had the foresight to imagine Dillinger taken alive—only to be coerced into giving information that damaged East Chicago. No. Dillinger would not be taken alive.

Anna Sage, the Woman in Red, ca. 1935.

Anna Sage was not a shadow woman, nor was she someone an inquiring reporter would need to research in a courthouse archive. She had been a newsworthy criminal in Gary for at least twelve years prior to 1934.

In 1923, when Leach was a Gary police officer and Gary was sin city, Anna was working for Big Bill Subotich in a place on Guthrie Street in East Chicago. Later she was arrested in a sensational night of raids on twelve vice resorts that resulted in multiple arrests. She was booked as "Kate Brown," for hustling on Jefferson Street. Three years later she was arrested on a robbery charge and held on $2,000 bail. She was rearrested and released constantly within the Lake County criminal court system. In 1932 she was pardoned on two criminal counts by the former governor Leslie.

Her criminal record notwithstanding, Anna, the mother of a son named Steven Chiolak, got involved with Alexander "Alex" Sage, a gambling den operator. In 1929 she married Sage. Two years later she faced conspiracy charges for intimidating a federal witness. Anna Sage was not a back-page item in Gary; she was the ingénue.

Anna Sage claimed she could not read or write. She always signed legal documents with an "X." Whether or not she was actually illiterate, her signature "X" reduced her accountability. In 1930 she was involved with a reporter named Harry Schmidt, who worked for the Chicago *Herald & Examiner*. Schmidt told Sage that she could operate the Kostur Hotel because he had a fix in. When Schmidt was tried on vice charges, Sage signed her witness affidavits against the reporter with the distinctive "X."[16]

In July of 1934, Leach was unaware that Gary madam Katie Brown aka Anna Sage was harboring Dillinger, and that one of her girls was serving as Dillinger's companion. The May-to-June cycle that marked Dillinger's dark period was Leach's dark period as well.

As Leach's voice faded from the general noise about Dillinger, the gangster, too, seemed to disappear. The two shared a parallel existence. The desperado went dark by choice while Leach acted alone in his work or with those troopers still loyal to him.

In June, Leach successfully formed a blockade against a group of thugs who were known in southern Indiana as the "Sheik Bandits." They were a trio of young men who hung around university towns and dressed in a fashion of the day called "collegiate." In between heists, they romanced college girls and attended frat parties. Leach led his men on the night of June 4th in patrols against the three desperate thugs, Lacell "Toots" Long, Robert Neal and Edward Coffin. They had just shot and killed John Pfaffenberger, an officer who stopped them during a routine traffic check on suspicion of driving a stolen car. Leach's blockade included a poorly rigged system of telephone and messenger communication, during which time the three shot and killed Deputy Sheriff Harold Amick and kidnapped a local named Ralph Shields to use as a hostage. Leach's posse captured the first of the three. Leach then requested the Bertillon files from the Indianapolis criminal identification bureau that identified him as Robert Neal, a Michigan City ex-con. Neal then identified his two friends as Coffin and Lacell. All three men were later convicted of first-degree murder. Coffin died in the electric chair. Long served life in prison. Neal, who had requested and received a separate trial, also served life in prison.[17]

The week before Leach pursued by posse the "Sheik Bandits," Dillinger had plastic surgery (on or around May 28th) in James Probasco's Chicago house located at 2509 North Crawford Avenue. Probasco was a Chicago friend of Piquett who had promised to harbor Dillinger. The attorney later stood trial, was convicted and lost his license for arranging the surgery for Van Meter.[18] While at the Crawford Avenue house, the gang planned what would be Dillinger's last significant public spectacle, the robbery of the Merchants National Bank in South Bend, Indiana. After Probasco kicked him out of his house, Dillinger went again to Piquett, who arranged that his client would move into a flat on Chicago's north side.

Polly Hamilton Keele, Dillinger's companion and housemate in Sage's Chicago hideout, ca. 1930s.

It was a neighborhood bustling with residential chic. Dillinger boarded with Anna Sage on Halsted Street. The Lakeview area boasted restaurants, bars and theaters along with grocery stores and dry cleaners. His new neighborhood was a short ride to Wrigley Field and walking distance to the Biograph Theater.

Location! Location! He had a new girlfriend. He'd lost Evelyn Frechette to arrest when the Chicago-based FBI picked her up based on an informant's tip. She was now serving two years in a federal prison for harboring. His new girlfriend, Polly Hamilton Keele, preened as his true love. She was no rare bird and considered their dates a business arrangement. She was divorced from Roy Keele, the Gary policeman who had been arrested with Leach back in Gary for bootlegging. She is believed to have also been Anna's manager at Gary's Kostur Hotel. After Dillinger's death, Leach would look up his connections in Gary to inquire into her affairs. What he would claim to know about Dillinger's death came partially through the Gary conduit.

While Polly was enjoying the nightlife with Dillinger, Anna's problems were escalating. Her long criminal record as a vice maven in Gary had caused the federal government to pursue deportation proceedings against her. This was a situation that eluded the fixer skills of Zarkovich.[19] His small-town payoffs didn't have any clout with the U.S. Department of Labor, the branch of government in charge of her deportation.

When she made the decision to surrender Dillinger in return for amnesty is not known. But it must have been clear to Sage that she could make Dillinger's presence pay in more ways than one. She met with the FBI to offer Dillinger up for target practice.

FBI records reveal that the arrangement was made on the night before Dillinger died. On July 21st, at 8 p.m., Captain Timothy O'Neill of East Chicago's police force met with Purvis and told him that it was

Dillinger made front-page news, July 22, 1934 (Bill Helmer collection).

believed that Dillinger would go to the Marbro theater. Those plans quickly changed, and without the knowledge of Leach or Stege, Cowley made haste to the Biograph. There he stationed himself, Melvin Purvis, Ed Hollis, and FBI sharpshooters Charles Winstead and Clarence Hurt, among other FBI agents. Alongside them stood East Chicago officers Peter Sopsic, Glen Stretch, and Captain O'Neill, along with two others. Altogether, twenty FBI agents and five East Chicago, Indiana, officers were at and around the theater. Dillinger had gone to see *Manhattan Melodrama*, starring Clark Gable, Myrna Loy and William Powell.

Purvis was stationed at the east side of the theater. A patron exiting the theater would enter the sidewalk going south. That placed Purvis on the southeast edge of the theater. As Dillinger and the women passed, Purvis, recognizing Anna Sage's orange skirt, shakily lit a cigar to identify the outlaw. Dillinger, not necessarily reacting to Purvis, became aware of several men closing in on him and started to run. Three agents fired five shots. Dillinger, who is believed to have been killed by bullets fired by agents Winstead, Hurt and Hollis, died twenty minutes after the end of the movie.

The hours after his death saw his body moved from the alley, where he lay for twenty minutes, to the lawn of the Alexian Brothers Hospital, to the Cook County Morgue and to McGready's Funeral Home in Chicago, before being taken home to his sister Audrey's house, and finally, to Crown Hill Cemetery in Indianapolis.

The week following Dillinger's death found Captain Stege and Leach both working behind the scenes. Stege reacted to his insulting exclusion from the ambush by arresting some of the women involved in the case. Captain Duffy, of the Sheffield Street and Marquette police stations, arrested Anna Sage. He was able to get her to speak of her Chicago activities of the prior two months.

At the same time that Stege was interrogating the women who had been part of Dillinger's circle, Leach travelled to Gary and Chicago. Given Anna Sage's connections to the two cities, Leach wanted to solidify his information on her. His roots in Gary served him well as he dug around his old precinct to learn a few things about the two women associated with Dillinger at the Biograph.

In spite of rumors that Leach was investigating Dillinger's death—what else had Leach investigated for the past thirteen months?—the

Crown Hill Cemetery, the site of Dillinger's funeral in Indianapolis. Photograph taken in 1989.

captain denied that his travels concerned Dillinger and insisted that he was investigating John Hamilton. Hamilton's death was unknown to police at that time.

Leach announced that he was going to investigate the issue of who "put Dillinger on the spot." The McNutt camp did not react happily to this. Feeney was becoming an FBI ally and didn't want Leach causing trouble. So Feeney announced, "The state police have no interest in the slaying of John Dillinger. If Captain Leach is making any investigation of the killing, I don't know it." Leach read that statement as a warning. He then retracted in his fashion.

> There are a million rumors floating around in Chicago and Lake County as to how and why Dillinger was put on the spot, but as far as I know there is absolutely no foundation to any of them.
>
> The East Chicago police department deserves a medal of honor for what the members did rather than an investigation as to why and how they did it. Regardless of what anyone may think of those men, they did a good job and congratulations are in order.
>
> The Chicago police department was working on the case from one angle and apparently the East Chicago police started from another and found him—in the gutter and broke.[20]

Leach's statement was made to appease Feeney, who was bowing to FBI demands to quiet down Leach and anyone else in the administration who ran counter to FBI policies. This collaboration manifested itself in a decision made regarding Anna Sage's statewide appeal for clemency on an Indiana vice conviction of February 8th, 1930. She was trying to clear her record in the deportation hearings by working from the ground up. Her grassroots efforts at local vindication were a waste of time. McNutt denied her request for a pardon on that Gary municipal conviction.[21]

The conspiracy at Crown Point continued to have lethal repercussions. Two months before Dillinger's death on May 24th, 1934, unknown persons fired in cold blood upon police officers Martin O'Brien and Floyd Mulvihill while they patrolled a back road near a cluster of pumping stations in the East Chicago area. Not only was the murder of these two police officers virtually ignored, but the Lake County Coroner's office later retained no record of their deaths.

Little to no information was published about this crime at the time. Although the East Chicago police made some arrests around Dillinger's old hangouts in Indiana Harbor, no solid motives for the double execution–style murders were ever revealed. After Dillinger's death, a few newspapers took a posthumous look at this occurrence. That gave rise to rumors that exist to this day. The most tenacious theory is that the two officers had overheard conversations among East Chicago cops about the conspiracy to spring Dillinger from Crown Point and demanded to be brought into the action. This episode epitomized the dark period in Dillinger's crime career. Possibly because the officers were not his men, Leach remained silent for the time being.[22]

In the days after Dillinger's death, a sinister atmosphere pervaded the office of the FBI in the Banker's Building in Chicago's Loop. On July 26th, James Probasco, who had hosted Dillinger's plastic surgery procedure, was pushed or fell through a window of the 19th floor. The FBI, claiming that it was a suicide, disavowed responsibility for the death of Louis Piquett's friend. Piquett, generally loquacious, kept silent. Perhaps the underworld lawyer sensed that his input would be futile.[23]

By the end of that dark month of Chicago's gangland, Leach made a mistake by generating insider information about Dillinger's death. He publicized the fact that East Chicago officials, mainly Zarkovich and

Captain Tim O'Neill, had been instrumental in bringing Dillinger into the scope of the FBI. O'Neill fought back, an eye for an eye, when he went to the press. O'Neill contacted Basil Gallagher, known as a newspaperman who covered Dillinger in the Indianapolis dailies as well as the *Washington Daily News*. Gallagher had always supported Leach. That was about to change.

In the article that followed, Gallagher accused Leach of failing in many facets of the Dillinger investigation. Leach, he wrote, was unable to unlock a number code that the Dillinger gang used in communicating. Leach was so incompetent, he opined, that it took him three months to decode the gang members' nicknames. Gallagher's article went back as far as the Michigan City escape, and claimed that information provided by William Shaw that would have thwarted the escape was ignored by Leach.[24] Leach brushed this scathing critique off. He was moving forward in a frantic attempt to expose the inside story on Dillinger's death.

In his usual bombastic style, Leach stormed the Division headquarters in the Banker's Building. He walked into the office of Sam Cowley and delivered an ultimatum. The inspector, who would himself become a martyr of the Dillinger campaign as a victim of Baby Face Nelson's machine gun, then wrote the words that would mark Leach as an antagonist.

CHAPTER 10

Obstructionists

The commander of the State Police is a man by the name of Matt Leach, who stood in our way throughout the entire Dillinger case.—
J. Edgar Hoover, memorandum for Mr. Tamm, November 1, 1934

A mere five days after Dillinger's death, Hoover confided to Inspector Cowley, "Leach has been the cause of a great deal of trouble." He then corroborated this by calling on his field agents for backup, and wrote, "Mr. Connelley informed me yesterday that he had had a great deal of trouble with him in Indiana." Hoover then ordered his Indianapolis team to interact with Leach. They would then list their complaints against him.

Leach generated the poison-pen campaign when he visited Cowley in the Chicago office, ostensibly on behalf of himself and Captain Stege. Leach demanded that Zarkovich be charged with harboring the outlaw. Leach then further demanded an investigation into the deaths of the two East Chicago police officers whose cold-blooded murders in June 1934 were commonly attributed to the Dillinger gang. In response, Inspector Cowley provided Leach with two concise answers: Sergeant Zarkovich had cooperated with the Bureau, and yes, the murder of the two policemen was a serious crime—over which the Bureau simply had no jurisdiction.

It was Cowley's honest reaction to Leach's query. Cowley then described Leach's attitude as a "frame-up," which was "possibly motivated by the jealousy" that both Leach and, by association, Captain Stege had felt at being excluded from the Dillinger apprehension.[1] Cowley's response provoked Leach, sparking a powder-keg reaction. After contacting a Mr. Duffield, Washington correspondent at the *Chicago Tribune*, Leach returned to Cowley's office.[2]

185

Leach then told Cowley that he had information that Zarkovich and Anna Sage had planned to take Dillinger's money from his bank robberies and were motivated to betray him to the FBI in order to have him killed. Leach also demanded that Zarkovich be charged with harboring Dillinger, and insinuated that Anna Sage and Polly Hamilton Keele each had had something to do with the deaths of the two East Chicago policemen.[3]

Leach followed with the charge that the FBI could have caught Dillinger months before he was killed, had the agency cooperated with the Indiana State Police. "They expect to obtain all sorts of information from us without giving any in return," he stated. "It's a matter of fact and record in our office and in the [Indianapolis field] office that I turned entire files of cases over to them."

The fact that Leach had leaked information to the *Chicago Tribune* made it difficult for the FBI to handle the resulting publicity. A week after Dillinger died, the *Tribune* published the news that the Indiana police were launching an investigation into Dillinger's death. The page featured photos of Anna Sage and Martin Zarkovich and revealed that there was more to the FBI version of Dillinger's death than had been revealed previously. The "Woman in Red," as Sage was now being called—this moniker stuck to her orange skirt like glue—was a close friend of Sergeant Martin Zarkovich. The sergeant was also the official from East Chicago who had led the Crown Point post-escape inquiries for Robert Estill.

This hefty investigative piece stated that after the escape, Zarkovich, in the words of Lake County Judge William Murray, "practically wore a path between the grand jury room and Estill's office." This prompted Zarkovich to deny charges that his assistance at Crown Point was a *quid pro quo* maneuver to obtain clemency for Sage in her revolving-door convictions in Lake County for prostitution. It also motivated the controversial Estill to deny that Zarkovich was there for any reason other than his detective abilities.

The article cited unnamed Gary police "officials" who confirmed that Dillinger knew both Sage and Polly Hamilton Keele while both were running disorderly houses in the neighborhoods where Dillinger was hanging out.[4]

It was at this juncture that Hoover went off the defensive and turned things around on Leach. This was the second major accusation that Leach brought against the FBI. Leach had registered his first complaint the previous March, when Mooresville locals misidentified FBI agents as gangsters.

Inspector Cowley would go on to the infamous Battle of Barrington, where he was killed alongside Agent Sam Hollis in a gun battle with Baby Face Nelson. The heroic agent's death occurred alongside that of Nelson, who died from seventeen slugs from the guns of both Cowley and Hollis.[5]

Three weeks before Cowley died in the fatal battle, Hoover solidified his enmity towards Leach. Sometime after

Slain agent Sam Cowley had worked closely with Melvin Purvis on the Chicago Dillinger campaign. Photograph ca. 1930s.

Dillinger's death, Leach began laying the groundwork for his own investigation into the Lake County police and officials and the killing. The FBI claimed they had planned to enter the ongoing series of inquests into the Crown Point escape.

It appears that Hoover was exploiting the Crown Point investigation without having any real interest in its outcome. He claimed that he would enter the case only if Indiana helped the FBI—and at the same time, stayed well away from the federal men. His rationale was that "the commander of the State Police is a man by the name of Matt Leach, who stood in our way throughout the entire Dillinger case, and Mr. Leach is a very good friend of the governor, but that Mr. Feeney, Commissioner of Public Safety, has been very cooperative with the Division."[6] Hoover's allusion to Feeney was due to the fact that the safety director had chosen sides in the week after Dillinger died with his statement that Indiana had no interest in the circumstances surrounding Dillinger's death.

Hoover revealed his practical side and, at the same time, his non-committal attitude toward internal Indiana politics. Regarding Crown Point, he wrote that "the matter could be satisfactorily 'cleaned up,' that for a few dollars we could get the whole story from the Pierponts." Sadly, the parents of Harry Pierpont were reduced to selling information once their son had exhausted his appeal.

Pierpont was on death row along with Makley in Columbus, Ohio, during the brief period of a stay of execution pending the appeal. During that time, Leach announced that Pierpont would issue a statement, ostensibly about the Michigan City break, in the days before he went to the chair. In response to that statement, Pierpont's attorney exploded. Jesse Levy, a Republican, was outraged at Leach's statement and "surprised that Captain Leach would resort to petty politics in an effort to find a feeble excuse for the 'rotten prison conditions' that resulted in the escape."[7]

Pierpont died in the electric chair on October 13th, 1934. Three weeks prior to that, on September 22nd, 1934, Makley died in an attempted escape from the Columbus, Ohio, death house. It is safe to say that no one in law enforcement in Indiana, Ohio or Illinois lamented the passing of these last members of the Terror Gang.

As 1934 faded into notoriety, a new year revitalized the Indiana politics that had caused all the trouble in the first place. Now there was a third-party agitator in the mix. The Division of Investigation, in 1935 called the FBI, began to influence legislation in Indiana. It reached into the state itself to mandate cooperation between the FBI and the Indiana State Police.

Matt Leach understood on some level that the FBI was building a defense against his accusations, and that his charges against them would hurt him professionally. So, he decided to fight them in a less overt way. He began a series of speaking engagements and took up writing. In 1936 his views on local policing were featured in *Startling Detective*: "It remains for the men on the firing line (I refer to the local law enforcement agencies) along that front to decide the issue, the men who go over the top a dozen times a day knowing they face death at every turn." Here Leach described his own theories of fighting crime. They were the very theories he used to fight Dillinger, by making him the head of the gang to the press: "The average crook is a natural egomaniac. Publicity is like wine to him."

It was statements such as this that kept Leach in the public eye. He asserted that he was against the state police owning machine guns, because "the lives of 5,000 criminals are not worth injury to a single child or citizen." He would live to regret that statement when one of his troopers was killed in 1937 by the machine-gunning Brady Gang. For now, Leach kept Dillinger in his vest, as he revealed his motivation for staying so close to the outlaw. Leach said of Dillinger, "What he feared was the alert, keen-minded detective who stuck relentlessly to his trail."[8]

When a character named Dr. L. E. Bracken started making statements about Dillinger's sex appeal, Leach jumped right in. Intimating that Dillinger had no sexuality, as he hung around with Evelyn Frechette "like a couple of playmates that never heard of

Matt Leach, who went on a lecture tour after Dillinger's death, pictured here ca. 1950s (courtesy James Stack).

sex attraction," he stated: "Can you imagine any girl, even after John had his $4,500 face lifting operation, skipping a heartbeat when he passed down the street?" Further, Leach claimed that Frechette and Sage "were not underworld characters." It is not known why he would have said that of Anna Sage, whose criminal history in his old precinct in Gary was common knowledge. Perhaps he was misquoted, or misunderstood due to his frantic linguistic pattern.[9]

As Leach went on more speaking engagements, his speech problems became apparent. A member of the Gillen Post No. 33, a fraternal organization in Bedford, Indiana, wrote a letter to McNutt commenting upon Leach's lecture to the group. Apparently the talk went on for three and a half hours. The review of Leach's lecture was caustic.

Twenty minutes after [Leach] warmed up, they completely forgot the impediment of his speech ... with a little more practice Matt will overcome his impediment and learn how to time his remarks and condense his talks to forty-five minutes. His subjects last night could be well divided into three speeches.

The critical letter writer did find something positive to say: "Matt was witty, had a keen sense of humor and impressed them with his sincerity and honesty."[10]

In another speech, Leach laid the entire blame for Michigan City on disgraced deputy warden Claudy. Leach took credit for making Dillinger the arch-enemy of the present age. "The Dillinger gang worked with precision," he said. "The gang was really led by Pierpont. Van Meter and Makley were the most cunning."

Throughout the lectures, his speech impediments could not be ignored. So he made a joke about it. A report on his talk to a Kiwanis Club mentioned that he started to use a word and couldn't "make it." Leach explained that he kept substitute words and switched to one of them. He just "[fought] it out" with the original word, if the substitute word didn't come out.[11]

More speaking engagements followed, most being clocked at three and a half hours. He spoke at venues such as the Kiwanis Club, the American Legion and Rotary Club. At times it appeared as though he was mimicking the Dillinger family's "Crime Does Not Pay" tours, in which the family, as well as molls Frechette and Kinder, spoke at theaters and carnivals about their notorious loved ones. "Finally, a letter came from the famous gangster with a 'ha-ha,'" Leach said at one such event. "John wasn't bad, he was cunning. He just had a swell time outsmarting the officers. And he did, too."

In his lectures, Leach covered every topic pertaining to Indiana law enforcement: Dillinger, the newspapers, the modern criminal and the old-time criminal. It must have been a difficult experience for the more intelligent audience members who felt he was advancing his own agenda. But it kept the captain busy in the period when the thirst for the now-departed Dillinger still fueled his every move.[12]

While Leach moved along in this manner, commenting on Dillinger whenever asked, less trivial matters presented themselves at the Statehouse. By June of 1935, the idea that police officers needed to have the right political affiliation had been thrown out. Al Feeney began making speeches decrying the practice of hiring policemen based on their political choices. This resurrected an old rivalry with Pleas Green-lee, McNutt's patronage secretary, which dated back to 1933 when Feeney fired Kokomo detective Harold Ware for being political—an act that was subverted when Greenlee rehired the detective. The feud continued into 1934 with Feeney still frustrated by the state's inability to implement his radio car network and the constant focus on politics, which he blamed on Greenlee.

By 1935, McNutt had grown weary of the war between Feeney and Greenlee. Feeney's constant carping about politics, not exactly an airy topic within McNutt's administration, had cast him as subversive as far back as 1933. More recently, the FBI's subjugation of the safety director exposed his lack of loyalty to McNutt and willingness to become a talking head of the FBI forces in Indiana. This was evident in the correspondence that Cowley had generated after Leach's startling visit. Cowley commented, "Although Leach is under Mr. Feeney, he seems to be more powerful." As a way to civilly oust Feeney, McNutt issued new guidelines for the state police and it began its reorganization. It was a polite way to fire his innovative safety director of the "New Deal for Indiana."[13]

Under the new safety director, Donald F. Stiver, the department appeared anxious to put its past behind. Stiver sought to establish himself among the voices that took credit for the police reorganization. In doing so, he resurrected some old platitudes. Maybe the public was ready for bland toast, because Stiver was instantly popular: "There is no substitute for work. Sweat will dissolve any problem. No organization can exist with any degree of efficiency unless individuals exercise some initiative," he said.

Stiver's first action was to order that one hundred and twenty-five recruits be chosen without having to state their political party. More importantly for the administration, it appeared that Leach's job was safe; Stiver agreed to keep the captain in his position.[14]

With the summer of 1935 following this pattern of reorganization for the Indiana State Police, an article appeared in the *Chicago Tribune* that hammered at the McNutt administration's prior conduct.

> The [Crown Point] escape shocked the country. U.S. Senator Arthur Robinson, Indiana, denounced the McNutt administration. "Dillinger's escape," Robinson said, "can be directly attributed to the McNutt administration.

For years neither party invoked the spoils system in state penal institutions, but the present administration has seen fit to disregard that custom with a vengeance.

However, the McNutt administration saw the Crown Point scandal as a cover up for the Michigan City affair, and promptly transferred the pressure there.[15]

Nineteen thirty-five signaled the beginning of the end of the era of Governor McNutt. Because the State of Indiana mandated that governors serve only one term, McNutt felt his political advantage would best be used by lobbying for a Democratic replacement for his desk in the Statehouse. More internal subterfuge surfaced with the revelation that Pleas Greenlee was planning to make a run for the office. To subvert Greenlee and another frontrunner named E. Kirk McKinney, McNutt reluctantly endorsed Lieutenant Governor M. Clifford Townsend.[16] The lieutenant governor had no special liking for Matt Leach or anyone within McNutt's clique. His election in 1936 meant that Leach could no longer count on gubernatorial leverage.

Finally, a shocking *Tribune* investigative piece solidified the East Chicago, Indiana, connection in Dillinger's death, which was labeled an "assassination." It revealed that the FBI and the East Chicago police had not notified the Chicago police of Dillinger's planned trip to the movies that night. It declared that East Chicago Sergeant Zarkovich had received reward money, as well as Captain Timothy O'Neill. Most damning was the revelation that the "mysterious murder" of officers O'Brien and Mulvihill was a matter of these two officers having seen and heard too much in one of three meetings held by East Chicago plotters to fund Dillinger's escape from Crown Point.[17] The article never mentioned Captain Leach as a source. It is highly probable, given Leach's connections within the *Tribune*, that he provided the background for much of the rumor. To the present time, many of these theories go unproven.

Another voice clamored to fill the void of information available on Dillinger. This article arose from the FBI's inner sanctum. Doris Lockerman was an FBI employee who had been an eyewitness to many of the interrogations that had taken place. She was intimately acquainted with the personalities of the era. She had well-placed contempt for the gang members and their women yet still appeared objective through a series of articles that appeared in October of 1935. There she told much of the story the way Leach had tried to tell it. She featured the shadowy image of Sergeant Zarkovich and his friendship with Anna Sage, along with the dealings of Louis Piquett and O'Leary in her series, which was written through the voice of an FBI insider. She wrote, "The government had put a price of $10,000 on Dillinger's head. Governors of five midwestern states had offered $1,000. In the background are the ugly rumors of the Crown Point escape. The outlaw was worth more dead than alive. And as always, in the underworld, there was someone willing to collect."[18]

Doris Lockerman went unscathed and was not censured by the FBI for her revelations. Leach, in contrast, was the subject of a damning conversation on December 13th, 1935, between the FBI and the ISP. Federal agents of the Indianapolis field office attended an ISP luncheon that was most likely a Christmas function. Over drinks and food, they complained about Leach's "hostile attitude" to everybody within earshot.[19] Two weeks later the tensions erupted again. On December 24th, the ISP arrested four men who were accused of robbing a National Guard armory in Wichita Falls, Texas. Although the FBI had obtained the suspects' license number, when the ISP apprehended them, they failed to notify the FBI in as timely a manner as the federal agency would have liked. Years later, during Leach's hearing, FBI Agent Reinecke admitted that Leach always stayed in contact with him in matters of federal offenders arrested in Indiana.

The issues no longer involved Dillinger. Yet earlier that year, in the summer of 1935, information surfaced in the mysterious case of John Hamilton. His painful death was detailed to the FBI by Barker Karpis gangster Volney Davis. According to Davis's revelations, Hamilton died as a result of gangrene when a bullet that hit him in the liver mushroomed, shortly after the Battle of Little Bohemia. He was buried in a gravel pit and covered by ten small cans of lye, ten miles south of Aurora. Hamilton's bones blended into the closeted skeletons of the Dillinger case which were, by 1935, all put to rest.[20]

On September 1st, 1935, an exciting event occurred in the Indiana State Police. A young man named Paul Vincent Minneman was admitted to the force. Assigned to the Lafayette Post, he performed the duties of a state trooper without coming to anyone's undue attention. He was destined to live only two more years. He would be shot and killed by a barbarous gang of thugs on May 25th, 1937. His death would directly pit

Leach against the FBI and would bring Leach to the conclusion that he would not in any way cooperate with the federal agency.

As the public enemy era receded, Leach's assignments changed. Some were routine, yet others packed the kind of melodrama for which the captain yearned. In the years following the Dillinger case, Leach continued to assert himself fearlessly through a series of altercations with the FBI.

One of these was the sensational 1936 murder case that would come to be known as the "Head and Hands" case. In his investigation of the murder of a retired Cincinnati fire captain Harry R. Miller, Leach again pushed the boundaries of his jurisdiction in the eyes of the FBI. The grizzly, tabloid affair became a battleground when agents allegedly hampered Leach's investigation.

The victim, Harry Miller, was a moderately wealthy, retired captain of the Cincinnati fire department. Miller was shot and beaten in or near his home in Indiana, after which his cottage was set on fire. After that, his head and hands were severed and dumped in Kentucky. His alleged torso was discovered in a culvert near Eminence, Kentucky. The body part was matched with Miller only because he had been reported missing, and was too damaged for a positive identification. That was the first problem with this puzzling case.

Miller's cottage in New Trenton, Indiana, put the murder into Leach's camp. He went out and arrested Flora Miller, the sixty-six-year-old sister of the victim, along with her chauffer and secretary, Heber L. Hicks. Hicks was fresh from serving eleven years in prison for murdering a Kentucky girl and severing her fingers. Flora Miller was the sole heir to her brother's $150,000 estate. So far, this was playing out like a paperback novel with movie rights.[21]

Behind the scenes, things were not as simple as a standard whodunit. Leach's arrest of Hicks caused the FBI to counter that Leach had not followed due process. This was a reference to the July 7th, 1936, arrest and interrogation of Hicks, during which the suspect confessed to Leach while a prisoner of a covert police procedure called "running the loop." Leach moved Hicks from one barracks to another as a way to keep lawyers and bondsmen away from him while he secured a confession. This scam was always challenged by defense attorneys but defended by police.[22]

During this confession, Hicks named his accomplices: John Joseph Poholsky, William A. Kuehlman and Frank Gore Williams. Hicks maintained that he did not participate in the murder. When Poholsky was arrested, he disputed that and insisted that Hicks was present for the act of severing Miller's head and hands, encasing them in concrete and throwing them into a lake. Kuehlman and Williams were eventually captured. All four were sentenced to death in the Michigan City electric chair.

The sister of the victim, Flora Miller, was curiously absent from all the interrogations. Initially, Leach had released her and formally arrested Hicks.

Kuehlman had tried to implicate "a woman," but Leach quickly put a stop to the story, calling it "hearsay." Later the defense charged that Flora had forged her brother's name at times in order to use his good credit, a charge the prosecution ignored. Most likely because Leach used her as a bargaining chip to get Hicks to confess, Flora escaped the fate that had befallen other females named in murder conspiracy cases, most notably Ruth Snyder in 1928 and Anna Antonio in 1934. Both of these women died in New York State's electric chair along with their co-conspirators in first-degree murder cases, convicted on the confessions of their co-defendants.

Matt Leach maintained that Hicks's arrest was made in "his" department, which also did the preliminary investigations. During the confession in which Hicks implicated the three alleged accomplices, Leach charged Hicks with murder and an indictment set the case for trial. Hicks confessed in the hope that Flora Miller would not be charged. There was circumstantial evidence that might have implicated her—she would inherit all of Miller's estate upon his death; she had a close relationship with Hicks.

Unknown to all but the ISP and the FBI, Leach knew at the time that he did not have sufficient evidence for a conviction. He later claimed to have gone to the Indianapolis office of the FBI to ask for help in bringing in Poholsky. The resultant stonewalling by the FBI and Leach's mounting frustration were all too familiar by then. The FBI claimed that the original agent to whom Leach had given his files was transferred and the files were lost. Leach became increasingly agitated as the case moved closer to trial. His calls to Agent Reinecke were blown off. The suspect Poholsky was later arrested in Warren, Ohio, by that police department with the help of two ISP officers, an Officer Stewart and John Barton. The FBI either sat on the case or just didn't feel it was worth their time.[23]

Later, when suspect Frank Williams was arrested in San Francisco, the Justice Department agents asked the arresting officers how they had gotten the information on his location. When the arresting officers told them it came from Leach, they grilled the San Francisco officers for hours as to just what Leach knew about the case.

The publicity resulting from this and other murder cases went directly to Leach. In an article published on the case, the *Indianapolis Times* said, "Solution of the 'head and hands' slaying of Harry R. Miller, retired captain of Cincinnati fire department ... was a feather in the cap of the Indiana State Police." Leach embellished his self-taught mastery of the criminal mind in a follow-up article published around the time of the executions of the accused killers. He detailed his strategies in getting the confessions out of the suspects. The tricks Leach used came out in the article. He had promised Hicks a light sentence and some money for his mother in return for a confession. The confession would keep his girlfriend, the sister of the victim, safe from prosecution. These techniques were later challenged as contrary to due process and possibly eliciting false confessions.

The spate of articles, strategically typeset around photos of Matt Leach, outraged the state police board. Back in 1935, the board had passed a resolution mandating that Donald F. Stiver, the superintendent, have the sole right to disseminate information on the activities of the state police.[24]

Leach's rebuttal was that his actions had resulted in arrests of suspects who were duly tried and convicted. It seemed to some, however, that the end result had not justified the means. Albert L. Rabb, an attorney on the Indiana State Police Board, publicly challenged Leach due to his handling of the case. Rabb's civil liberties critique of the captain formed a basis for the FBI's accusations of the same nature.

One year later, in 1937, they challenged Leach on his methods. The main issue was that Leach had moved the suspects around to get their confessions under fire, that he was violating the suspects' constitutional rights. Leach wrote off the charge by saying that Hicks could not easily have his constitutional rights violated. He made this statement based on Hicks' record, which had been to murder a girl and cut off her fingers to get her rings. Unofficially, Leach believed that these questions about his methods were being made by police board people who had no practical experience in actual police work. Later he admitted, however, that he lacked evidence against his suspects:

> Charges of murder were filed against Hicks. His case was set for trial.... I realized at that time that with the information that we had and evidence that we had concerning Hicks, it would not be sufficient evidence, that we would have to have material evidence or one of these men who took part in this killing must be apprehended.[25]

The end result was four people sentenced to the death penalty and Leach having been accused of failing to follow due process in securing these convictions. Although he was criticized for his aggressive, narrowly focused prosecution, Leach's conduct was typical of the 1930s.

The year of the Miller "Head and Hands" case, 1936, witnessed a law-and-order dynamic develop. The post-desperado era marked the height of the morality movement in the United States that went by the catchphrase "Crime Does Not Pay." Hoover and the FBI led this targeted campaign, aimed at demystifying the violence of the Depression-era crime wave.

Hoover was nearly successful in his attempt to dilute the effects that the gangster years had had on law and order. Then a new gang appeared. The Brady Gang served a challenge to Hoover and compromised his anti-crime campaign.

PART III

The Mutineer

CHAPTER 11

The New Dillingers

I accuse the Department of Justice of deliberately seeking to confound state and local law enforcement authorities for the purpose of advancing the ambition of Mr. Hoover.—Matt Leach, in the *Gary Post-Tribune*, September 4, 1937

The Brady Gang were wanton desperadoes who went into history as skid row thugs. Most people today do not recognize their faces.[1]

A trio of Indiana ex-cons composed of Al Brady, Clarence Shaffer and James Dalhover had started out in 1935 as armed robbers targeting two jewelry stores, one of which they hit twice. After a Chicago fence foiled them by hijacking their cache, they abandoned jewel thievery and dropped into the ghetto of grocery store stickups. With an ego that winced at the thought of small-town jobs, leader Al Brady executed several bank robberies with the occasional help of a fourth man.

In their bank jobs they tried to conjure up the memory of John Dillinger. He was the dead guy whose cardboard shoes they hoped to fill. They made this fact known by announcing to the shivering citizens caught in their holdups that they were the "new Dillinger gang."

Although the Brady Gang claimed to make "pikers" out of the Dillinger gang, it was not going to happen. This was not because of any mistake on the part of mastermind Al Brady, or mechanical genius Rhuel James Dalhover or the misguided Clarence Schafer, Jr. This gang never usurped the mythological stature of the Dillinger Gang because that era had passed.

The FBI had entered the chase early in 1936. At the time, Al Brady was still pulling small stickups. He stepped out of his predictable pattern by stealing a car belonging to FBI Agent Oliver Salinger in Chicago. During the stickup of the federal agent, Brady stole $40 and Salinger's service revolver. Salinger confided to the SAC of the Chicago office, D. M. Ladd, that the robber had compared himself to Dillinger during the robbery.

The episode of Salinger and Brady's confrontation and the announcement that Brady was the new Dillinger became the basis for the FBI's interest in the case. That was the incident that brought the Brady Gang to prominence within law enforcement circles. It pulled many police agencies into the case, which ended up covering a vast geographical area in the Midwest and Northeast.

Shortly afterwards, the gang, along with a fourth member, Charles Geisking, heisted three jewelry stores, the last of which was Kay's Jewelry Store in Lima, Ohio. During a gun battle in Lima, Sergeant Richard Rivers was killed. The jurisdiction of Ohio kept Leach out of the case, as detectives from Dayton began an investigation. At the same time, the FBI was actively monitoring the case.

The Bradys crossed into Indianapolis to fence the jewels, but had ambitions to meet Chicago fence Jack Becker. It was the Brady Gang's activities in Chicago that brought Detective Sal Corsi as well as captains Stege and Egan into the case.

The gang struck again in Ohio, with the March 4th robbery of the Roy O. Wieland jewelry store in Greenville. Their new Chicago fence, Jack Becker, sized the gang up as the very thing they didn't want to be— a bunch of "pikers." Becker hatched a scheme with "Dago Jack" Ventucci to stage a jewel robbery of the gang. The gang, seeing this as a betrayal, left Chicago. They reverted to grocery store stickups, again in Ohio. During the robbery of a meat market, a twenty-one-year-old clerk named Edward Lindsay was shot and killed. This brought federal agents into the area of Piqua, Ohio, where they worked with Sheriff Kenneth Miller in investigating the robbery.

By May of 1937, the states of Indiana, Illinois, Ohio, Connecticut and Maryland formed an interstate nesting ground for the Brady Gang. Police officers who had made names for themselves during the Dillinger investigations, such as captains Egan and Stege in Chicago, Chief Michael Morrissey in Indianapolis and Inspector Yendes in Dayton, were handling investigations in their own jurisdictions without garnering publicity. One of the Pinkertons was also involved in the Brady case. E. S. Clark, who had penned many investigative memos during the

$1,500.00
REWARD

On June 15, 1937, Homer Cummings, Attorney General of the United States, under authority vested in him by law, offered the following rewards:

$500 for information furnished to the Federal Bureau of Investigation resulting in the apprehension of **ALFRED BRADY;**

$500 for information furnished to the Federal Bureau of Investigation resulting in the apprehension of **JAMES DALHOVER;**

$500 for information furnished to the Federal Bureau of Investigation resulting in the apprehension of **CLARENCE LEE SHAFFER.**

The photographs and descriptions of the above named persons are hereinafter set out.

A complaint was filed at Cleveland, Ohio, on October 13, 1936, charging the above named individuals with the interstate transportation of stolen property. These men are also wanted in the State of Indiana upon murder charges and are sought for several bank robberies.

No part of the aforesaid rewards shall be paid to any officials or employees of the Department of Justice. The right is reserved to divide and allocate portions of said rewards as between several claimants. The offer provides that all claims to any of the above described rewards and all questions and disputes that may arise as among claimants to the foregoing rewards shall be passed upon by the Attorney General and that his decisions shall be final and conclusive.

ALFRED BRADY, with aliases: J. A. BARTON, JAMES BARTON, JOHN BARTON, JOHN A. BARTON, EARL GENTRY, JAMES REID, JOE REID, AL BORDEN, ELMER BORDEN, JAMES A. REED.

DESCRIPTION - Age, 26 (born October 25, 1910, in Indiana); Height, 5 feet, 7 inches; Weight, 160 pounds; Build, medium; Eyes, gray; Hair, light brown; Complexion, ruddy; Nationality, American.

JAMES DALHOVER, with aliases: JAMES WILLIAMS, JAMES MILLER, JACK KING, TED STEWART, ALBERT GOINS, JAMES DALHOBER.

DESCRIPTION - Age, 30 (born August 24, 1906, Madison, Indiana); Height, 5 feet, 4½ inches; Weight, 134 pounds; Build, medium small; Eyes, blue; Hair, light brown; Complexion, ruddy; Nationality, American.

CLARENCE LEE SHAFFER, JR., with aliases: LEE JACKSON, CLARENCE LEE SHAFFER, AL C. LAYTON.

DESCRIPTION - Age, 20 (born 1916, Indianapolis, Indiana); Height, 5 feet, 5 inches; Weight, 123 pounds; Build, medium; Hair, brown; Eyes, gray; Complexion, dark; Scars, small scar back of right hand; Occupation, laborer; Nationality, American; Marital Status, single.

Information may be communicated in person, or by telephone or telegraph collect, to the undersigned, or to the nearest office of the Federal Bureau of Investigation, United States Department of Justice, the local addresses and telephone numbers of which are set forth on the reverse side of this notice.

JOHN EDGAR HOOVER, DIRECTOR,
FEDERAL BUREAU OF INVESTIGATION,
UNITED STATES DEPARTMENT OF JUSTICE,
WASHINGTON, D. C.
TELEPHONE, NATIONAL 7117.

June 15, 1937.

The New Dillingers, June 15, 1937. Al Brady (*top*), James Dalhover (*center*) and Clarence Shaffer (*bottom*), had nothing to do with Dillinger. They emulated the outlaw and formed a copycat gang.

Dillinger hunt, complained of lack of cooperation by Chief Morrissey and the Indianapolis police.

After they were arrested in Chicago, Shaffer, Brady and Dalhover were returned to Indianapolis to stand trial for the murder of Sergeant Rivers. On October 11th, they escaped from the Hancock County Jail at Greencastle, Indiana. They embarked upon a reign of terror in Indiana, raiding police arsenals and building up their machine gun power by converting a World War I belt-fed, 200-round Marlin for modern use.

The unpublicized nature of the Brady hunt changed on May 25th, 1937, with the robbery and murder of State Trooper Paul Minneman and wounding of Deputy Sheriff Elmer Craig. The gang, fresh from robbing a bank in Goodland, Indiana, passed Officer Paul Minneman and Cass County Deputy Sheriff Elmer Craig on what is now called State Road 16. Brady, Shaffer, Dahlover and an unidentified fourth man shot at the officers, who then chased them.

The officers were armed only with .38 Special Colt revolvers. A 12-gauge pump shotgun was kept tethered to the trunk of the car, which one unnamed source said was done according to department regulations. Leach had announced years before that troopers would never carry automatic weapons.

In the ambush of May 25th, the Brady Gang had armed themselves with the 30–06 belt-fed machine gun. The deadly weapon was a Marlin that Dalhover had revamped from its original use in the First World War.

Officer Minneman was shot twenty-three times. He took sixty-four hours to die in agony. Paul's partner, Deputy Elmer Craig, recovered from the ambush.

Officer Minneman's death brought Matt Leach into the case publicly when the captain told the press that he promised a quick end to the Brady Gang. Leach was parochial in believing that the Brady Gang jurisdiction belonged to his department because Minneman's death had occurred in Indiana. He felt assured, as did other law enforcers, that the job of catching Minneman's killers was the responsibility of the local police. It was an emotional idea that never materialized. Federal jurisdiction would be applied in bringing Minneman's only surviving killer to justice. James Dalhover would be captured, convicted in a federal court for the slain trooper's murder and sentenced to death in the electric chair.

Hoover immediately issued a statement that the FBI was going to formally enter the hunt for the Brady Gang. The statement appears to have been timed just as Leach was claiming it was his jurisdiction. The FBI had maintained an active file on the Brady Gang for months. Due to the interstate nature of the Brady Gang, the FBI would naturally have been involved.

This raised Hoover's ire like nothing that had occurred since 1934, when the director had accused Leach of being a troublemaker. Hoover actually feared the onslaught of another Dillinger Gang. The director could not afford the romantic news copy that would bring the Brady Gang into

Officer Paul Minneman, slain by the Brady Gang. Photograph ca. 1935 (courtesy Indiana State Police Museum).

the public sphere. Hoover was aware that Leach had been instrumental in garnering the publicity that had launched the Dillinger myth. Now the director kept one step ahead of Leach in the hopes of averting the kind of hype that had catapulted Dillinger to fame.

Hoover was aware that journalist Basil Gallagher, with a readership extending outside of Indiana, was quoting Leach.[2] Unless the FBI stepped in to quiet the newsman, Al Brady would get his wish of leaving an iconic legacy such as that which followed Dillinger.

With the Depression crime wave ended and the late thirties anti-crime campaign in full swing, Hoover was putting the finishing touches on his amazing rise to national prominence. At that pinnacle point in Hoover's growth spurt, he fought to stifle anything with the potential to cast the Brady Gang as an object of glamour or sympathy. Leach rose to the status of being the most credible local police chief in the Brady campaign. The FBI was exploiting his involvement and running to him with questions about details as mundane as the spelling of the names of suspects and associates of the Brady Gang. They also depended heavily upon the fact that he knew a great deal about these associates, including the wives of the gang members.

Until this point there had been many police officials involved in the Brady case. For that reason, it was never a matter of Hoover versus Leach.

Hoover adopted a new strategy in dealing with the enmity between himself and Leach. Rather than tackle Leach head-on as in earlier times, he quietly built a case against him. The opportunity arose when Leach went to Baltimore, Maryland, to investigate the gang. The captain left himself wide open by traveling so far out of his jurisdiction.[3]

Leach was about to repeat his patterns from the Dillinger era and involve himself with the molls of the gang. In May of 1936, Leach had arrested Mary Kinder's recently paroled brother. Charles "Chuck" Northern had been paroled the previous November after his 1929 arrest and ten-year prison sentence in the Indiana State Prison for robbing a filling station. Leach's position in arresting Northern was to question him concerning the Brady case. Brady had just been arrested in Chicago and charged with the murder of Indianapolis police sergeant Richard Rivers in a holdup. Leach charged Northern and had him held on a $20,000 bond on a charge of vagrancy. Northern was released for lack of evidence.[4]

Leach's escalating flamboyance was just the opening his enemies were waiting for. And once again he became a target of the very gang he was facing. Al Brady announced that he was going to kill Matt Leach, and so stated under interrogation in Chicago.[5]

Undeterred, Leach continued to make rash statements to the press: "We will blast the Brady gangsters off the face of the earth if they ever again attempt to kill and rob in Indiana." This boast masked the fact that Leach was not making progress in the Brady case. He'd been led into a sandpit by the sudden reticence on the part of his witnesses. Leach claimed that the FBI had told people not to speak to him. The FBI countered by accusing him of the very same thing, of telling his witnesses not to speak to the FBI.[6]

The federal agency went on to slam Leach over his handling of the Christine Puckett affair. Miss Puckett was the mother of Brady Gang member Clarence Lee Schaffer's child, who was born out of wedlock.

Leach had visited Puckett. Puckett's relationship with Schaffer had ended when the outlaw refused to marry her. She was considered by the FBI to be a potentially good source on the gang. Leach decided to visit her unannounced. He instructed her to laugh at the FBI agents if they came to interview her about the gang's whereabouts. Leach countered that the agents had gotten to her first, and told her that she should not speak to him.[7]

Soon the Brady case shifted to Baltimore, Maryland. The Bradys had been hiding out there with three women who were serving as wives and claiming to be unaware of their true identities. When they were almost captured in a gun battle near Baltimore, the near miss brought the FBI head to head with Matt Leach.[8]

Baltimore was the turning point in the Brady case. There the gang members had put down roots by marrying, joining clubs, taking self-improvement lessons and visiting doctors for issues ranging from sexually transmitted diseases to male pattern baldness. Baltimore opened the quirks and personalities of the three members of the gang to the FBI. Al Brady apparently was a fanatical roller skater who took figure skating lessons while living in Baltimore. He was known to carry a pair of roller skates in a black bag. He had also purchased ice skates in Baltimore, and had joined a skating club under the guise of a businessman. As a member of the skating club, he went on bus trips to other cities to skate in rinks outside of Baltimore.

The arrest of the wives and a search of the Brady premises revealed this bizarre facet of Al Brady's personality. His dedication to roller skating had prompted him to join the skating club at the Carlins Park rink in Baltimore. Something prompted Leach to release the skating story to the press. The FBI then declared their ice skating investigation aborted. Despite their claim, the FBI avidly visited roller skating rinks in cities as diverse as Philadelphia and Baltimore, and in states ranging as far to the west as Nebraska and as far east as Philadelphia.

In August of 1937, Leach went to Baltimore to interview the two women who had married Brady Gang members James Dalhover and Clarence Lee Shaffer, Jr. The marriages had occurred back on November 30th, 1936, in a double wedding ceremony. The two desperadoes had married the women, Mary and Minnie Raimondo, under assumed names while posing as businessmen. Minnie Raimondo was wed to

Clarence Lee Shaffer, Jr., and Mary Raimondo had married James Dal-hover. The women denied knowing that the men were notorious crim-inals. Leach interviewed their brother, Anthony Raimondo, as well as their sister Josephine Raimondo aka Josephine Economidis, who lived with the women. "We didn't know anything about their business," she said. "Now we are cooperating with the police."[9]

Leach went to the Baltimore State Police to check on sterling sil-verware that Dalhover and Shaffer had given to their brides as wedding presents. The silverware originated at the robbery of the Carthage, Indi-ana, State Bank the previous December. On August 20th, 1937, the Bal-timore police released the silverware to Leach to return to its rightful owner, Mrs. Vera Hill of Cartage, Indiana. It had been stolen from a safe deposit box during the robbery of the State Bank of Cartage. Leach later confided to Tubby Toms that Mrs. Hill had berated him for one missing spoon.[10]

After Leach obtained the silverware for return to Mrs. Hill, he vio-lated an edict that Stiver had brought in back in 1935. Called the Pub-licity Resolution, it gave the superintendent, Stiver, the sole right to release information to the public. When Leach leaked the clue of Brady's roller skating to the press, he challenged that resolution. The article was the size of an obituary yet blew up in his face. After living on the peak of the Indianapolis dailies, he was brought down by two suburban dailies. Leach said glibly that Brady liked to roller skate.[11]

Agent Myron E. Gurnea, of the Indianapolis field office, prepared a report at this juncture of August of 1937. Things weren't good, he inti-mated; the FBI had run down all leads in Indiana. With the Brady Gang's whereabouts still unknown, tension mounted in other police stations. In Chicago's Maxwell Street Stationhouse, Detective Sergeant Corsi and Sergeant Eugene Spain had been investigating Jack Becker, the fence in the Brady Gang's Lima jewelry robbery. The sergeants received a tip that the gang was hoping for amnesty by turning themselves in there. After working night and day on the case, Corsi learned that he and his team had followed a false lead.

Corsi and Spain, along with Stege, refrained from making state-ments against Leach. It was obvious that they preferred to work without him, as they had not included Leach in their interrogation of Brady at the Maxwell Street Stationhouse on April 30th, 1936. That deposition had been taken in the company of Captain Egan and Chief Morrissey, along with Corsi and Stege in the presence of William Crawford, the assistant state attorney. The only public disagreement had been over a disclosure by Leach that Al Brady had been identified as the killer of Indianapolis policeman Sergeant Richard Rivers. This disputed what George Whitley, a former bootlegging partner of Brady, had told the Chicago detectives. Leach stated that Whitley had named Brady as the killer. City detectives then stepped up to dispute Leach, saying that Whitley didn't know who had killed the officer. The result, which may have vindicated Leach, was that Stege and Egan of the Maxwell Street station, along with Morrissey in Indianapolis, reported that Al Brady had admitted to being the killer of Sergeant Rivers.

The Chicago police kept their opinions of Leach out of the papers during the Brady hunt. The interstate Brady chase continued without Leach. It later culminated in a shootout in Bangor, Maine, on October 12th, 1937, during which Brady and Shaffer were killed and Dalhover taken alive. By then, Leach would be out.

To rid the case of Leach, the FBI had some strategic moves to make. They first needed to figure out who in Chicago was on their side. Shortly before September 1st, an FBI inspector visited the offices of James Allman, who was Chicago's long-term reform police commissioner.

Agents Harold H. Reinecke and Myron Gurnea, of the Indianapolis field office, took this information to the Indiana Police Superintendent Donald Stiver on September 1st. They had arranged to meet Albert L. Rabb, the Indiana State Police Board attorney.[12]

Rabb was an opponent of Leach due to his handling of the "Head and Hands" murder case of Harry Miller, during which Leach had "looped" the suspect, Heber Hicks. With Rabb already rabid over Leach, he was one of the more aggressive members of the board in moving forward for dismissal.[13]

The meeting started a momentum that took on a life of its own. The federal agents announced that they would no longer work with the Indiana State Police unless and until Matt Leach was forced to step down. They had already broken off all working relations with the ISP and refused to communicate in the case of the Brady Gang. The FBI supplied their reason: that Matt Leach had refused to cooperate and exchange information.[14] At the same time, Leach kept criticizing the bureau, claiming that his 1934 letter to McNutt criticizing the FBI was the basis for the dismissal.[15]

In his outspoken remarks, he gave the FBI exactly the entry they needed to start a proceeding against him. With his unwitting help, they were able to proceed in the way that came naturally to this straight-laced bureaucracy. They went by the book. Federal agents from the Indianapolis field office conferred with the Indiana State Police Board members: Major Claude L. Crooks of Lebanon, chairman; Albert Rabb of Indianapolis; Clarence Gramelspacher of Jasper; and William Bell of Decatur. These four board members concurred in charging Leach with misconduct.

Backing their accusations was the generalization that Leach had challenged Chapter 299 of the Acts of the Indiana General Assembly of 1935, which mandated cooperation between the Indiana State Police and the FBI.[16]

On September 4th, the Indiana State Police Board relayed its wishes to Donald Stiver. The superintendent entered the Statehouse office of Matt Leach and asked him to resign. Stiver reminded Leach of the new assembly acts, which forbade noncooperation between law enforcement agencies. As far as the enforced resignation, Stiver told Leach that there were thirteen to fourteen charges pending against him. These included the disclosure of confidential information to the press without a superior's permission. It amounted to insubordination and acts unbecoming an officer of the law.[17] Then Stiver dropped the stink bomb in Leach's lap. Captain Walter Eckert, of the Seymour barracks, had already been hired as the new captain of the ISP.[18] When the ousted captain prepared for his scheduled hearing, he came up against a barrage of charges, many of them reworded and redundant.

Leach already knew about his fate. Tubby Toms later wrote, "Leach was in Lake County … when it was decided to fire him peremptorily. Two of his reporter friends got word to Leach. By the time he arrived back in Indianapolis at dawn, they had whipped off a statement for the soon-to-be-deposed officer. When Leach walked into the door of his office he was handed a note of formal discharge."[19]

Toms, always a supporter of Leach, got some facts wrong. These articles appeared some eighteen years later, and his memory must have been vague. Most accounts claim that the members of the police board themselves had given Leach the advance notice. Regardless of who told him, Leach had prepared an answer and a demand for a hearing.

As they handed Leach the memorandum, he demanded his day in court. According to Toms, "Without even looking at the paper, he handed the other man his answer. It was some time before the state police brass knew just how Leach had kept up with them at so great a distance."[20]

Then, in a characteristic move, Leach issued a press release:

> I have refused today to resign as captain of the Indiana state police as requested by the state police board on the complaint of J. Edgar Hoover, director of the Federal Department of Justice.
>
> My sole reason for refusing to resign is the record of our department through the period of going on five years in which I have been the active head of the state police. I cite the ascending record of achievement of the department since the time of its creation in 1933 as the best defense I have to offer. In this position I have been fortified by public endorsement of the work of the state police department.

Leach went on to list the cases recently solved by his department. He outlined his distress over the FBI's methods in several cases concerning FBI agents in routine investigations as well as the Dillinger case:

> These foolhardy methods of J. Edgar Hoover made it necessary for me to lodge formal complaint with the Governor of Indiana against the policies of the department of justice as now operated, such being in the interest of the safety of the citizens of Indiana, the law enforcement authorities of this state and the subordinates of Mr. Hoover assigned to Indiana.

Leach mentioned the lack of cooperation in the murder of Indiana State Trooper Paul Minneman and accused the FBI of telling persons associated with the Brady Gang not to assist him:

> Four months ago one of our own men was killed in the performance of his duty. In the pursuit of the murderers our department solicited the cooperation of the Department of Justice and other agencies. What assistance have we received from the Department of Justice?
>
> This attitude on the part of the department of justice now passes beyond the point of refusal to cooperate—it becomes definite antagonism. I will not surrender to an authority from without which lacks authority within.
>
> In turn, I accuse the Department of Justice of deliberately seeking to confound state and local law enforcement authorities for the purpose of advancing the ambition of Mr. Hoover.
>
> I shall ask that the United States Senate proceed with an investigation of Mr. Hoover's methods and motives and expect, accordingly, to amplify the foregoing statement [sic].

In the unsettled aftermath, Leach spoke candidly to the press. If it was his attempt to return to law enforcement, he did a poor job.[21]

> I would like to know the real reason why I was dismissed. I am given no notice of dismissal until I arrive at my office this morning. The board held a secret meeting and voted my dismissal without giving me an opportunity to be heard or to defend myself. There is something behind it besides lack of cooperation with federal authorities.[22]

Donald Stiver added his voice and said, quite honestly, that "a representative of Mr. Hoover had threatened to sever relations with the Indiana department unless Leach was removed." As the fight played itself out in the papers, Leach got his parting shot when he said, "[I am] glad to surrender my position as a step toward clearing up the situation surrounding this Hitler—by which I mean Hoover."[23]

The charges were an upsetting mélange of generalities. They said in essence that he had to go. It must have wounded his pride to read the charge that he had conducted himself in a manner unbecoming to a police officer, and that he had failed toward the end of "achieving greater success in preventing and detecting crimes and apprehending criminals."

At the hearing scheduled for September 17th, the former captain hoped to further sway public opinion. He planned to countercharge that the FBI had withheld information in the Brady case, and would illustrate this with statements from witnesses who had been intimidated by the FBI into not speaking to the Indiana State Police. It became a moot point with devastating results. The moment the Indiana State Police Board fired him, the FBI had delivered the Brady files. Leach was not informed of this and remained ignorant of this fact until his hearing date.[24] He gathered his evidence and wrote endless rebuttals, as he put his world on hold until the morning of September 16th, 1937. It would be a day that would put to death his career and whatever was left of his good reputation.

CHAPTER 12

Kangaroo Court

I will not surrender to an authority from without which lacks authority within.—Matt Leach, in the *Indianapolis Times*, September 4, 1937

On the day Leach was fired, everybody seemed to be out of town. Governor M. Clifford Townsend could not be reached, nor could his secretary Dick Heller. When Townsend finally made a statement, he said merely that there were no other reasons behind the dismissal other than those reflected in the charges presented against Leach. In Washington, Hoover was not available for comment. Even Harold H. Reinecke, SAC of the Indianapolis field office, would not remark on Leach's dismissal.

Leach's crony Pleas Greenlee had visited Townsend personally to hear the charges. Back in 1936, Greenlee had tried to run for the Democratic nomination to succeed McNutt. Governor Townsend defeated him. But Leach had backed Greenlee in his failed gubernatorial bid—and was identified as being a member of the "Greenlee Cabinet." The problem was that Greenlee lost, which sent all of his backers scurrying to resign when Townsend won the election. The move was called "Going the Way of All Greenlee Boys" in the press. Leach, who had refused to resign simply because he had backed Greenlee, should have seen that eventually he would be out.[1]

Leach had supported Greenlee, but his loyalty meant nothing now. Greenlee approached the Leach situation with a shrug and an attitude of "what have you done for me lately?"

Leach, who paid homage only to McNutt, had defaulted on his Hoosier Democratic "2 Percent Club" dues to Townsend. It did not help that Leach's photo of McNutt hung in place of a photo of the new

213

governor. Given these obvious snubs, Townsend had no reason to support Leach.

Stiver was clear in his opinion that Leach was a liability. The new safety director had a reputation for disliking the bastions of 1933. He'd written them off as "bureau old timers" who "owed their jobs to ranks and politics."[2] With the full blessing of the governor, Stiver released twelve formal charges against Leach in the hours after the captain was fired.

The first charge referred directly to Chapter 299 of the recently enacted Acts of the Indiana General Assembly of 1935, which mandated cooperation between the Indiana State Police and the FBI. The second reiterated the first, that Leach "willfully disobeyed the rules and regulations of the Department of State Police in that he willfully failed and refused to cooperate and exchange information [with the FBI]." The third declared that Leach had committed conduct unbecoming to an officer by publicly criticizing the FBI and its members. The fourth and fifth charges concerned the Brady case by stating, "Leach ... has communicated or given police information to the public at large ... confidential police information concerning one Al Brady." These two charges included the fact that Leach had released the "skating proclivities of said Al Brady, the same being information given said Captain Leach for use in the arrest or apprehension of [Brady] and not for publication."

The sixth charge stated that Leach had attempted to prevent witnesses from cooperating with the FBI. Likewise, the seventh charge invoked Chapter 299 of the Acts in accusing Leach of preventing witnesses from cooperating with the FBI. The eighth charge was more loaded in that it accused Leach of preventing FBI witnesses from working with ISP officers. The ninth accused Leach of publicly slandering officials and members of the FBI. The tenth elaborated on the fourth and fifth charges, in the sense that it accused Leach of giving information to the press about the affairs of the ISP. The eleventh claimed that Leach conducted himself in a manner unbecoming to a police officer for refusing to cooperate with the FBI. The twelfth repeated charge number eleven, with the addendum that his lack of cooperation went counter to the "end of achieving success in preventing and detecting crimes and apprehending criminals."[3]

It seemed like Leach had no friends left. His actions had pushed the state police into a difficult position. Two weeks earlier, on September 1st, the FBI had broken off all working relations with the ISP by refusing to communicate in the case of the Brady Gang. The FBI supplied their reason: that Matt Leach had refused to cooperate and exchange information. In his outspoken remarks, Leach gave the FBI exactly the entry they needed to start a proceeding against him.

When the ousted captain appeared for the hearing at nine o'clock in the morning on September 16th, his face was drawn and thin. He was dressed in his customary neat, dark suit. As he walked into the House of Representatives chamber in the state capitol building, he sensed that he was outnumbered by complainants from both the State Police Board and the FBI.

Leach was already aware of the barrage of charges, many of them redundant. Worse, the blue wall of support he had expected was nowhere to be found. "I feel sure," he had said, "that police officers throughout the country will

Captain Matt Leach, September 4, 1937 (Harry Ransom Center, the University of Texas at Austin).

be with me in my stand." That wasn't to be the case. Leach was, however, backed by the American Legion Gary Post, whose members voted on a motion to protest the firing. A true brotherhood, its members had lodged their protest over Leach's objections. He had tried to protect his fraternal organization by asking them not to get involved.

Three members of the Indiana State Police Board appeared as complainants. They were Patrick J. Smith, assistant attorney general representing the State of Indiana and the Indiana State Police Department; Albert Rabb, who had accused Leach of unconstitutional maneuvers in the case of the "Head and Hands"; and Claude Crooks, a board president from Lebanon who assumed the role of the bench in this proceeding. The latter two appeared hostile to Leach. They fired out interrogatories that Leach would later characterize as leading questions. In this proceeding, the state police board complainants were free to ask their questions in any form they chose to.

The FBI appearance of Harold Reinecke, head of the Indianapolis field office and the agent who had demanded Leach's termination, was a startling remnant of the Dillinger era. Reinecke bore the distinction of having earned placement on John Dillinger's hit list for having slugged Evelyn Frechette, Dillinger's moll, during her interrogations in April of 1934. Dillinger had taken his rant only as far as pen to paper and no further. Ironically, Leach shared an equal spot on Dillinger's hit list.[4] But Reinecke's mere presence at the hearing conjured up Dillinger's ghost.

Reinecke was now going to testify against a fellow lawman. He had helped the State Police Board file its exhaustive list of allegations on September 1st.[5] It had been Reinecke who told Superintendent Stiver, "We are not here to tell you how to run your organization, but to tell you how we are running ours."

During the tedious, six-hour hearing, Leach defended himself against the testimony of Reinecke and three of his fellow federal agents. Representing Leach was former Attorney General Philip Lutz, Jr., who was the Interstate Crime Commission board chairman and its former president. Leach seemed to have this one supporter that day. He was buoyed when Lutz announced, "I regard Captain Leach as one of the best police officers in the country, and have been assured that he is so regarded by other police officials."

The hearing was conducted without jurisprudence. It made up its structure as it went along. Lutz asked that the rules of court evidence be observed. The board overruled the objection. This kangaroo court commenced in view of a spectator section comprised of state employees on coffee breaks and lunch hours. Pat Smith, who was the deputy attorney general representing the state, acted as the proceeding's *de facto* judge. He suggested that Leach take the stand. But Leach's attorney Lutz disagreed, claiming that Leach was unaware of the charges pending against him. The state attorney then retorted that he would be happy to dismiss the proceeding altogether. That did not bode well for Leach. But Smith did agree to have Reinecke take the stand first.

Reinecke recalled the many instances between 1935 and 1937 when Leach did not completely cooperate with protocols set by the FBI. Then Lutz, realizing that there was no jurisprudence directing the proceeding, asked if Leach could examine Reinecke. The bench objected. Rabb permitted it, and Leach was permitted to question his long-standing opponent:

LEACH: In four years, there has been no cooperation?
REINECKE: There just hasn't been any, Mr. Leach.
LEACH: How do you define "cooperation"?
REINECKE: We cooperate with agencies in which the officials are honest, attempting to do their duty and not publicity mad.

"I'm afraid that is your head man," Leach retorted. Leach's reaction clashed markedly with Reinecke's studied anonymity. "I'm not here," the agent responded, "to engage in any personalities, but merely to state the department's policies." Leach pressed on, regarding Brady:

LEACH: Mr. Reinecke, you said I told those relatives not to tell your men anything and to laugh at them?
REINECKE: We have an affidavit to that effect.
LEACH: We'll go elsewhere…. You said in a certain city I criticized your men.
REINECKE: You have, publicly and privately.
LEACH: What, specially, did I say to that chief of police?
REINECKE: You said we were not cooperative; that our work was not particularly important. I would not use some of the words you used about our personnel.

Reinecke's recollections took him back to 1935, with no mention of the name of Dillinger. The agent's testimony was vague and nonresponsive: "On August 26, 1937, a chief of police told us Matt Leach had libeled the federal bureau of investigation. His attitude was described as 'contemptuous.'"[6]

Leach had his opportunity to answer these vague allegations. While on the stand, the exiled captain defended his actions in the individual cases that had been the courses of conflict: Dillinger, the "Head and Hands" murder case, the lesser-known Center Point robbery in which Leach accused federal agents of pushing ISP officers around, and the Brady Gang. Leach's answers unfolded in a rambling manner, revealing his agitation.

Agent Kenneth Logan, a co-complainant, denied during testimony that agents ever pushed ISP police officers around, as Leach had maintained. In the aftermath of the Center Point, Indiana, bank robbery, Rockville barracks officers who arrived before the FBI claimed that the agents were pushing them around. Agent Logan denied the whole episode. Leach would not be put off. On the stand he testified:

I dispatched two men from our office to make the preliminary investigation in connection with this robbery. After they got there, they phoned me, and the officer that phoned me, his voice quivered to such an extent that I thought he was injured ... "the Department of Justice are here, pushing us around and we can't interview them because they said that it was their case."

While Reinecke and his co-complainants seemed unconcerned with the Dillinger case, Lutz wanted the altercations of the Dillinger era brought into the record. He determinedly brought the questioning back to 1934. Lutz wanted to reveal the white elephant in the room, the unspoken conclusion that Dillinger was the true reason for Leach's dismissal. When he examined Leach, he brought the matter up.

"Will you tell the Board," asked Lutz, "what [the FBI] has said, and what you have said regarding Mr. Hoover of the Federal Bureau of Investigation or any of the personnel?" He was referring to that day in 1934 when federal agents drove into Mooresville, unbeknownst to the ISP. The event had prompted citizens to report Dillinger sightings.

Leach was anxious to elaborate. "I thought, 'I've got to spend my time and effort because of insane policies to protect these individual members of the Department of Justice.'" Leach claimed that he was "justified in filing a complaint." He repeated his previous statements that he had not publicly criticized any individual member of the FBI, but the "tactics used."

Mr. Lutz pressed on. "You can't think of any instance where you publicly criticized Mr. Hoover other than this instance that you have related?"

"Publicly, no," said Leach. In conducting this line of questioning, Lutz had tried to hand Leach a way to ameliorate the damage—Leach may have said disparaging things about Hoover, but privately to the governor and not for public distribution. Still, the ground was laid for the assumption that Dillinger and not Brady lay at the heart of the dismissal.

Prior to the day's hearing, Leach had been widely quoted as saying that Hoover was deliberately seeking to "confound state and local law enforcement agencies, for the purpose of advancing his own ambitions." That classified Leach, before the proceedings even began, as having a vendetta of his own. His threat to demand a United States Senate investigation into Hoover's "methods and motives" further alienated the assembly, which was composed mainly of Leach opponents. Try as he might, Leach was unable to persuade the body that he had been justified. Under cross-examination, Rabb asked him pointedly, "How long prior to September 4, [1937], did you entertain this attitude?"

Leach replied, "In 1934, my attitude was based on their attitude. It is not my original attitude. I did not originate this notion. It is not my notion. I have stated that every attitude was for the protection and safety of the department. I am not the originator of it. I didn't start it. That is a matter of record."

In spite of Lutz's attempts to make it a Dillinger-centric hearing, the issues centered around 1937 and the Brady case. Agent J. S. Johnson testified about Leach's tampering in the federal investigation of the Brady case by repeating that Christine Puckett, whom he referred to as "the informant," would not speak to the FBI about the case after Leach instructed her not to. Agent Johnson also denied Leach's allegations of keeping Puckett out of the reach of his department.

Under examination by Lutz, Leach maintained that the FBI had obstructed his investigation:

> I detailed one of our officers to go there and interview [Christine Puckett]. Three hours later or more, our officer, after a brief interview with this person, phoned me. He said, "I am helpless … the Department of Justice had been there and informed this person not to give Indiana officers any information concerning this case."
>
> I again walked into Mr. Stiver's office and stated all of these facts, and that we should register an official complaint against these activities and interference on [their] part in connection with the killers of my own police officer. Again, Mr. Stiver, in his diplomatic way (I was of course hostile and irritated a little bit. He is more of a diplomat than I am), said, "Hold on a little bit and maybe this thing can be ironed out and perhaps make it easier." But I am of a different notion.

Leach later admitted that he became vindictive after that event. "That prompted me to advise not to relay any information to the Department of Justice, was the fact that they advised this relative not to give me information. I suggested that the information should be given to us instead of the Department of Justice, if that is their attitude."

The Brady-inspired breach to the newspapers about Al Brady's roller skating habits—which had been a footnote-sized entry in small-circulation newspapers—lay at the heart of the testimony provided by complainant Gurnia, of the Indianapolis field office:

Immediately after that article came out in the newspaper, both Mr. Reineke and myself contacted each agent and put that question to them ... whether or not at any time they had made any statement to any informant or any other person, not to give any enforcement organization information ... every agent had denied ever trying to intimidate a witness by telling them not to speak to Indiana officers.

In his convoluted testimony, Leach admitted to blocking the FBI's access to witness Christine Plunkett. This gave the complainants the evidence they sought to cast him as an obstructionist. Along with Kenneth Logan, J. S. Johnson, and Agent Gurnia, Agent Reinecke had produced the credible witnesses to substantiate his claims.

The Brady Gang's killing of Officer Minneman, which should have elicited a modicum of sympathy for Leach and his positioning of the ISP, lacked resonance. Leach was, by this time, in a rambling mode.

Every effort was made by individual officers, including myself, to apprehend the killers of our brother officer ... after I talked to a relative of one of the men who was wanted.... I was told that "an agent of the Department of Justice instructed this person not to give the Indiana officers anything concerning his habits."

The afternoon went along those lines. To every question, Leach responded with a long answer that attempted to deflect the accusations of obstructionism onto the FBI. With the "Head and Hands" case, Leach insisted that he had asked the FBI for assistance in assembling material evidence to help his case in court. This statement was seized upon by complainant Pat Smith: "At that time, was the case of Hicks set for trial? He had been arrested and charged with murder but you didn't have the evidence to convict him?" Leach had always claimed that the FBI had tricked him by absconding with his files in the Hicks case. He couldn't have invented an answer like this, and replied with frustration, "Three days later ... [the FBI] said, 'I would like to have the information on that. I said, 'Your man was in three days ago and has all the information.' And he said, 'He was transferred out of the Indianapolis office and we don't have the information here.'"

Leach, who was unwilling to pull any ISP officers into his messy problem, had no back-up witnesses to match the barrage of agents and their damning testimony. After all four testified, Leach conceded that he had no witnesses to corroborate his version of events.

It is an embarrassing situation to bring these men in here to state and testify to substantiate my statement that those are the facts. Yes, I am sorry but I am going to be a sport, a good sport. For the good of our department. Take this as is. I am not going to ask and I can't ... ask those boys to come up and testify ... it would hurt the Department.

Mr. Crooks responded by asking, "Do you mean to infer that if one or more officers came up here to testify, it would jeopardize their futures?"

Realizing that he was getting deeper and deeper into incriminating statements, Leach let it go. After another long and rambling reiteration of what he'd said before, he concluded, "I mean that I would be creating dissention within the department and, for that reason, and for that reason alone.... I am going to let it end as is."[7]

And end it did. After the ruling confirmed Leach's dismissal, Agent Gurnia let a bomb drop. He admitted that all federal evidence in the Brady case was handed to the ISP on September 4th, the day that Leach was fired. The ousted captain was astounded to hear that the moment the Indiana State Police Board had fired him, the FBI had delivered the Brady files.

"Do you mean to tell me," he cried, "that since I've been retired, this information has been made available to the state police?"[8]

As abruptly as the proceedings began, they ended. Attorneys snapped their briefcases shut and headed for their own offices. Most were gone within minutes. Matt Leach rose along with them. It was to be a long exile.

PART IV

The Landowner

CHAPTER 13

Reveille

He's back in the army again.—*Hoosier Sentinel*

Since the 1920s, Leach had measured the value of his life through his police work. Getting fired was a crack in the face. The hearing and its outcome dumped him into a flattened world with no peaks to climb. In the unsettled aftermath, he led a lifelong attempt to return to law enforcement.

His work on the Brady case was overturned by his dismissal. His own positioning as the officer of record was gone. Sal Corsi, the Chicago sergeant who had worked on the case, was awarded a contract to feature himself within a series of ghostwritten articles on the Brady Gang for *True Detective*.[1]

Corsi affirmed that the Brady Gang was a "band of young desperadoes whose deeds were no less fantastic than the career of the former farm boy whose lawlessness they strove to outdo." That analysis was published in 1938, a year after Brady and Shaffer were killed in a violent ambush in Maine, with Dalhover condemned to die in the electric chair.

Now Leach was unemployed and living in an overpriced Indianapolis apartment with Marion, his wife. From all angles, the marriage was strained. Leach had been observed by FBI agents as far back as 1934 visiting a woman "not his wife" in a hotel in Indianapolis.[2]

While still in Indianapolis, Matt found a job as a beer salesman. This afforded him an income as he started the real work of figuring out the next step.[3]

Of all the losses that Leach sustained that day, the greatest demerit was his stripped-down retirement. He was not, after all, a graying denizen from the old days, a mellowing old cop. There were no buddies in warmer climates whose Christmas cards would replace the urgent telegrams of the Dillinger hunt.

Leach's peers, men such as Art Keller and Harvey Hire, still manned the desks, files and phones. Some of his colleagues, such as *Indianapolis News* reporter Tubby Toms, had been subtly demoted because of association with him. Toms was eventually assigned to a fishing and hunting column.

With one or two exceptions, his fellow officers were still the detectives, sergeants and lieutenants who had staffed the Indiana State Police in the years of Dillinger. They were officers of the caliber of Mike Morrissey and John Stege. They still wore their collar brass. They continued to pack their .38 service revolvers.

Pulling himself together, Matt sought the shelter of his fraternal organization, the American Legion. There was a convention planned in New York. He told his brother, Mahlon, that he was going to take a "real vacation."[4]

The first years were the hardest. Census records indicate that Matt and his wife, Marion, went back to Gary to join the crowded apartment at 756 Delaware and lived with Matt's three grown siblings, Marshall, Mahlon and Mildred Stack, along with their respective spouses. That arrangement provided temporary shelter for the shell-shocked Matt. It allowed him a period to recover among his trusted loved ones.

The couple soon picked up and moved again. There had always been a kinetic quality to their marriage. Records indicate that Marion lived in Chicago for a while in 1935. They obviously had some problems, with Matt being seen in the company of another woman in an Indianapolis hotel, and the fact that they were estranged in 1935.

To her credit, Marion did not leave Matt after he was fired. The two remained a couple and tried to stay together. They left Gary in late 1937 and moved back to Indianapolis. There they struggled. The diminishment of their social status was a painful reality. The glory days of Captain Matt Leach had been a large distraction, and had provided a glamorous existence for Marion. After those days ended, the veneer of their marriage cracked apart. He wasn't invited to any golf outings. She was no longer the wife of an important man who could expect to see famous people while in his company. Yet at their heart, Matt and Marion were hardscrabble, the second-generation children of immigrants. Having no choice, Matt and Marion Leach started over. The only caveat was that their relationship was strained to the point where both were considering divorce. In spite of their personal problems, they continued to work. From 1938 to 1942, Matt honed new skills as a salesman. One of his goods was beer. In 1939 he worked for sixteen weeks as a beer salesman, which earned him $640. The census records for that year list Matt as having no other income, showing that he was not receiving pension or other compensation for his military and police service.

While Matt worked in beer sales, Marion had employment as a saleswoman in a dry goods store that specialized in housewares. She had slightly more formal education than Matt, having graduated from the eighth grade. She earned $180 in 1939. After the dismissal from the ISP, Marion and Matt found their circumstances so reduced that they had to live as lodgers. It was common, during the 1930s, for people with large apartments to rent out a portion to someone else. This was the type of situation they needed if they were going to remain in Indianapolis. They lived as lodgers in a house owned by Samuel and Dorothy Zine at 3316 Sherman Drive in Indianapolis.[5]

Living in Gary was more feasible economically. Back in the old hometown, the extended family moved once again. It was an era before security deposits, and apartments were cheap and plentiful.

Mahlon and his wife moved to 523 Washington, while Marshall and his wife moved to 131 East 5th Avenue. With the late thirties economy bringing America out of the Depression, every member of the family could live up to his or her potential. Mahlon was the chief hearing judge in the Indiana Department of Motor Vehicles. Marshall was a detective in the Gary Police Department.

Matt's sister, Mildred, moved with her husband, Joseph Stack, to 539 E. 7th Avenue. Joining Mildred was her mother, Mila.[6] The matriarch now went by the Americanized name of Mildred, "Milly" for short. Vujo had moved back from Steelton, near Harrisburg. Mildred took care of her parents. Vujo passed away from natural causes in 1943. It could be said that although there was ambivalence about this difficult man within the family, they always took care of him.[7]

It had been many years since Matt had had time to focus on his extended family. He enjoyed a close relationship with his brothers and sister. Their support helped him to build back his confidence. Among his family, he could speak the truth about the things he held so dear—what really happened that night at the Biograph Theater; what J. Edgar Hoover's true sexual orientation was (a closeted and hushed topic in the late 1930s); and what he would reveal in his own book, which he always kept in the back of his mind. On the day he was fired, having had advance notice that he was out, Matt had grabbed his ISP files and gotten them out of his office at the Statehouse. These files and

Matt Leach enjoys a family meal with his beloved sister, Mildred, ca. 1950s (courtesy James Stack).

his collection of news clippings formed the building blocks of his dream of writing a book about Dillinger.

With the continued help of his family, Matt slowly healed. He started to reach for new levels. He contemplated a career as a real estate agent. He put that idea on hold because the marriage was an issue that no longer could be ignored. In 1942, Matt moved back to Gary. While Marion visited Gary and was seen with Matt that year, she was maintaining a separate residence at 2236 North Alabama in Indianapolis.[8]

Their divorce was finalized in 1945. Matt Leach was serving in the military at the time of the divorce and was forced to waive consent and ask for a court appointed surrogate to represent him. Their marriage had almost made the twenty-year mark.[9]

After Mildred Stack took the apartment at 539 East 7th, Matt moved back in with his sister. He shared the apartment with their mother, along with Mildred's husband, Joseph. This was the address that Matt provided when he re-enlisted for military service at the onset of World War II.[10]

The "Men from Lika," ca. 1950s (*left to right*): Mahlon, Matt and Marshall. The brothers all joined the military in World War II (courtesy John Leach).

By 1942, the Second World War was changing American life. The Leach brothers dug deep into their military heritage as descendants of fighters from the Military Frontier of Austria-Hungary. All three brothers enlisted in the armed services.

Marshall joined the Marines at the age of 36 as a warrant officer. He was transferred to Montford Point, Camp Lejeune, North Carolina. It was during the segregated era of Jim Crow laws, and Marshall was assigned to manage an 1,800-man "Negro" troop as a physical training officer. Marshall, like Matt, was back in the news. The local Gary papers wrote of Marshall, "For the ex-boxer who in 1931 came within an ace of winning the world's middleweight championship, life in the Marine Corps is 'just what the doctor ordered.'" Mahlon became a sergeant with an American ordinance company, and went on to fight at Utah Beach in Normandy.

The War created a renaissance for Matt. He was commissioned a first lieutenant in the Army Air Corps on June 6th, 1942. His re-enlistment kicked off the kind of publicity he had enjoyed back in 1933.

News photos of the newly emboldened Matt Leach reveal an effervescent soldier. Yet Leach soon found out he was too old for active duty. "This is my third 'war,' and I wouldn't have missed it for anything," he told the press.

He was transferred to a post in Wichita, Kansas. Once away from the cramped Gary apartment, he galvanized into a military machine. There he organized, directed and drilled civilian protective forces at airplane factories, testing and ferry command bases for more than a dozen states. He rose in rank to captain, then major, while maintaining this military job as director of training for plant protection forces in the aircraft industries. He had a peak moment while in the service, when he

was invited to the East Room of the White House. There he stood in the audience as President Harry Truman presented an award to Admiral William F. Leahy.

Military service made Matt his old self. For several years he was once again an officer. He wore a uniform.

Left: Matt Leach, always happy to be wearing a uniform. *Right:* Matt Leach served in World War I, the Mexican Conflict, and World War II. Photographs ca. 1942 (both courtesy James Stack).

His life was ordained by his service. Yet, if he felt any pangs about return-ing to civilian life, he didn't show it. During a postwar interview with a local Gary paper, he belied any anxiety about the future. "Plans? Who wants to bother about plans at a time like this? Heck, who knows? I may wind up as a newspaper reporter, maybe operating a crossroads filling station!"[11]

The dark side of his past, the life associated with Dillinger, Brady and the FBI, came back to haunt him. Once transferred to Wichita, Leach came again to the attention of the FBI. In December of 1942, an agent from the Houston field office, SAC Abbaticchio, met Leach and found him to be "very cordial." The agent contacted the FBI headquar-ters to ask how Leach was regarded now that he was a "Captain in the Army Air Corps." The reply was cryptic: "Mr. Ladd advises Leach absolutely no good. SAC Abbaticchio advised."[12]

The security he felt as a commissioned officer continued through the American Legion. In the postwar years, he held a job as manager of the dining room of the Gary Memorial Post. Once again, this organi-zation helped him to make the necessary career moves. It started to look like he would be offered a state job. It occurred to Matt that he might try to reconcile his old differences with the FBI and its director.

On October 31st, 1952, Leach visited a branch office of the FBI in Hammond. He identified himself, said he was in the employ of the Elks Lodge, and began to make his pitch. He told the SAC there that he had "developed increasing respect for the director of the FBI." Any "ill feel-ings between his first State Police organization and the FBI have certainly been healed by the passing of time and the splendid work of each depart-ment."[13]

Hoover was not ready to forget his old grudge against Leach. Later, after Leach's death, Hoover would order surveillance on newsman William "Tubby" Toms of the *Indianapolis News*. The reason was that Toms had shown the audacity to write a series of articles celebrating Leach's work in the Dillinger campaign.

On March 4th, 1954, Matt returned to an official position. Governor George N. Craig named him a Democratic investigator for the Indiana Alcoholic Beverage Commission for eight northern counties.[14]

The appointment was controversial. The prior investigator, Charles R. Swaim, claimed he was fired so that Leach could have the job: "It's just another case of an American Legion crony getting a job, that's all." Could it be that the patronage plague of 1933 was dogging him all over again?

The woman who became Matt Leach's second wife wasn't looking for a sugar daddy. She had her own job as a buyer with Pearson's Department Store in Gary. Her income amounted to a small salary with vacation and sick pay. She was beyond childbearing, at age 45 at the time of their marriage. Like Matt, she had never had any children. Their marriage would be that of two mature people. They were both divorced, and wise to life.

In a chance at a second career, Leach had an I.D. photograph taken for a job on the Beverage Commission in March 1954 (Calumet Regional Archives).

Matt proposed to Mary Heddens with a five-diamond ring, 13-karat white gold with a ½-carat center stone of good quality, with two marquise diamonds and two more round diamonds. When they married on April 9th, 1950, in a civil ceremony in Crown Point, Indiana, he gave her a wedding band with five diamonds in matching 14-karat white gold. After the ceremony, they returned to Mildred Stack's home for cake and champagne.

For the marriage ceremony, Mary wore a conservative suit and a corsage. Matt dressed in his usual suit and tie. Both looked happy as they cut the cake.

For a time they shared an apartment at 477 Hayes, in Apt. B-6.

It was the postwar boom period of the 1950s. Mahlon and Margaret had their own place at 544 Harrison. Marshall and Jean lived at 546 Johnson. Everybody had their own apartment now. It was like television, where Lucy and Ricky, Fred and Ethel, and even Alice and Ralph, lived as young marrieds, on their own, independent of extended family. Mothers-in-law were visitors, and not quite welcomed into the homes

Matt Leach with his new wife, Mary Heddens, April 1950 (courtesy James Stack).

of these television couples. Yet the Leach family continued to provide care to the aged Mila, who lived with her daughter and Matt's sister, Mildred Stack. Mary and Matt had the best of everything. They had their own place, with extended family members all in the same neighborhood.

TV was defining a new way of life. Matt went out and bought a 17-inch Motorola black and white television set to put into the new apartment. The fifties had arrived. With the postwar boom came new credit and mortgage services. 1955 was the best year ever. The couple decided they could afford to buy a house. With Mary a "career girl," as working women were called at that time, they had enough income to apply for a VA mortgage. On March 15th, 1955, they took out a mortgage for $10,000 and purchased a two-bedroom ranch house at 1226 Montana Street in a suburban subdivision of Gary.

They furnished their new home as any older couple would, though, with acquired pieces and some things new. Their night table was damaged, and completed a set made up of a maple bed and five-drawer chest and mirror. Mary hung curtains and favored drapes that could be pulled back and forth. She and Matt furnished the home with mahogany pieces and small hooked and scatter rugs. They favored pastoral paintings and pottery pieces. As befitted the smoker's culture of the 1950s, their house had several ashtrays and a cigarette box.

Their wedding gifts were modest and serviceable candlesticks, a bonbon tray and silver sugar tongs. Yet their china service was incomplete, as was their plated flatware, which was missing pieces of its original service for eight. Perhaps they did not entertain friends or family very often, as family gatherings always took place in Mildred Stack's home.

In their new home, they hoped to live a comfortable and studious life. There were 100 books of fiction and biography, the television, a magazine rack, a spinet desk and matching chair. They enjoyed the convenience of a gas dryer, GE refrigerator and gas stove.[15]

The purchase of this home left the couple in a mortgage-poor condition. Like all first-time home buyers, they expected to recoup their investment. After they bought their house, they were left with Mary's jewelry and black Persian lamb coat, and $180 dollars in the bank.

With very little cash but dreams coming to the surface of his stoic mind, Matt Leach began to put the pieces together to finally tell the story of John Dillinger from his perspective. Common sense should have dictated that Dillinger was in the past and his life was resting comfortably in the moment with his new wife and home. His second-stage life, though a perfect vision of the American Dream, contained one major flaw. It lurked beneath the surface of everything he did. Leach could not rid himself of Dillinger.

CHAPTER 14

Milepost 107.5

A lot of grief that day.—John Leach

As he settled into life with Mary Heddens, Matt went into a renaissance. He felt the time had come for his book about Dillinger. That was naïve, as Hoover still exercised control in Washington. Matt, who had saved the news articles and other papers from his years with the ISP, was not thinking of Washington and his enemy in FBI headquarters.

With his memory acute and facts straight on some issues, most notably the relationship between Sage and Zarkovich, he nevertheless lacked editorial skills. He was a cop's cop but no Mickey Spillane. With notes, drafts and documents substantiating his outspoken memories, he went in search of a ghostwriter.

In the years over which he'd organized his collected newspaper clippings, he had made an attempt to write a book about Dillinger. He now reached into his address book and contacted one writer who had been helpful to him in the past, reporter William "Tubby" Toms. The reporter had written pieces on Dillinger for the *Indianapolis News*, including a first-hand report from Tucson. Twenty years later, Toms was one of the few people around from the Dillinger crowd who mattered to Matt. Toms viewed the case as central to Indiana. Matt gave Toms some sample chapters to read. Toms, who always believed that Leach was the most important lawman in the case, nevertheless could not help with the project.[1]

Matt deepened his search for a ghostwriter, one who would develop his notes and ideas into a book-length work. He turned up two candidates for the job. One was Al Spiers, a former Michigan City *Dispatch* writer. He had been a cub reporter at the time of the Terror Gang escape from the state penitentiary. While taking an interest in Matt's project, he declined the offer to ghostwrite, claiming he had no time. This left Matt without the book collaboration he was searching for.[2]

Matt next approached Alan Hynd, a true-crime writer who wrote in the tough-guy style of dialog popular at that time. Leach visited Alan Hynd in or around 1955. Noel Hynd, the son of the writer, recalled that Leach had visited his home.

"Matt Leach came to our home in Connecticut and had a meeting with my father. I was seven years old and met him very briefly. He drove like a wild man if I recall, and could put back a few drinks," recalled Noel Hynd.[3]

Mr. Hynd politely refused the request to write Captain Leach's book. In reaching out to two writers in his tenacious way, Matt did generate some press from behind the scenes. Mr. Hynd's product of this meeting would be an article, "Dillinger's Strange Career in Crime," which Matt did not live to see published.[4]

Matt Leach had now influenced the work of two journalists who would promote his point of view on Dillinger. This was more than he'd been able to do in the twenty years since the outlaw's death. The ex-lawman felt buoyed enough to make a giant leap and approach the publishing industry. He made plans to go to New York City, ostensibly to meet with a publisher or agent. It was a large move, a bold move. He was a Midwestern man at heart and had only traveled once or twice to New York in his lifetime.

He and Mary set off in their car in or around the second week of June 1955. Mary had her own plans for hitting New York City's pavement. A buyer with Pearson's Department Store, she was looking forward to visiting the garment district to purchase inventory.

With something possibly akin to a manuscript but most likely notes and his sample chapters, Matt brought his fabled gift of gab. It was a time predating the Xerox machine, and photocopies hadn't been invented yet. That staple of the modern office, the carbon copy, was probably not made by this 1930s cop who would have considered that a secretary's job. If there was a carbon copy of his work left in his home on Montana Street, it was never found. The publishing company and the results of this meeting have never been determined.[5]

Mary Heddens Leach had her own career as a buyer in Pearson's Department Store.
Ad from June 1955.

As the couple prepared to leave New York on June 14th, 1955, people
were talking about the new James Dean movie, with co-stars Julie Harris
and Raymond Massey. *East of Eden* starred Dean as a new, sensitive type
of teenager. He was a film nonconformist, struggling for autonomy while
crying to his conflicted parents. Dean's characters must have seemed weak
to Matt. He remembered the young outcasts of the thirties whose mis-
deeds resulted in hard jail time. Men such as Pierpont and Dillinger had
misguided parents who either defended them or ignored their problems.
To Leach, looking back on the changing times, it was amusing. Dean's
films depicted the new model of a teenaged outcast, a suburban kid beg-
ging for love. The standards of manhood had evolved since the thirties.

It was June of 1955. The Cold War was a grim reminder that world peace might not last. Mary and Matt left New York hours before a scheduled air raid test. Had they extended their stay, their itinerary would have featured a trip to a fallout shelter. There they would have been told to stay for ten minutes from 2:05 until 2:15 p.m., and leave on the public "all clear" announcement.

There was postwar prosperity. Newspapers brimmed with ads for shiny appliances and solid family cars. It was exciting to be in the city.

Matt and Mary were anxious to reach Gary for the 1955 graduation party of his niece, Patricia Jean (courtesy James Stack).

New York had always been a destination for Matt. His first glimpse of America had taken place from the steamship *Patricia* as she moved tentatively towards the dock at Ellis Island. He had once run away to New York and tried to lose himself in its cavernous streets in the tortured days after he was fired back in 1937.

Now, his mind was on going home to Gary.

His family was planning a party. Mildred's daughter and Matt's niece, Patricia Jean, had just graduated from high school. Matt was anxious to get home for the celebration. Mary was anxious to see Pearson's advertisement showcasing dresses and lingerie in her hometown newspaper. The goods she was bringing home from New York's garment district might be showcased in the next advertisement.

The house on Montana Street was bursting with promise as she thought about her plans for decorating and transforming the Montana Street house into a home.

Either Matt did drive like the wild man so described by Noel Hynd, or they left very early. By 8:30 a.m. they had made it onto the Pennsylvania Turnpike, one exit east of Uniontown. The New York morning papers had predicted overcast skies and cool temperatures at 70 degrees. The only rain forecast was scattered light showers in some areas of Pennsylvania.[6]

Matt and Mary drove in the Pennsylvania rain, the panorama of the Allegheny Mountains surrounding the highway. Narrow and winding, the turnpike had taken the form of an overpass for miles as the car approached Somerset. The tight feel of the road contrasted sharply with the farmland abutting the highway.

Matt and Mary passed Exit 110, known as the Somerset Interchange, and drove another two miles. Suddenly, an eastbound Buick 2-door flipped over the median. The car, boasting a formidable, waterfall-style grille, pushed the Leach car off the highway. It crashed down the sides of a thirty-foot-deep ravine to the right of the road.[7]

The Buick was carrying four members of the Sewell family of

A car like the one that hit the Leach car on the Pennsylvania Turnpike. A 1949 Buick Sedanette 51, it was streamlined and fast.

Uniontown. They were bound in two cars for a family gathering in Harrisburg. The first of these two automobiles was being driven by thirty-year-old Barbara Graves. Her father followed in the second car. The first Sewell vehicle, when it jumped the median, went into the westbound side of the turnpike and came to a stop. The impact propelled the Leach car into the bottomless tangle of brambles and treetops. The car careened into the thirty-foot labyrinth. Matt and Mary flew out of the car and disappeared into the thicket. There they lay in shock, with multiple fractures, lacerations and contusions, twenty-five feet from the wrecked car.

After the horrific crash, turnpike ambulances rushed to the scene. Responders and rescue crews, guided by the Pennsylvania State Police and Pennsylvania Turnpike Police, had no idea who was in the ravine or how many people to search for. The Sewell car, although visible and on the highway, was smashed along the front end with the doors pushed in upon the passengers. By the time rescue crews were able to get the injured to the hospital, almost two hours had passed.

One factor that might have saved two occupants of the other car who survived was that Somerset Hospital was situated less than ten minutes away from the scene of the accident. But it was too late for the people who died that day.

There had been three passengers in the car operated by Mrs. Graves. All of the occupants were African-American. Her sister, 19-year-old Shirley Boone, who was pregnant, died first. She was, with the others, in the emergency room of the Somerset Community Hospital. Like dominoes in a macabre table game, four victims died in rapid succession. Shirley Boone died at 10:30 a.m. of a fractured skull. Her unborn child died with her.

Matt Leach was the next to die, at 11:10 a.m. He'd suffered a crushed chest, fractured right wrist, a skull fracture, multiple lacerations of the face, hand, ears and tongue, and shock. The driver of the other car, Barbara Graves, died at 11:35 a.m.

Mary Leach died at 1:25 p.m. during emergency surgery. She was afflicted with multiple fractures of the skull, fractured jaws, a crushed chest, lacerations of the face, ears, chin and head, and shock.

The passengers who survived were the teenaged Shirley Taylor and James Sewell. The 16-year-old James suffered from shock but was discharged from the hospital two days later.[8] Sadly, the father of the two women, Shirley Boone and Barbara Graves, witnessed the accident. The Reverend A. L. Sewell, a Church of God minister, had been traveling in a car behind them, en route to the family gathering in Harrisburg.

The bodies of Matt and Mary Leach were transferred from the Somerset Community Hospital in caskets to be taken to the B&O Railroad in nearby Rockwood. There, at a lonely junction surrounded by railcars and unused track, their bodies were boarded on the last train home. It was an unintended end to a month of graduations and new beginnings. Each looked forward to returning, Mary to her job and Matt to his continuing plan for a book about the John Dillinger case. The coroner's report mistakenly listed Mary as a retired housewife, but listed Matt as a retired state policeman and real estate broker.[9]

Their bodies were returned to Gary. They had paid $1,000 down on their new home, purchased only four months earlier.[10] The down payment had left them poor of pocket yet rich with the promise of the American Dream. Now the house stood empty. The Leach and Stack families awaited the return of the bodies. "My father was crying like crazy. The family was there. A lot of grief that day," recalled Marshall's son John Leach."[11]

In the wake of the disaster, Mildred Stack made funeral arrangements for the couple. At the same time, in a move all-too-typical of death and its aftermath, a rift developed between the two families. Unaffected in death by conflict, Mary and Matt were viewed and buried together.

Jim Stack was a young teenager when his uncle Matt died. Although there was a highly publicized viewing at Gary's Williams & Burns Funeral Home, Matt's nephew did not attend. "My mother said to me, 'You don't want to see him like that,'" Stack related.[12] A Protestant minister delivered the eulogy in the funeral home on the night before the funeral. Matt Leach and his wife were buried in the Protestant section of the Calumet Park Cemetery on Friday, June 17th. The same newspapers that carried the story of the funeral also featured the Pearson's department store's ads, a cheerful array of dresses and lingerie.

The car remained in the deep ravine and its fate is a mystery. Nothing was ever salvaged from inside the wreck. Had there been items recovered, they would have been shipped home with the bodies. "It would have been at the discretion of the coroner," said a representative of the funeral home that supervised the shipment of the bodies through the B&O Railroad. The coroner's report, however, contained no mention of the personal effects of the Leaches. "The personal items of the deceased persons would have been shipped along with the bodies," said an unidentified member of the coroner's family.[13] Among the collection of papers kept by Leach nephew, Jim Stack, nothing was found. No manuscript was ever seen by a member of the family.

After Leach's death, his old friend and booster Tubby Toms wrote a short series of articles about the role that Leach had played in the Dillinger case. This prompted an angry response from Hoover, who ordered a report generated on Toms.

"Toms is obviously an old admirer of Matt Leach and obtained all of his information from Leach. The three newspapers in Indianapolis thrive on controversies.... Leach 'leaked' constant stories to the newspaper men, and undoubtedly Toms was one of several newsmen involved with Leach during those days. Indianapolis [field office] has never had any occasion to have any contact with Toms ... since his columns have dealt solely with fishing and hunting in Indiana."[14]

This meant that Toms was on the radar and a possible candidate for a Hoover-style blacklist and witch hunt. Bravely, the journalist typed out his postscript. An insider who could have revealed a great deal more, Toms was limited by the era and the FBI control over the Dillinger story. Throwing away caution, and moved by the reality that Leach was gone, he published a prophetic article in the *Indianapolis News*. It was a rebellious act in that era of FBI sovereignty over Dillinger's death.[15]

"It was Leach's opinion," Toms wrote, "that the FBI attached itself to the O'Neill-Zarkovich team as a face-saving gesture. If, and when Leach's book on the Dillinger story is published, it will say that the FBI played second fiddle to the East Chicago team."

In death, after all, Matt Leach got the last word.

Appendix A.
Indiana Police Board Charges Against Matt Leach, Charges Drafted by Indiana State Safety Director upon Request of FBI Director J. Edgar Hoover, Dated September 4, 1937

1. Captain Leach has willfully violated the 1935 state law in that he has willfully failed and refused to cooperate and exchange information with federal police forces, to wit, the Federal Bureau of Investigation, in the prevention and detection of crimes and the apprehension of criminals.

2. Captain Leach has willfully disobeyed the rules and regulations of the state police in that he willfully failed and refused to cooperate and exchange information with the Federal Bureau of Investigation.

3. Captain Leach has committed conduct unbecoming to a police officer in that he has publicly criticized the FBI and members and officers thereof.

4. Captain Leach has communicated or given police information to the public at large concerning business of the state police department to the detriment of the department, to wit: that he made public confidential police information concerning Al Brady, fugitive from justice … for use in the arrest and apprehension of said Al Brady and not for publication.

5. Captain Leach has communicated to the public at large information which may aid a person, namely one Al Brady and associates,

to escape arrest or to delay their apprehension, namely information concerning the skating proclivities of said Al Brady, the same being information given said Captain Leach for use in the arrest or apprehension of said Al Brady and not for publication.

6. Captain Leach has conducted himself in a manner unbecoming to an officer in that he has attempted to prevent witnesses having information of value in the detection and apprehension of criminals from transmitting such information to police forces cooperating in such detection and apprehension, namely the Federal Bureau of Investigation.

7. Captain Leach has willfully violated the provisions of Chapter 299 of Acts of the Indiana General Assembly of 1935 in that he has attempted to prevent witnesses having information of value in the detection and apprehension of criminals from transmitting such information to a police force with whom the Indiana state police force was cooperating, namely the Federal Bureau of Investigation.

8. Captain Leach has willfully disobeyed the rules and regulations of the Department of State Police in that he has attempted to prevent witnesses having information of value in the detection and apprehension of criminals from transmitting such information to police forces with whom the Indiana State Police force was cooperating, namely, the Federal Bureau of Investigation.

9. Captain Leach has conducted himself in a manner unbecoming to a police officer in that he has publicly slandered officials and members of the Federal Bureau of Investigation.

10. Captain Leach has willfully disobeyed the rules and regulations of the Department of State Police in this, namely that he has given statements to or for the public press and its representatives about the affairs and activities of the Department of State Police of the State of Indiana without the specific authorization and without any authorization of the Superintendent of State Police, in violation of state law.

11. Captain Leach has conducted himself in a manner unbecoming to a police officer in that he has advised, requested and ordered members of the State Police of the State of Indiana not to cooperate or exchange information with the Federal Bureau of Investigation or its officials or members.

12. Captain Leach has conducted himself in a manner unbecoming

to a police officer in that he has failed and refused to cooperate and exchange information with the Federal Bureau of Investigation, its officials and members, toward the end of achieving greater success in preventing and detecting crimes and apprehending criminals.

Appendix B.
Matt Leach's Rebuttal
to State Police Board Charges,
Indianapolis Times,
September 4, 1937

To the Press:

I have refused today to resign as Captain of the Indiana State Police as requested by the State Police board on the complaint of J. Edgar Hoover, Director of the Federal Department of Justice.

My sole reason for refusing to resign is the record of our department through the period of going on five years, in which I have been the active head of the State Police.

I cite the ascending of a record of achievement of the department since the time of its creation in 1933 as the best defense I have to offer. In this position I have been fortified by the public endorsement of the work of the Indiana State Police Department.

I have only to mention the following cases which have been solved recently by the department:

Apprehension and conviction of a number of murderers including the apprehension and conviction of the four murderers of Captain Harry R. Miller, a retired Cincinnati Fire Department officer, apprehension and conviction of the two men who robbed and killed William Bright, an Indianapolis druggist and numerous other cases with which the public is familiar, and courteous service rendered by the entire department to the citizens of the State of Indiana.

We have enjoyed complete cooperation of all law enforcement

agencies within and without the state except that of the Federal Department of Justice, which has antagonized all of the local enforcement agencies in the country. No. 1, our department averted slaughter of the members of the Department of Justice through a routine investigation of a citizen's report that an automobile load of armed bandits were speeding eastward through northern Indiana during the height of the Dillinger chase. Failure of the Department of Justice to cooperate with the police authorities in Indiana put us in the position several times of not knowing whether a carload contained bandits or federal men.

No. 2, Once again I dispatched the State Police reserves in quest of Dillinger when a citizen reported the outlaw and his gang were bound for Mooresville in two machines. Those machines were found loaded with armed members of the Department of Justice. The fact that I answered call and ascertained facts before acting and communicated same to local authorities prevented federal officers from being mistaken for bandits.

These foolhardy methods of J. Edgar Hoover made it necessary for me to lodge formal complaint with Governor Paul V. McNutt against the policies of the Department of Justice as now operated, such being in the interest of the safety of the citizens of Indiana, the law enforcement authorities of this state and the subordinates of Mr. Hoover assigned to Indiana.

Four months ago one of our own men was killed in the performance of his duty. In the pursuit of the murderers our department solicited the cooperation of the Department of Justice and other agencies. What assistance have we received from the Department of Justice?

Persons associated with the operation of the Brady gang informed us that they had been advised in advance by agents of the Department of Justice to refrain from telling the Indiana State Police anything concerning the whereabouts of the Brady mob. What we have learned has been in spite of the Department of Justice. This attitude on the part of the Department of Justice now passes beyond the point of refusal to cooperate and becomes definite antagonism.

I will not surrender to an authority from without which lacks authority within. In spite of stated facts I have never failed to cooperate with the Department of Justice. In turn, I accuse the Department of Justice with deliberately seeking to use state and local law enforcement agencies for the purpose of advancing the ambition of Mr. Hoover.

I ask the United States Senate to proceed with an investigation of Mr. Hoover's methods and motives and except accordingly to amplify the foregoing statement. I am justified in making this request against Mr. Hoover for the reason that he has in the past refused to cooperate with this Department.

Appendix C.
The Lost Manuscript:
Matt Leach's Ghostwriters
Weigh In

The pervasive rumor of Matt Leach's mythology is his missing manuscript. The rumors began during the terrible week after his death, when newspapers printed misinformation that he was in New York seeking a publisher for his book on Dillinger. In the horrendous car crash that ended his life, his car was destroyed as it careened into a thirty-foot-deep ravine that shouldered that section of the Pennsylvania State Turnpike.

The personal articles that were contained within the car were destroyed in the wreck or lost to salvage in the recovery of the vehicle. Yet no record exists of any recovery effort of this motor vehicle, either by the Pennsylvania Turnpike authorities or local salvage companies. We do know that the bodies of Mr. and Mrs. Matt Leach went home to Gary, Indiana, in a boxcar on the B&O Railroad. Queries to the funeral director in Somerset, Pennsylvania, who took responsibility for their remains from the hospital emergency room to the train depot, had no record of their personal effects from that long-ago day in 1955.

Since then, Dillinger researchers and readers alike have pondered the fate of Leach's "lost manuscript." There are a few clues to the fate of this holy grail.

Indianapolis News reporter William "Tubby" Toms, in an article written in the week after Leach's tragic death, wrote: "[Leach had] eternal hope that someday he would be vindicated. That was what prompted him to write a book on the Dillinger subject. Much of the script this writer proofread some years ago."

Toms, in this ambiguous statement, does not say specifically that there was a finished manuscript. "Much of the script" leaves us guessing as to what exactly Leach was showing around to his friends in newspaper and magazine writing circles. Rather than point to a narrative that ran a specific number of pages, with photos and illustrations like a typical finished book, all signs point to a work in progress.[1]

By the year 1955, Matt Leach had gotten his life together. With a new foundation of health and happiness enabling him to pursue his dream, Matt searched for a ghostwriter. What he shopped around to at least two writers—who were both coincidentally named "Al"—was a collection of notes and segments of sample chapters. During that year, Matt approached Alan Hynd and Al Spiers, and asked them individually to ghostwrite his book.

Leach paid a visit to the Connecticut home of writer Alan Hynd, pitched his project and asked for Hynd's assistance in ghostwriting his book. According to Noel Hynd, his son, Mr. Hynd declined the request but followed up with an article about Leach and Dillinger. His published article points to the fact that Leach influenced him in his portrait of Dillinger.[2]

Al Spiers also verified that Leach was looking for a professional writer. In an article that he wrote for the Michigan City *Dispatch*, Spiers confirmed that Matt Leach had not actually written a book:

> When Leach subsequently left the Indiana State Police, he took with him an elaborate file and all his personal notes on Dillinger, intending some day to write a book.
> In 1955, he asked me to collaborate with him on the book. The subject was fascinating, but other work interfered at the time and, regretfully, I had to decline.
> So Matt and his wife drove to New York to consult publishers and seek another ghost writer. Coming home, they were both killed in a Pennsylvania Turnpike crash.[3]

Spiers concludes with a mention of the legendary Dillinger historian, Joe Pinkston (now deceased). This dates this article and ties it to the period when Mr. Pinkston actively assembled a collection of Dillinger artifacts, which was the 1970s to the 1990s.

Chapter Notes

Addresses and locations for the Licanin/ Leach family, as well as occupants of the various dwellings listed, were taken from the annual Gary City Directories, 1913–1943 (intermittent years), Calumet Regional Archives, Indiana University Northwest Library.

Abbreviations

RECORDS DEPOSITORIES

CRA   Calumet Regional Archives of Indiana University Northwest

BRAGA   FBI, "History: Famous Cases: The Brady Gang," https://www.fbi.gov/history/famous-cases/the-brady-gang

FBI   Federal Bureau of Investigation (Freedom of Information FOIA), John Dillinger file "JODIL," are frequently filed under the file numbers 62–29777 but not exclusively under this numerical designation. Historical FBI memoranda can be searched through https://www.fbi.gov/services/records-management/foipa

ISA   Indiana State Archives

LOC   Library of Congress, Reproductions from the Collections of the Manuscript Division

NARA   National Archives and Records Administration

NEWSPAPERS

CT   *Chicago Tribune*
GPT   *Gary Post Tribune*
IN   *Indianapolis News*
IS   *Indianapolis Star*
IT   *Indianapolis Times*

Introduction

1. Purvis to Cowley, July 25, 1934, FBI, JODIL, File No. 62-29771-23.

2. Fred J. Cook, *The FBI Nobody Knows* (New York: Macmillan, 1964), 172.

3. Oct. 27, 1937, L. A. Tamm to Hoover, FBI, JODIL, (prefix missing)-6932.

Chapter 1

1. Record of Aliens Held for Special Inquiry, Hamburger Passenger Lists, Port of New York Passenger Lists, Arrived Aug. 21, 1906, 1850–1934, Vol. 373, VIII A1 Band 181, http://www.ellisisland.org; http://www.ancestry.com.

2. *Ibid.*

3. Philip D. Hart, "Captain Matt Leach: Dillinger's Nemesis," *Serb World U.S.A.,* May/June 1992, 47; Statement of Applicant, Report of Physical Examination, Regular Army, Organized Militia or Volunteers, Indiana State Archives, Indiana Commission on Public Records. Leach listed his birthplace as Austria here and Serbia in his enlistment papers to the National Guard.

4. Carl Jancarich (St. Sava Serbian Orthodox Church, Merrillville, Indiana), in a telephone conversation with author Ellen Poulsen, informally discussed the culture and the church and the theory that records of birth were not kept in civil courts in the late 19th century but were

recorded by the Orthodox churches, many of which have been destroyed in the wars of the 20th century. Lichanin is pronounced with the soft "c-h," as in "chuck." Lika is pronounced with the hard "k" sound, as in "key."

5. Michael D. Nicklanovich, "The Military Frontier: Serbs of No Man's Land, 1500–1918," *Serb World U.S.A.*, March/April 1988, 14; "Names of Our Forefathers," *Serb World U.S.A.*, July/Aug. 1999 (the authors acknowledge the contributions of John Macut and Nicholas Kosanovich), 54. Then 38 years old, Vujo (often misspelled "Vugo" in official records) listed his country of origin as Brograd, Servia (Beograd, Serbia; Beograd is now called Belgrade). Misspellings were changes and generalizations by records clerks. Mildred Stack informed Philip Hart in an interview that her father came from Vrginmost.

6. Leach's most accurate recorded date of birth was written by Leach himself. Matt Leach, World War II draft registration card, n.d. He recorded different dates of birth at various times.

7. Leach's siblings' ages (approximate) were calculated from the 1930 U.S. Federal Census, http://www.ancestry.com (accessed Jan. 9, 2015); Marshall's date of birth is listed as May 1, 1906, Gary/[Marshall] Leach, Boxing's Official Record Keeper (courtesy James Stack), http://boxrec.com/en/boxer/84631 (accessed 10/01/201?, n.d.). Note: Mila and Vujo are listed in the Steelton City Directories for the years 1926–1929, 1931. (They appeared to live in Steelton and Gary, and Vujo may have maintained the Steelton address for purposes of employment.) Vujo is simultaneously listed in Gary in 1927, Mila simultaneously in Gary in 1930 at the Grant address. The consistent Steelton address is 717 So. 4th. Vujo Licanin, Northwest Indiana Genealogical Society, Lake County, Indiana Naturalization Records 1854–1932, Vujo Licanin Naturalization, 1912, 183; Philip Hart, "Becoming Americans," *Serb World U.S.A.*, May/June 2002, 50; "Naturalization Records," NARA, https://www.archives.gov/research/naturalization/naturalization.html.

8. James Stack, in telephone conversation with Ellen Poulsen, Oct. 2012 (quote used with permission).

9. R. Taylor Graham, "Creating the Newest Steel City," *The Survey*, April 3, 1909, CRA, Box 10, File 54; "Gary: One of America's Youngest Cities," *Bell Telephone News*, 1922, CRA, Box 10, File 93. Leach family address: Report of Physical Examination, Regular Army, Organized Militia, or Volunteer, ISA.

Leach's siblings' ages (approximate), 1930 U.S. Federal Census, http://www.ancestry.com (accessed Jan. 9, 2015); Marshall's date of birth is listed as May 1, 1906, Gary/[Marshall] Leach, Boxing's Official Record Keeper (courtesy James Stack), http://boxrec.com/en/boxer/84631 (accessed 10/01/201?, n.d.). While some records state the family address as 2194 Broadway, Leach listed 2200 Broadway on his enlistment papers as the domicile of himself and his mother, "Amillia Leach" (clerk's misspelling), http://www.ancestry.com.

10. "List of United States Citizens for the Immigration Authorities," S.S. *Leviathan*, Cherbourg, Oct. 11, 1927, to Port of New York, Oct. 17, 1927. There Leach listed his naturalization as having taken place at Forest County, Mississippi, April 15, 1918. New York Passenger Lists, 1820–1957; http://www.ancestry.com; Matt Leach later listed his naturalization as having occurred while he was in the armed services in Forest County, Mississippi; "Citizenship Through Military Service," NARA, Naturalization, https://www.archives.gov/research/naturalization/naturalization.html. It was common for World War I veterans to apply for naturalization while in the armed services. Matt Leach listed his citizenship as having taken place in the military.

11. Vugo [*sic*] Mike Licanin, World War I draft registration cards, 1917–1918, Birth date, "7 (or 17) January, 1874," FHL Roll No. 1851307, Draft Board 1, United States, Selective Service System, NARA,

M1509, 4,582 rolls, http://www.ancestry. com (accessed Nov. 1, 2009).

12. Stack to Poulsen (quote used with permission).

13. *Ibid.*

14. Leach listed his education as fifth grade in the 1940 census, http://www. ancestry.com.

15. Report of Physical Examination, Regular Army, Organized Militia, or Volunteer, ISA. Matt Leach listed his occupation as "electrical."

16. Indiana National Guard 1898–1940, Ref. #GUAO32477, ISA, Box 312, Location 40-F-3; Indiana State Digital Archives, Box 312. Indiana Guard Website, "Our History," http://www.in.ng.mil/AboutUs/ History/tabid/214/Default.aspx. Matt Leach was enrolled in the National Guard on July 19, 1915; enlistment information, "Report of Physical Examination, Regular Army, Organized Militia or Volunteers," ISA.

17. Vugo [*sic*] Mike Licanin, World War I draft registration cards, http://www. ancestry.com.

18. Leach's military service details are confirmed in Hart, "Captain Matt Leach"; Indiana's 150th Field Artillery Regiment fought with distinction as part of the new 42nd (Rainbow) Division; "Who's Who in the State House," *The Hoosier Sentinel*, n.d., lists Col. George Healy as Leach's commanding officer; Indiana National Guard's history correlated with Matt Leach's newspaper biographies published at the time of his death; Leach's activity with the AEF as a bayonet instructor, "Former Gary Police Lieutenant Is Now Air Force Captain," *Hoosier Sentinel*, n.d., published in 194? at the time of Leach's reenlistment into military service.

19. Calumet Regional Archives, Indiana University Northwest, Library, Gary City Directory.

20. Gary Police Yearbook, 1934; Fraternal Order of Police Official Program, Aug. 1933, "Gary's First Hundred Years," *Steel Shavings*, col. 37, James B. Lane, ed., CRA, Box 10, http://www.iun.edu/~cra/steel_ shavings/.

21. *Ibid.*

22. "14 Get Jobs, and 14 Are Let Out by Gary Mayor," *Gary Post-Tribune*, Feb. 1, 1922.

23. Report of Physical Examination, Regular Army, ISP.

24. Gary Police Yearbook, 1934.

25. Gary City Directory, CRA.

26. GPT, June 1, 1927.

27. Vujo to Louis name change, "Louis Leach (Licanin)," Coroner's Certificate of Death, Indiana State Board of Health, Bureau of Vital Statistics. Marriage of Matt Leach, Application for Marriage License, Female, Marion Brancis, State of Indiana, Lake County, No. 77400, Feb. 27, 1925; Application for Marriage License, Male, Matt Leach, State of Indiana, Lake County, No. 77400, Feb. 27, 1925; Certificate of Marriage, State of Indiana, Lake County, Matt Leach and Marion Brancis, Feb. 27, 1925, Clerk Lake Circuit Superior Court, Lake County, Indiana.

28. Gary City Directory, CRA.

29. Marshall Leach, GPT, Nov. 27, 1929.

30. Stack to Poulsen (quote used with permission); Gary/[Marshall] Leach, Boxing's Official Record Keeper (courtesy of James Stack), http://boxrec.com/en/boxer/ 84631 (accessed 10/1/201?, n.d.).

31. *Ibid.*, Marshall Leach's boxing chronology, GPT, April 25, 1929; Nov. 27, 1929.

32. "Crime Bureau in Operation; Appoint Aids, Galloway and Leach Are Named as Acting Lieutenants," GPT, June 1, 1927.

33. List of United States Citizens for the Immigration Authorities, S.S. *Leviathan*, Cherbourg, Oct. 11, 1927, Port of New York, Oct. 17, 1927. Debra Brookhart, curator-archivist, Library Division, American Legion Headquarters, provided a blank "Official Certificate of Inspection, The Second A.E.F." This would have been the passport Leach used.

34. "Gary's First Hundred Years," *Steel Shavings*, CRA, Box 10. "The Bucket of Blood" was listed, and is not to be confused with the establishment of the same

name that was managed by Anna Sage, "the Woman in Red." Anna Sage's establishment, the Kostur Hotel, 654 Washington Street in Gary, GPT, Dec. 21, 1933.

35. John Binder, *Al Capone's Beer Wars: A Complete History of Organized Crime in Chicago During Prohibition* (Amherst, NY: Prometheus, 2017), 202.

36. Leach's prior involvement with Roy Keele: *Hammond Daily* (unidentified), Dec. 8, 1929, collection of Tom Smusyn.

37. Leach's termination, GPT, Jan. 1, 1930. Leach's occupation was listed in the Gary City Directories during the years of the 1920s and is used to pinpoint the years of his promotions in the department.

Chapter 2

1. Stack to Poulsen (quote used with permission).

2. Marshall title of "Steel City Middleweight," GPT, April 25, 1929.

3. "Hammond Jury Frees Six Men, Policeman and Two Bootleggers Are Convicted," *Hammond Daily*, Dec. 8, 1929; GPT, Jan. 1, 1930.

4. "Linn and Leach, Former Gary Police Officers, Are Named Deputy Sheriffs," GPT, Feb. 18, 1930, 1.

5. Debra Brookhart, curator-archivist, American Legion, Library Division, email to author Ellen Poulsen, Feb. 3, 2013.

6. Philip Von Blon, "The Hoosier Schoolmaster," *American Legion Monthly*, American Legion, Library Division, Jan. 1929.

7. Dean J. Kotlowski, *Paul V. McNutt and the Age of FDR* (Bloomington: Indiana University Press, 2015), 120.

8. Frank Mayr rally, "Leech-Feeney Showdown Up to Governor," unidentified clipping, Indianapolis, July 4, 1935, collection of Tom Smusyn.

9. Letter, McNutt to Leach, Nov. 15, 1932, Library of Congress, Manuscript Division, Dillinger, John.

10. "Patronage Trouble," column, "They Tell," n.p., Jan. 10, 1933, collection of Tom Smusyn.

11. Text of Leach's legislative doorkeeper award, unidentified clipping, n.p., Olsen collection.

12. Lori Hyde, "Captain Matthew Leach, Lawman and Man of War: John Dillinger's Nemesis," *On the Spot Journal*, Winter 2006; "State Police Post to Leach," *Herald Examiner*, Feb. 28, 1933.

13. Frederick Van Nuys approval of Feeney, "Leech-Feeney Showdown Up to Governor," Indianapolis daily, n.p., July 4, 1935; Mayr backers dismissed, IS, March 15, 1933.

14. Pleas Greenlee, IS, June 11, 1935; IN, Nov. 11, 1932; Greenlee suicide, *Evansville Press*, Sept. 29, 1954, Genealogybank.com; Gary Police Department Year Book 1934 would identify the Indiana State Police "as reorganized by Gov. Paul V. McNutt." CRA, Box 10.

15. Salary, "State Police Post to Leach," *Herald Examiner*, Feb. 28, 1933.

16. U.S. City Directories, 1930 U.S. Federal Census, http://www.ancestry.com.

17. Marion Leach, U.S. City Directories, 1821–1989, http://www.ancestry.com (accessed Jan. 9, 2015).

18. Grott, "Who's Who in the State House," *Hoosier Sentinel*, n.d.

19. Chester Butler, lieutenant, district chairman, district meeting to organize ISP, "Tipton Host to Twenty-Two State Police," *Kokomo Tribune*, n.d.; Stack ISP firing and reappointment, GPT, March 15, 1933.

20. IS, Feb. 4, 1933. McNutt reorganization bill, Indiana Acts 1933, Chapter 4, Senate Bill 130, approved Feb. 3, 1933, "State–Executive–Administrative Act." Reorganization was the consolidation of the State Fire Marshall, State Motor Police, and Bureau of Criminal Identification and Investigation into the Division of Public Safety. The Highway Commission was also reorganized.

21. William "Tubby" Toms, Dean J. Kotlowski, *Paul V. McNutt and the Age of FDR* (Bloomington: Indiana University Press, 2015), 147.

22. Leach publicity, *Herald Examiner*, Feb. 26, 1933, May 3, 1933; IS, April 4, 12,

May 1, 1933; IT, May 5, 31, 1933; GPT, May 26, June 3, 10, 1933.

23. Philip Hart to Ellen Poulsen, telephone conversation (quote used with permission).

24. Ralph L. Brooks, "State Police Tuned to Noble Creed, Start Patrol—and, Oh, Those Uniforms," IS, May 1, 1933.

25. "Leach Locked in Office, McNutt Merely Chuckles," IS, April 12, 1933.

26. "State Police Get Barracks at Tremont," GPT, June 3, 1933.

27. Lack of funding, GPT, June 10, 1933. State Trooper Eugene Teague would be killed as Dillinger and his gang were on the loose, before the radio system was implemented. The ISP was still releasing statements that "the department is engaged at the present time in planning a state-wide radio system that will be of great help to all law enforcement agencies." "Dillinger Issue Perils Governor McNutt," *Daily News*, May 5, 1934; backlash on political appointees, "Bar Politicians on State Police Force," IT, Nov. 8, 1933.

28. Michigan City appointments, *Daily News*, May 5, 1934.

Chapter 3

1. "Callahan Not to Run for Mayor," *Hammond Times*, Jan. 27, 1925; "12 Alleged Ill Fame Resorts Raided, 27 Held," GPT, n.d.

2. "Big Bill Gets More Bad News," *Hammond Times*, March 1, 1921; "Big Bill Again in Custody," *Hammond Times*, May 13, 1921, collection of Tom Smusyn

3. "Governor, Can You and Matt Do Anything About This Mess," GPT, Dec. 21, 1933.

4. The East Chicago meeting of Eddie Bentz and Baby Face Nelson was noted in Huntington to File, Sept. 13, 1933, Pinkerton's National Detective Agency, Library of Congress, Manuscript Division; Long Beach, Indiana meetings noted in FBI, "Lester Joseph Gillis, Part 01 of 03, "Edward Wilhelm Bentz," April 11, 1936, File No. 91-57-9.

5. Visit of Poulsen to Indiana State Penitentiary, 1988.

6. John Dillinger, Indiana Reformatory, Notice of Arrival of New Inmate (Sandy Jones Collection).

7. *Ibid.*

8. John Herbert Dillinger: Paroled May 5, 1933, Record of Indiana State Penitentiary, LOC, Manuscript Division, Dillinger, John.

9. Visit of the authors Poulsen and Hyde, individually, to Mooresville farmhouse.

10. A list of White Cap gang members and associates is fragmented, as members of the assorted groups that composed the Dillinger Gang during the "White Cap Gang" period varied. The nuclear members of the group that has historically been called the "White Cap Gang" were William A. Shaw, Noble Claycombe, and Paul "Lefty" Parker. The next wave included Hilton Crouch and "John Vinson," who was identified by F. Huntington as "John Vincent." Memo, F. Huntington to File, Pinkerton's National Detective Agency, Inc., Sept. 13, 1933, LOC, Manuscript Division, Dillinger, John. Post–White Cap activity involved Clifford Mohler, Sam Goldstine, Harry Copeland, and Homer Van Meter. Later there were James Kirkland, Maurice Lanham, and Frank and George Whitehouse (Lebanon, Kentucky). While the New Carlisle robbers were in Dillinger's presence daily, doubt lingers among historians, who believe that the New Carlisle, Ohio, job of June 21, 1933, may have been the work of the others, not including Dillinger.

11. Homer Van Meter, Record of Indiana Reformatory, Pendleton, Indiana, LOC, Manuscript Division, Dillinger, John.

12. Robert Cromie and Joseph Pinkston, *Dillinger: A Short and Violent Life* (New York: McGraw Hill, 1962), 36.

13. Shaw's charge that Copeland was "yellow," "F. Huntington to File," Pinkerton's National Detective Agency, Inc., Sept. 13, 1933, LOC, Manuscript Division, Dillinger, John.

14. Harry Copeland, Record of Indiana State Penitentiary, LOC, Manuscript Division, Dillinger, John.

15. Samuel Goldstine, Record of Indiana State Penitentiary, LOC, Manuscript Division, Dillinger, John.

16. FBI, "JODIL," File No. 62-29777-115, March 12, 1934; Shaw's revelations and Dillinger's vindication from Lebanon involvement: FBI memo, "Connolley to File re. James Kirkland et al.," 3, 1934, FBI, "JODIL," File No. 62-29777, 26-34560-6.

17. World's Fair, IT, May 27, 1933; June 5, 1933.

18. Clifford "Whitey" Mohler, "Principals in Double Killing Wednesday Night," March 11, 1926, n.p., Collection of author Lori Hyde.

19. Witnesses picked Lanham out of a selection of police mug shots. Police promptly picked him up and held him in the Jefferson County Jail pending his trial at Lebanon. Lanhan was also held in connection with the Gravel Switch robbery in the Jefferson County Jail; "U.S. Agents Plan to Quiz Man Held in State Robbery," *Louisville Times*, Aug. 16, 1933.

20. "F. Huntington to File," Sept. 13, 1933, LOC, Manuscript Division, Pinkerton's National Detective Agency. This memo claims that Shaw denied ever meeting Van Meter. Long Beach, Indiana meetings noted in FBI, "Lester Joseph Gillis, Part 01 of 03, "Edward Wilhelm Bentz," April 11, 1936, File No. 91-57-9.

21. Mohler, "Prison Gates Clang Behind Mohler Again," GPT, Aug. 21, 1933. Officers Edmunds, Zarkovich, Cheranko, Whelan and Sopsic participated in the raid, which was led by Captain Tim O'Neill, "East Chicago Police Arrest Foxy Criminal," *Hammond Times,* Aug. 23, 1933; "State Police Nab Paroled Convict Here," GPT, Oct. 1933. Arresting officers, Edward Knight, Officer [first name missing] Edmunds, Martin Zarkovich, Officer [first name missing] Cheranko, Officer [first name missing] Whelan, and Peter Sopsic, in a raid led by Captain Timothy O'Neill.

22. "Bank Bandits Confess Crime to Police," *Hammond Times,* Aug. 19, 1933.

23. "F. Huntington to File," Sept. 13, 1933, LOC, Manuscript Division, Pinkerton.

24. Physical layout of Baring and 144th, authors visit, 2013. Leach's trail to Baring Street, Smusyn research.

25. Officer George W. Daugherty, "Recalls 1930s' Manhunt," unidentified article, Olsen Collection.

26. "F. Huntington to File," Sept. 13, 1933, LOC, Manuscript Division, Pinkerton.

27. *Ibid.*

28. Letter, Della Mohler to Matt Leach, June 18, 1935; Leach's response, Leach to Della Mohler, June 24, 1935, LOC, Manuscript Division, Dillinger, John.

29. Sam Goldstine was also known as "Sam Goldstein." For purposes of consistency, this text refers to him as "Goldstine." Arrest, GPT, Aug. 23, 1933, Oct. 1, 1933; IS, Sept. 1, 1933; Leach's recollections of the Gary arrest were recorded by Al Dunlap, "Why Dillinger's Gang Is Doomed," *Liberty Magazine*, Oct. 37, 1934.

30. Russell Girardin and William J. Helmer, *Dillinger: The Untold Story* (Bloomington: Indiana University Press, 1994), 25.

31. "F. Huntington to File," LOC, Manuscript Division, Pinkerton.

32. Leach to Sam Burk, chief of detectives, Terre Haute, Sept. 18, 1933; Leach to Daniel T. Wolfe, chief of police, Toledo, Aug. 30, 1933, LOC, Manuscript Division, Dillinger, John.

33. "Leach Tells of Plot to Flee Prison," *Indiana* [masthead illegible], Sept. 29, 1933. The existence of such an offer would have led police to surmise that a prison break was in the planning stage. This is an indication that there was no concern raised by Leach, Huntington or other police officials before the breakout.

34. Dillinger transferred about $27,000 to Pearl Elliot (Mike McCormick, "Historical Perspective," *Terre Haute Tribune Star,* Aug. 2, 1998, 7); Letters [two in number], Omar F. Brown, Kokomo, to Lena Pierpont, n.d., Brown to Lena Pierpont,

July 8, 1933, letters contained in LOC, Manuscript Division, Dillinger, John.

Chapter 4

1. IN, Sept. 9, 1933; IT, Sept. 27, 1933.
2. IT, Sept. 30, 1933.
3. IT, Nov. 3, 1933. Angered over his discharge, Claudy openly condemned Governor McNutt and Warden Kunkel, blaming them for the prison escape.
4. Board of Trustees Inquiry, ISA, Sept. 28, 1933. It claimed Claudy gave an interview to the *Chicago American* and *Michigan City Dispatch* stating he had heard rumors about a breakout to take place on Sept. 27, and apparently, he never told Kunkel beforehand. In his pre–1962 papers, late Dillinger researcher Joe Pinkston wrote that Claudy also believed the escape was planned for a date in October, which gave him more time to investigate than he had originally thought. The fact that Pierpont moved the breakout date to late September to avoid the possibility of Claudy's betrayal would reinforce the idea that Claudy had prior knowledge of the breakout. This does not, however, advance the theory that Claudy was a party to the breakout.
5. Michigan City Board of Trustees escape inquiries, ISA. Although it is highly doubtful that Claudy aided Pierpont, the interviews of Northern, O'Leary and Brehen appear to be almost rehearsed.
6. Walter Detrich State Police Interview, Indiana State Archives.
7. Some biographical details, Mike McCormick, "Historical Perspectives," *Terre Haute Tribune-Star*, Aug. 2, 1998; Walter Detrich State Police interview, ISA.
8. Estella Cox research.
9. Board of Trustees escape inquiry, ISA.
10. Board of Trustees escape inquiry, Floyd Back Register #11125, interview, ISA.
11. Board of Trustees escape inquiry, Thomas Register #12453, interview, ISA.
12. Detrich, State Police interview, ISA; GPT, Jan. 10, 1934; IN, Jan. 10, 11, 1934; CT, Jan. 11, 1934. Interrogated by Matt Leach,

the outlaw admitted that "an elephant could have been smuggled into prison if a box had been large enough." Leach avoided any questions that referred to the theory of NcNutt's political spoils and steered the interview toward blaming older prison officials, namely Claudy.
13. Board of Trustees escape inquiry John J. Cunningham interview, ISA.
14. Board of Trustees escape inquiry Albert Evans interview, ISA.
15. Prison escape, Board of Trustees, 64-page transcript interviews with actual participants and Walter Detrich State Police interview, ISA; Board of Trustees escape inquiry Albert Evans interview, ISA.
16. IN, Sept. 29, 1933; *Herald Examiner,* Sept. 30, 1933. After DeMont and five officers were charged by the broadcasting station with aiding in the gun battle hoax, Leach denied that any of his men participated and said an investigation would clear their names.
17. Sheriff Neel's statements after release, *Chicago Herald,* September 29, 1933; IN, Sept. 30, 1933.
18. IN, Sept. 28, 1933. Leach appeared doubtful that the home invasion actually had happened, or about which group of convicts descended on the Werners, if it had. With Sheriff Neel documenting Detrich's movements after the escape, apparently Pierpont had held the family hostage.
19. Cromie and Pinkston, *Dillinger: A Short and Violent Life,* 64.
20. *Ibid.* Huntington went to great lengths not to share informers with the state police captain, including him only when necessary. Leach most certainly found this annoying due to his determination to catch the gang.
21. Edward S. Cook to Inspector Yendes, Aug. 25, 1933, Sept. 4, 1933, Library of Congress, Manuscript Division, Pinkerton's National Detective Agency.
22. *Dayton Journal,* Sept. 23, 1933.
23. Cromie and Pinkston, *Dillinger: A Short and Violent Life,* 54–55.
24. IN, Sept. 27, 1933; GPT, Oct. 27, 1933. Leach told newspapers that if he had

been permitted to view documents found on Dillinger, the prison escape could have been prevented. Yendes insisted that Matt had been warned and even urged to make copies, but had dismissed the papers as unimportant. Forrest Huntington, who was present with Leach, verified that Yendes did do this. The matter was dropped when Indiana feared alienating Ohio and loosing Dillinger.

25. Michigan City prison escape report, Oct. 13, 1933, ISA.

26. *Ibid.*

27. Hamilton hideout, Report of E.S. Clark to S.H. Brady, March 3, 1934, LOC, Manuscript Division, Pinkerton.

Chapter 5

1. Cromie and Pinkston, *Dillinger: A Short and Violent Life*, 55.

2. *The Dayton Journal*, Sept. 23, 1933.

3. Lima Lodge No. 21, Inc., Fraternal Order of Police, 1983 yearbook.

4. E. S. Clark, Ohio Bankers Association, Oct. 10,1933, Library of Congress, Manuscript Division, John Dillinger File. Brown had convinced Sheriff Sarber to allow him to see Dillinger and furnished credentials as a former sheriff of Howard County, Indiana. Another inmate stated that Brown spoke in code to Dillinger and could make no sense of the conversation. HFS Report, First National Bank, St. Mary's Ohio, Holdup, Oct. 24, 1933, LOC, Manuscript Division, Pinkerton Detective Agency.

5. E. F. Connelly, Bureau of Investigation report, Oct. 14, 1933. Dillinger released his Terraplane to his lawyer in Dayton, who transferred it to Dillinger's brother Hubert. Hubert then transferred it to a Mrs. John Dillinger (probably Mary Kinder) of 1052 S. 2nd Avenue, Hamilton, Ohio. This was the automobile Pierpont was driving.

6. Interview with Fred Pierpont, Bureau of Investigation report, Oct. 14, 1933. John Hamilton was thought to have been with the gang in Ohio, but he is never mentioned in the interview.

7. Lima Lodge No. 21, Inc., Fraternal Order of Police, 1983 yearbook.

8. *The Lima News*, Oct. 19, 1933. The identity of the third man is questionable. First news accounts listed Pierpont, Copeland and Clark. Later accounts changed Clark to Makley, then finally said Pierpont, Makley and Clark.

9. The gang went to Hamilton, Ohio, to live in a cottage supplied by a relative of Russell Clark. Report of E.S. Clark to S.H. Brady, March 3, 1934, LOC, Manuscript Division, Pinkerton.

Chapter 6

1. Midwest Crime Wave overview, ca. May/June 1933, Harvey Bailey, escape from Kansas State Pen, IT, May 31, 1933, June 2, 1933; accused in Urschel kidnapping, IT, Sept. 19, 1933, Sept. 21, 1933; biographical, Lori Hyde, "Harvey Bailey, Dean of the American Bank Robbers," *Oklahoma Hombres*, winter 2009; Hyde, http://www.geocities.ws/harveybailey 2002/index-2.html (accessed Oct. 28, 2017).

2. Kansas City Massacre, IT, June 17, 1933.

3. "Laws of Congress," statement by the Federal Division of Investigation, IT, Oct. 24, 1933. The federal printing of 35,000 circulars of the gang in secret agreement with Ohio officials, Forrest S. Huntington's three-page internal report, dated Oct. 24, 1933, Library of Congress, Pinkerton File, Manuscript Division.

4. Kidnapping of William Hamm, IT, June 17, 1933.

5. Al Feeney's request to the Indiana Bankers Association, IT, July 8, 1933.

6. "Faked Radio Battle Brings Complaint," unidentified newspaper clipping, n.d., collection of Tom Smusyn.

7. Cessation of paroles in Indiana, IT, Oct. 28, 1933; reinstatement of paroles, IT, Nov. 6, 1933.

8. "Claudy Asserts Kunkel Assigned Factory Guards," unidentified newspaper clipping, Nov. 3, 1933, collection of Tom Smusyn.

9. McNutt administration, William

Shinnick, "Dillinger's Happy Hunting Ground, a Record of Murder, Robbery, and Indiana Politics," *Chicago Sunday Tribune*, Oct. 9–38 (collection of Tom Smusyn); "Investigate State Police," IN, Oct. 4, 1933.

10. Mike Morrissey versus Leach dispute, IS, June 17, 1933; IT, Oct. 5, 1933. Note that the name of Mike Morrissey, Indianapolis police chief, is spelled with one "s" or two in various newspaper articles. The Indiana State Library confirmed that the City Government pages of the City Directory gave the spelling as "Morrissey," with a double "s."

11. Background on Daniel McGeoghegan, "Brand Culver Bandit," IT, May 31, 1933.

12. "Leslie Gave Hint of Prison Break," IN, Sept. 28, 1933

13. Letters and notes found on Dillinger, "Leach Thinks Letters Would Have Been Aid," GPT, Oct. 27, 1933.

14. Dayton controversy, *Sharon Herald* (Pennsylvania), Sept. 27, 1933; *Dayton Journal*, Sept. 28, 1933; Al Dunlap, "Why Dillinger Gang Is Doomed," *Liberty*, Oct. 27, 1934. Dunlap wrote that Leach was given the map of Michigan City on Sept. 30, 1933, and that Leach then notified Sheriff Sarber.

15. Letter generated from Ohio office of the Pinkertons, who were then authorized to get word to Sarber.

16. Letter, Oct. 4, 1933, E. S. Clark to J. L. Sarber; LOC, Manuscript Division, Pinkerton Detective Agency.

17. Egan's counsel of Dillinger, Pinkston papers, collection of Tom Smusyn.

18. The Hamilton raid, George Daugherty, "Recalls 1930s' Manhunt."

19. Huntington's refusal to "out" McGinnis was based on underworld rumors, later confirmed by alleged bank robber Leslie Homer (arrested soon after the Dillinger gang Racine holdup) that the "gang planned to murder McGinnis as soon as they could find him." Quotes taken from the notes of Joe Pinkston, 132, collection of Tom Smusyn.

20. Mary Kinder's family members,

"Identified as Amo Bank Robbers, William Robert Behrens, Margaret Ann Behrens, Claude E. Parker," IS, June 2, 1932.

21. Pierpont family and Mary Kinder's family, IT, Oct. 7, 1933; Theodore Rahutis restaurant, IT, Oct. 18, 1933.

22. Ellen Poulsen, *Don't Call Us Molls: Women of the John Dillinger Gang* (Little Neck, NY: Clinton Cook, 2002), 295. Opal Long was unable to prove she was married to Clark. After he was arrested in Tucson in 1934 and sent to the Ohio State Penitentiary, Opal Long was not granted visitor's rights based on the fact that she could not prove that she was Clark's legal spouse.

23. Leach's statements on Frechette and Longnaker, Frank A. White, "State Police to Concentrate on Rural Districts, New Strength to Stop Criminals in Small Communities, Explanation Given by Captain Leach, IS, Oct. 4, 1935, Leach's reply to a statement of Dr. L. E. Bracken of Columbus, speech, American Association of Orificial Surgeons, Chicago, that "sex appeal was responsible for the late John Dillinger's life of crime."

24. Dillinger's letters and postcards mailed to Matt Leach, as confirmed by the Leach family; "How to Be a Detective," IN, Jan. 31, 1934. Contradicting the IN article, in his memoir, author Irving Leibowitz attributed the mailing of the book to International News Service reporter Jack Cejnar in Irving Leibowitz, *My Indiana* (Englewood Cliffs, NJ: Prentice Hall, 1964), 181.

25. Greencastle, "Indiana Officers Quiz Copeland," *Evansville Courier*, Nov. 20, 1933.

26. Informant McGinnis' and Huntington's relationship, as well as excerpts from Huntington's letters of complaint about Leach, Pinkston notes, collection of Tom Smusyn.

27. Chicago Dillinger Squad and killing of Louis Katsewitz, Charles Tatelbaum and Sam Ginsburg, "Robbers Killed in Gun Battle in Rogers Park," "Slain Gunmen Identified in 3 More Crimes," and "Mayor Kelly Praises Police for Killing of Three Criminals," CT, Dec. 18–19, 1934.

28. Leach's use of plainclothesmen in Chicago, Kellner, Esther, "Fifty Years of Service, The Story of the Indiana State Police for their 50th Anniversary," Pamphlet, CRA, Box 10.

29. Irving Park Blvd, IT, Nov. 16, 1933.

30. Copy of wiretap actual conversation Nov. 15–17, 1933. Mary Kinder talking, transcripts from Chicago Police wiretaps, authors' collection.

31. Ibid.

32. Huntington and his memoranda issued internally and externally to other law enforcement agencies, including the letter to Sheriff Sarber, LOC, Manuscript Division, Pinkerton Detective Agency.

33. Racine holdup, *Racine Journal-Times*, Nov. 2, 1933 (collection of Tom Smusyn); *Milwaukee Journal*, Nov. 2, 1933.

34. Arrest of Leslie "Big" Homer, "Wisconsin and Indiana Officers Vie for Dillinger Gang Held Here," Jan. 29, 1934; Arizona, ca. Jan. or Feb. 1934 [masthead missing], newspaper clipping file, Arizona Historical Society.

35. Letters written by Leach, Leach to J. W. Cook, police chief, Lima, Nov. 27, 1933; Frank S. W. Burk, assistant superintendent, commanding Detective Bureau, Washington, D.C., Nov. 8, 1933; Warden (unnamed), Michigan City, Oct. 31, 1933, LOC, Manuscript Division, Dillinger, John.

36. The entry of Cincinnati Field Office of the FBI, Cincinnati FBI to Leach, Nov. 14, 1933; Leach to Cincinnati FBI, Nov. 28, 1933, FBI JODIL, 62-(file no. missing or illegible).

37. Feeney and Copeland's discussion of football, IT, Nov. 22, 1933.

38. Chief Mike Morrissey's opinion regarding Matt Leach, Huntington's behind-the-scenes role in the disposition of Copeland, and Huntington's statement that state police were under fire, Pinkston papers. Details on Dillinger's indictment by Marion County grand jury for the Massachusetts Avenue bank robbery, IT, Sept. 29, 1933. Early evidence of lack of cooperation between city and state, "Mum's Word, State Cops Not Let in on Bank Robbery, Says Captain Leach," IT, Aug. 4, 1933.

39. "Bought their way out," IT, Nov. 21, 1933.

40. Progression of Copeland's status, *Lima News*, Nov. 20, 1933; IT, Nov. 21, 1933; IS, Feb. 8, 1934.

41. Hamilton's killing of Sergeant William Shanley, CT and *Chicago Times*, Dec. 15, 1933.

42. Robbery attributed to Ed Shouse, *Fort Wayne News-Sentinel*, Dec. 18, 1933. Death of Officer Eugene Teague and arrest of Ed Shouse, CT, Dec. 21, 1933; IN, Dec. 21, 1933. Police strategy in using a relay approach, Pinkston notes.

43. Arrest of Detrich, CT, Jan. 7, 1934; interrogation of Detrich, Jan. 11, 1934, IT, Jan. 10, 1945. Statement to Matt Leach relative to prison break from Indiana State Prison, provided in 1934 by Walter Detrich, GPT, Jan. 10, 1934.

44. Huntington and his memoranda, Library of Congress, Manuscript Division, Pinkerton File.

45. Correspondence between Omar Brown and Mrs. Pierpont regarding H. D. Claudy's cooperation, Letters [two in number], Omar F. Brown, Kokomo, to Lena Pierpont, n.d., Brown to Lena Pierpont, July 8, 1933, letters contained in LOC, Manuscript Division, Dillinger, John.

Chapter 7

1. William Patrick O'Malley, IS, Jan. 16, 1934; IN, Jan. 16, 1934.

2. The Naomi Hooten (Hamilton, Ohio), connection to the arrests, Report, S.H. Brady to E.C. Clark, Cleveland, Cincinnati, OH, March 3, 1934, LOC, Manuscript Division, Pinkerton Detective Agency; quoting the *Cincinnati Enquirer*, Sunday, Jan. 28, 1934.

3. Chief C. A. "Gus" Wollard, "Clark! Makley! Pierpont! Dillinger! Captured," *True Detective*, June 1934, is one of the best sources of the arrest narratives that gives the viewpoint of the firemen. The salesmen's assertions that "questionable characters" were in town was drawn from an author interview with retired Tucson police officer and police historian Stan

Benjamin in 2004. The salesmen's version was also published in the *Arizona Citizen*, Jan. 26, 1934.

4. Wollard, "Clark! Makley! Pierpont! Dillinger! Captured," *True Detective*, June 1934. The account of the arrests was compiled from a vast collection of newspaper originally held in the Tucson Historical Society, classified under "Dillinger." Dillinger's arrest and quotes, *Arizona Star*, Jan. 28, 1934; Pierpont's arrest and quotes, *Arizona Star*, Jan. 30, 1934. Further details of the Tucson officers and their arrests, Stan Benjamin, "Without a Shot Fired, the 1934 Capture of the Dillinger Gang in Tucson," *Smoke Signal*, no. 80, Dec. 2005; arresting officers in Tucson, booking slip and supporting documents, Tucson City Jail, courtesy Andy Dowdle.

5. Matt Leach's arrival in Tucson, IN, Jan. 27–31, 1934.

6. Robert Estill's arrival in Tucson, IN, Jan. 27, 1934.

7. Estill used his own warrant to bring Dillinger back to Lake County. Fight between Makar and Leach, *Arizona Citizen*, Jan. 29, 1934.

8. Racine, Wisconsin, extradition attempt, *Arizona Citizen*, Jan. 29, 1934. Issues surrounding proposed Wisconsin extradition, Al Dunlap, "Why Dillinger's Gang Is Doomed," *Liberty*, Oct. 27, 1934. Leslie Homer controversy, *Arizona Daily Star*, Jan. 29, 1934.

9. Benjamin to Poulsen, 2004. Mr. Benjamin's source was a detective of the Indiana State Police, Det. Harvey Hire, whose commanding officer was Matt Leach. According to Mr. Benjamin, Det. Hire spoke him at length on April 25, 1974.

10. Allegations of Leach's drunkenness, *Post-Tribune*, "Tucson Has No Use for Matt Leach, Declare Arizonans," n.d., 1934, 2, and "Tucson Policeman Will Call on Leach to Make an Apology," n.d., 1934, 2–7.

11. Arresting officers' reward as later reported, *Arizona Star*, May 29, 1934.

12. Fred Pierpont's revelations, Library of Congress, Pinkerton files, Manuscript Division.

13. Mary Kinder, Basil Gallagher, *IT* staff writer, Jan. 26, 1934; "Affable Mary," IT, Jan. 26, 1934. "Pierpont Confesses He Murdered Sheriff in Jail Delivery at Lima," Basil Gallagher, IT, Jan. 29, 1934.

14. Record of Marriages, Marriage License, Pima County, State of Arizona, Jan. 29, 1934. A record of the divorce of "Dale R. Kinder v. Mary Kinder" was filed previously in Indiana on the 5th Judicial Day, June 9, 1933.

15. Extradition to Ohio, IS, Feb. 8, 1934.

16. Revelations that Shaw called Copeland "yellow," "F. Huntington to File," Pinkerton's National Detective Agency, Inc., Sept. 13, 1933, LOC, Manuscript Division.

17. Dillinger's extradition to Lake County, *Arizona Star*, Jan. 30, 1934.

18. Leach's thoughts on Estill's actions regarding flying Dillinger out of Tucson were published in the IS after Leach's firing on Sept. 9, 1934.

19. Mark Robbins' statement regarding the reward, *Arizona Star*, Jan. 30, 1934.

20. Leaving Tucson, IN, Feb. 1, 1934. Leach's handing of $100 each to officers, "Police at Tucson Divide Rewards," IN, Feb. 1, 1934.

21. Leach's reaction to insults from Sherman and Eyman, Al Dunlap, "Why Dillinger Gang Is Doomed," *Liberty*, Oct. 27, 1934.

22. Pierpont and Mary Kinder conversation regarding Leach, transcript of prison visit between Mary Kinder and Harry Pierpont, filed in Indiana State Library.

Chapter 8

1. Movement of Pierpont, Clark and Makley from Tucson to Michigan City, *Arizona Citizen*, Jan. 29, 1934; IN, Feb. 1, 1934; IN, Feb. 1, 1934; IT, Feb. 1, 1934.

2. Robert Estill and East Chicago in Tucson, IN, Jan. 27/16; Fee Book No. 25, Lake Criminal Court; unidentified news article, Feb. 2, 1934.

3. Piquett, IN, Feb. 1, 1934.

4. Lillian Holley, *Lake County Star,* Jan. 2, 1933.

5. Estill, IS, Feb. 1, 1934; "Governor, Can You and Matt Do Anything About This Mess?" GPT, Dec. 21, 1933.

6. Eyman's allegations of Leach's intoxication in Tucson, IT, Jan. 6–7, 1934.

7. Prohibition background article, IN, Jan. 2, 1934.

8. Dillinger's claim to have mailed "How to Be a Detective," IT, Feb. 1, 1934.

9. "Marie Grott Seriously Hurt in Auto Crackup; Leach Also Is Injured," IT, Feb. 3, 1934, "Who's Who in the State House," *Hoosier Sentinel,* n.d.

10. Kinder grand jury, IN, Feb. 1, 1934; IT, Feb. 3, 1934; IT, Feb. 15, 1934.

11. Copeland, IS, Feb. 10, 1934; IT, Feb. 15, 1934.

12. The escape, CT, March 10, 1934; IS, March 7, 1934; Testimony of James Posey, cellmate of Herbert Youngblood, to Edward J. Barce, deputy attorney general, IS, March 3–11, 1934, CT, Mar 4, 1934, with diagram and photos. Dillinger FBI, JODIL, File No. 62-29777-115. Judge Murray's statement, "a hundred men couldn't release the outlaw from such a jail," gave rise to the erroneous term "escape-proof county jail."

13. Stege's re-commissioning of the Chicago Dillinger Squad, IS, March 5, 1934.

14. Blunk and Cahoon taken into custody, IS, March 6, 1934, IS, Marvh 17, 1934, CT, Oct. 30, 1934.

15. *New York Sun,* Dec. 19, 1934. Lovemaking remarks, GPT, March 5, 1934.

16. Estill's East Chicago four-man investigation into Crown Point, IS, March 9, 1934; GPT, Jan. 18, 1930, IS, March 9, 1934.

17. William Shinnick, "A Record of Murder, Robbery and Indiana Politics," *Chicago Tribune,* Oct. 9, 1938.

18. Division of Investigation (later known as the FBI), the Five-State Pact, William J. Helmer and Rick Mattix, *The Complete Public Enemy Almanac* (Nashville: Cumberland House, 2007).

19. Tucson arresting officers and the FBI, JODIL, File No. 62-29777-16.

20. Matt Leach would later testify at his inquest pending his 1937 firing that he had always sought to give the FBI agents the entirety of his files. FBI, JODIL, File No. 62-29777-6932.

21. Lebanon connections of Lanham, Zoll, Kirkland and Whitehouse: FBI, JODIL, File No. 62-29777-115, March 12, 1934; White Cap–era associates found in FBI, JODIL, File No. 62-29777-16; Leach's recommendation to shadow Hubert Dillinger, FBI, JODIL, File No. 62-29777-447.

22. Leach's status in Lima as an officer, IS, Feb. 10, 1934.

23. Leach's relationship with the federal agents, FBI, JODIL, File No. 62-70407, Dec. 3, 1942.

24. Letter, Ernest Cummings to Matt Leach, FBI, JODIL, File No. Missing, March 12, 1934.

25. Warsaw, "Scene of Dillinger's Latest Raid," *Frankfort Times,* April 15, 1934; *New York American,* April 14, 1934.

Chapter 9

1. The account of the Lima trial was compiled from a vast collection of newspapers originally held in the Tucson Historical Society, classified under "Dillinger." "Pierpont Goes on Trial in Ohio," *Tucson Citizen,* March 6, 1934, "Sarber's Son Retells Death of His Father," *Arizona Star,* March 8, 1934.

2. "Makley Sent to Death Row by Lima Jury," IS, March 17, 1934; Tom Hunt, *Wrongly Executed? The Long-Forgotten Context of Charles Sberna's 1939 Electrocution* (Whiting, VT: Seven Seven Eight, 2016), 2–3, 140, disputes the general juror understanding of the 1930s recommendation of mercy option in sentencing.

3. A phrase that has been misquoted many times, this is the original source as reported in IS, March 18, 1934.

4. Shouse/Coy, Feb. 3, 1934; IN, Feb. 3, 1934. Shouse at Lima trial, "Makley's State Witness Balks," IS, March 15, 1934. Convictions, "Clark Is Convicted, Gets Life Term; Makley and Pierpont Deaths

Set for June 13," IS, March 24, 1934. Clark's life term and release from prison, "Ohio Releases Last of Dillinger Gunmen," *Star*, Aug. 16, 1968. Indiana Biography, Dillinger, John, Marion County Public Library. Clark was suffering from lung cancer at the time of his release and died shortly afterward in the family home (interview with a member of Clark's family).

5. Leach and Louis Piquett in Lima, *New York Daily News*, March 19, 1934; IS, March 18, 1934; FBI, JODIL, File No. 62-29777-1804.

6. Tim Mahoney, *Secret Partners: Big Tom Brown and the Barker Gang* (St. Paul: Minnesota Historical Society, 2013), 17.

7. Paul Maccabee, *John Dillinger Slept Here: A Crooks' Tour of Crime and Corruption in St. Paul, 1920–1936* (St. Paul: Minnesota Historical Society, 1995), 8–12.

8. "Raid Iowa Bank, Get $52,000 and Shoot Way Out," unidentified clipping, March 13, 1934, Lori Hyde Collection; "Dillinger Shot Twice, Revealed by His Doctors," *Star*, April 27, 1934. Joseph "Fatso" Negri ("In the Hinges of Hell," *True Detective*, Jan.–Dec. 1941) alleged that Nelson had helped fund Dillinger's escape from Crown Point and that Dillinger was an underling in Nelson's gang. Nelson's role in Crown Point is unconfirmed.

9. Leach on Mason City, "Leach Scorns Dillinger Tip," IT, March 17, 1934.

10. Beth Green revelations, H. H. Clegg to Dir., April 11, 1934, FBI, JODIL, File No. 62-29777-407.

11. Huntington dropped out of public scrutiny. His obituary, "Forrest C. Huntington Dies, Ex-Adjuster and Investigator," unidentified clipping, April 16, 1970, Lori Hyde Collection.

12. "Dillinger Aide Dies in Fight with Deputies, Youngblood Death Leads to Belief," IS, March 16, 1934; *Citizen*, March 16, 1934.

13. "W. A. Rorer to Director," April 1, 1934, FBI, JODIL, File No. 62-29777-387, FBI, JODIL, File No. 62-29777-2340.

14. "St. Paul Clegg to Director," May 15, 1934, FBI, JODIL, File No. 62-29777-462;

"W. Hanni to Director," May 22, 1934, FBI, JODIL, File No. 62-29777-1753.

15. Re. Hoover to Tamm, Matt Leach, FBI, JODIL, File No. 62-29777-6932, Oct. 27, 1937.

16. Leach's prior knowledge of Anna Sage, *Evansville Courier and Journal*, July 31, 1934. Background on Anna Sage's criminal career, GPT, Feb. 13, 1923; July 24, 1926; Nov. 15–30; CT, July 29, 1934.

17. The Sheik Bandits, "Trailing Indiana's Sheik Bandits," *Startling Detective*, Feb. 1935.

18. Probasco's address, CT, July 27, 1934; "Piquett Accused as 'Master Mind' of Dillinger Gang," *Wisconsin State Journal*, Sept. 2, 1935.

19. *The Chicago Tribune* published a pre-dated photo of Sage and Zarkovich posing together on July 30, 1934.

20. "Leach Denies Any Probe in Killing of John Dillinger," *Evansville Courier and Journal*, July 31, 1934. Sage's arrest by Captain Duffy, Hoover to Tamm, July 27, 1934, FBI, JODIL, File No. 62-29777-2966; Dillinger's death, Purvis to Cowley, July 25, 1934, Lockerman and Cowley, "Dillinger File-Part 2 of 3," FBI, JODIL, File No. 62-29777-23. In this memo, Cowley stated that Agent Winsted fired the fatal shots, affidavit sworn to on July 28, 1934, by Agent Purvis and Inspector Cowley. Agent Hurt and Agent Hollis also verified that the Chicago police were not involved in the shooting.

21. *New York Times*, Oct. 1, 1935.

22. Murdered police officers Martin O'Brien and Floyd Mulvihill, letter, Lake County Coroner's Office to Tom Smusyn, Collection of Tom Smusyn; *New York Daily News*, May 26, 1934; *New York Herald*, May 26, 1934.

23. Probasco's death, Report of E.S. Clark, Cleveland, July 29, 1934, p. 2., LOC, Manuscript Division, Pinkerton Detective Agency; "Dillinger's 'Hospital' Host Dives to Death," *New York Daily News*, July 26, 1934.

24. Basil Gallagher, *Washington Daily News*, Aug. 11–15, 1934.

Chapter 10

1. Allegation of a frame-up, Hoover to Tamm, July 27, 1934, FBI, JODIL, File No. 62-29777-2966. Although Captain Stege was mentioned as being in Leach's faction, Stege never went officially on record of being slighted because Dillinger was apprehended and slain by the FBI with the East Chicago, Indiana, police in attendance.

2. Duffield, *Chicago Tribune*; Hoover to Acting Attorney General, July 31, 1934, FBI, JODIL, File No. 62-29777-3079.

3. Leach blame of Sage and Keele for East Chicago Policemen's death, Hoover to Tamm, July 27, 1934, FBI, JODIL, File No. 62-29777-2966.

4. Sage and Keele, "Links in Mystery of Dillinger Shooting" (photos with captions only), CT, July 29, 1934. Zarkovich, "Indiana Police Launch Quiz on Dillinger's Death," CT, July 30, 1934. "I turned entire cases over to them," "Leach, to Be 'Good Sport,' Drops Case," [Indianapolis] Sept. 16, 1937.

5. Richard Emery, *Sam Cowley: Legendary Lawman* (Springville, UT: 2004) 59–63.

6. Al Feeney and Matt Leach, Hoover to Tamm, Nov. 1, 1934, FBI, JODIL, File No. 62-29777-434.

7. *Ibid.*; "Pierpont Politics Charge Re-Echoes," unidentified newspaper article, collection of William Helmer.

8. Leach publicity, Matt Leach, "The Public Enemy and Crime Suppression," *Startling Detective*, Oct. 1936.

9. Leach's rebuff to a statement of Dr. L. E. Bracken of Columbus, speech, American Association of Orificial Surgeons, Chicago, Frank A. White, "State Police to Concentrate on Rural Districts, New Strength to Stop Criminals in Small Communities, Explanation Given by Captain Leach," IS, Oct. 4, 1935.

10. R. E. Winne to Governor Paul V. McNutt, Jan. 30, 1935, unidentified masthead, n.d.

11. He just "fights it out," unidentified news article, collection of Tom Smusyn.

12. "Captain Leach Speaker Here," "Lions Learn of Dillinger Case," *Osgood Journal*, n.d.; Publicity, "Criminal Activities Are on Move to More Remote Area," IS, Oct. 4, 1934.

13. Indiana internal affairs, police hiring practices, IS, June 7, 1935; "Feeney Wins Battle with Greenlee," unidentified newspaper article, Nov. 8, 1933, Olsen Collection; "Feeney to Ask End of Politics in State Police," *Plymouth* (Indiana) *News*, March 3, 1934; power structure of Feeney to Leach, Hoover to Tamm, July 27, 1934, FBI, JODIL, File No. 62-29777-2766; firing of Feeney, "Feeney Ousted as Police Head," IS, June 7, 11, 1935, Oct. 6, 1935.

14. Stiver quotes, Indiana State Police retrospective; "Pick 125 Men for Indiana State Police," unidentified article, June 27, 1935, Collection of Lori Hyde.

15. Frank Cipriani, "Records Shed New Light on Dillinger's Assassination," *Chicago Tribune* (Sunday), July 21, 1935, part 7, 10.

16. Election of M. Clifford Townsend, Kotlowski, *Paul V. McNutt and the Age of FDR*, 194–197.

17. Frank Cipriani, "Records Shed New Light."

18. Doris Lockerman, "A Girl Among Manhunters." CT, Oct. 15, 1935.

19. ISP luncheon of Dec. 13, 1935, "E. A. Tamm to Director Re. Matt Leach," Oct. 27, 1937, FBI, JODIL, File No. 62-29777-6932.

20. Death of John Hamilton, Aug. 26, 1934, FBI, JODIL, File No. 62-29777-6334. Note that Bruce Hamilton, the nephew of John Hamilton, has written an alternative ending to the life of John Hamilton. It states that John Hamilton survived the Dillinger era and escaped to Canada. Bruce W. Hamilton, "John Hamilton, the Other Side of Dillinger," (published magazine).

21. "Head and Hands" murder case, CT, July 7–9, Nov. 19, Dec. 8–9, 15–16, 1936; "Mutilation Key to Solution in 'Head-Hands' Case," IT, June 9, 1936; "Leach Avoids Talk on Crime," IT, Dec. 18, 1936. Leach's rebuttal to the FBI charge of

deviating from protocol, "E. A. Tamm to Director Re., Matt Leach," Oct. 27, 1937, FBI, JODIL, File No. 62-29777-6932.

22. Police loop or "The Loop," Leach's method of moving Hicks was called "running the loop," Paul R. Kavieff, *The Purple Gang: Organized Crime in Detroit, 1910–1946* (Fort Lee, NJ: Barricade, 2000), 8.

23. Rebuttal to charges of failure to follow procedure, L. A. Tamm to Hoover, FBI, JODIL, File No. 62-29777-6932.

24. Stiver's exclusivity in giving out information to the press on the activities of the ISP, untitled article, *Indianapolis Daily*, Sept. 9, 1937.

25. Tamm to Hoover, FBI, JODIL, File No. 62-29777-6932.

Chapter 11

1. Brady gang synopsis was compiled from the following, Chicago sergeant Sal Corsi, "Yellow Rats, Blasting the Brady Gang. (as told to Raymond Ruddy)," *True Detective Mysteries*, Feb.–Oct. 1938, LOC, Manuscript Division; Al Brady Gang; FBI, BRAGA. "Paul Minneman," Pamphlet, Indiana State Library.

2. Basil Gallagher, "The Truth About Dillinger," *Washington Daily News*, Aug. 11, 15, 1934.

3. "Leach in Baltimore Probing Brady Clue," IT, Aug. 18, 1937.

4. Arrest of Charles "Chuck" Northern, CT, May 3, 1936.

5. Brady's threat to kill Leach, "H. S. Boone to File, Statement of Alfred Brady," FBI, BRAGA, April 30, 1936, p. 1.

6. In spite of the critique, Leach was assisting the FBI with information gathering, "J. J. Meehan to File, Brady Gang Synopsis of Facts," Oct. 26–36, 1937, FBI, BRAGA.

7. "Christine Puckett, Memorandum for the Director Re, Matt Leach," Oct. 27, 1937, FBI, BRAGA, File No. (prefix missing)-6932.

8. "Gun Gangsters' Wives Arraigned, Charged with Obstructing Justice," *Baltimore News-Post*, Friday evening, Aug. 13, 1937.

9. Interviews with Mary Schwartz, wife of James Dalhover, and Minnie Riley, wife of Clarence Lee Shaffer, Jr., *Baltimore News-Post*, Aug. 10–13, 1937.

10. Leach's interview of the wives of Dalhover and Shaffer, which linked Officer Minneman's shotgun and the silverware given to the women as wedding presents with the Carthage robbery, IT, Aug. 11–18, IS, Aug. 18, 1937; Leach's receipt of the silverware, D. B. Davies, Aug. 28, 1937, Brady Gang, Synopsis of Facts, FBI, BRAGA.

11. Stiver's publicity resolution, "Leach Says States Rights Are Invaded," GPT, Sept. 9, 1937. Brady roller skating story, "Police Learn Brady Exhibited as Skater in Baltimore," *Evansville Courier & Press* (Indiana), Aug. 24, 1937, p. 1. "Gangster Brady a Skating Star, Police Reveal," *Rockford Illinois Morning Star*, Aug. 24, 1937, p. 3. Roller skating memo generated by the FBI, "Memo for All Agents," Aug. 18, 1937, BRAGA. One inaccuracy was published by IN reporter Tubby Toms, "When the Brady Gang was on the loose, after the Carthage bank robbery, Leach confided to reporters that they were in Baltimore. One reporter couldn't keep the secret, and from this leak came the demand from the FBI that Leach be fired" ("Matt Leach Fired on Demand of FBI," IS, June 18, 1955).

12. Gurnea, Reineke to Stiver, "Fires Leach as Police Captain," unidentified article, n.d., ca. Sept. 1937, Collection of James Stack.

13. Rabb's contention of civil liberties dispute in Hicks case, Frank A. White, INS news correspondent, "State's Rights Invaded, Reply of Capt. Leach," unidentified article, n.d., ca. Sept. 1937, Collection of James Stack.

14. FBI's break with Indiana over Leach, "Officer Removed on Charges of Refusing to Work with G-Men," IN, n.d., ca. Sept. 1937, Collection of James Stack.

15. Charges against Leach, "Fires Leach as Police Captain," unidentified article, n.d., ca. Sept. 1937, Collection of James Stack.

16. Acts of Indiana General Assembly, "E. A. Tamm to the Director Re, Matt Leach," Oct. 27, 1937, JODIL, File No. 62-29777-6932, p. 1.

17. Stiver fires Leach, "E. A. Tamm to the Director Re.: Matt Leach," Oct. 27, 1937, FBI, JODIL, File No. 62-29777-6932, 2.

18. Eckert hired, "Oust State Police Captain Leach," *Chicago Herald & Examiner*, Sept. 5, 1937; "Officer Removed. Lt. Walter Eckert of Osgood Is Successor," IN, n.d., ca. Sept. 1937.

19. William "Tubby" Toms, "Matt Leach Fired on Demand of FBI," IN, June 18, 1955.

20. *Ibid.*

21. Leach's press release, IT, Sept. 4, 1937, 1, provided the published press release. Leach's original letter contains the unexpurgated version. For the full text of the letter as originally written by Leach, see Appendix A.

22. Brady files, "Board Upholds Leach Ouster," unidentified article, n.d., ca. Sept. 1937, Collection of James Stack.

23. Hoover/Hitler remarks, "Leach Moves to Fight Back Over Ousting," unidentified article, n.d., ca. Sept. 1937, Collection of James Stack.

24. Transfer of the Brady files to the ISP, E.A. Tamm, Memo for the Director, FBI, JODIL, File No. 62-29777-6932, 29. This document contained excerpts of verbatim testimony in the hearing of Matt Leach.

Chapter 12

1. Pleas Greenlee's relationship to Leach, "Does Efficiency of Politics Rule State Police Force?" unidentified article (Indianapolis?), n.d., ca. Sept. 1937; "Charge No. 10 … alleges Mr. Leach gave statements to the press about police activities without authorization of the state police superintendent—in other words, that he didn't consult 'the boss' every time he had a matter of news interest…. Mr. Leach was friendly to Pleas Greenlee in the democratic convention fight of 1936; M. Clif-ford Townsend was the victor and was elected governor." Greenlee boys, "Charge Politics in Leach Ouster," unidentified article (Indianapolis), n.d., ca. Sept. 1937, Collection of James Stack.

2. Stiver's attitude toward the "1933 Old Timers," Al Spiers, "It's Like This," ISP commemorative piece, Olsen Collection.

3. Charges and transcript of Leach Testimony, L. A. Tamm to Hoover, Oct. 27, 1937, JODIL, File No. 62-29777-6932.

4. G. Russell Girardin with William J. Helmer, *Dillinger: The Untold Story* (Bloomington: Indiana University Press, 1994), 140–141, 184.

5. "Leach Denies G-Men Charges"; "FBI Executive Accuses Matt," unidentified article (Indianapolis), n.d., possibly Sept. 16, 1937, Collection of James Stack.

6. *Ibid.*

7. L. A. Tamm to Hoover, Oct. 27, 1937, FBI, JODIL, File No. 62-29777-6932.

8. Brady files, "Board Upholds Leach Ouster," unidentified article, n.d., ca. Sept. 1937, FBI, BRAGA.

Chapter 13

1. Sergeant Sal Corsi, "Yellow Rats, Blasting the Brady Gang," *True Detective*, Feb.–Oct. 1938.

2. Bryan Burrough, *Public Enemies: America's Greatest Crime Wave and the Birth of the FBI* (New York: Penguin: 2004), 416.

3. 1940 United States Federal Census; Gary City Directory, CRA; www.ancestry.com (accessed Oct. 28, 2012).

4. Lori Hyde, "Captain Matt Leach," *On the Spot Journal*, Winter 2006; "Police Board O.K.'s Removal of Matt Leach, Gary Man to Take Two Weeks' Rest Before Disclosing Plans," GPT, Sept. 17, 1937.

5. 1940 United States Federal Census.

6. Gary City Directory, CRA.

7. Death of Vujo/Louis Licanin, conversation with James Stack. Vujo is last seen in public records in 1941, and died in Gary in 1943. "Louis Leach (Licanin)," Coroner's Certificate of Death, Indiana State Board of Health, Bureau of Vital Statistics.

8. Marion's Indianapolis address, 1940 census and concurrently listed in a publicity article about Leach, "Former Gary Police Lieutenant Is Now Air Force Captain," unidentified article (*Hoosier Sentinel?*), n.d., ca. 1942, Collection of James Stack.

9. *Marion Leach vs. Matt Leach*, Divorce Decree, City County Building, Indianapolis, May 25, 1945.

10. Matt Leach, World War II draft registration card, 1942, www.ancestry.com (accessed May 11, 2009). Leach listed his date of birth as Aug. 1, 1984. This contradicts earlier dates of birth provided by Leach but is considered the most accurate.

11. Hyde, *On the Spot Journal*; Leach was featured in local newspapers during the war years, "Leach Back; Says Training a Life Saver"; "Matt Leach Advanced to Major's Rank"; "Leach on Trail of Wartime Public Enemy—Sabotage!"; "Tokyo and Berlin Tremble as Matt Leach Joins Up," "Major Leach Goes to White House," "Axis Papers Please Copy, Matt Leach on the Prowl," n.p. (GPT?), *Hoosier Sentinel*, n.d. All held in clipping file, collection of James Stack.

12. "Memo to Mr. Ladd," JODIL, File No. 62-29777-70407.

13. Memo, FBI, JODIL, File No. 62-70407-2, Oct. 31, 1952.

14. "Matt Leach Named ABC Investigator," IN, March 4, 1954.

15. Mary Heddens, Application for Marriage License, April 5, 1950, Lake County, Indiana, No. A117065, 159; Certificate of Marriage, Matt Leach and Mary Heddens, April 9, 1950, filed in Office of the County Clerk, Lake County, No. A117065. Personal possessions and Gary home address, "In the Matter of the Estate of Mary Leach, Deceased, June 24, 1955, State of Indiana, Lake County, Petition for Issuance of Letters of Administration."

Chapter 14

1. Tubby Toms, IN, June 1955.
2. Al Spiers, "John Dillinger, America's Scourge of the Thirties," *News Dispatch*, n.d.

3. Authors email interview with Noel Hynd, July 31, 2013 (quote used with permission).

4. Alan Hynd, "Dillinger's Strange Career in Crime," *True, The Man's Magazine*, Sept. 1956. It should be noted that the FBI memorandum on Dillinger does not mention the trip that Matt Leach allegedly made to the office of SAC Melvin Purvis. This may have been the result of the blackout of Purvis' role in place at the time.

5. It was conjectured by a researcher who wishes to remain anonymous that the publisher Leach visited was Bantam.

6. Advertisements by Pierson's, June 14, 1955; weather report, *New York Herald Tribune*, June 14, 1955; weather map; "What to Do in Air Raid Test Today," *New York Herald Tribune*, June 14, 1955; "Television," *Evening Standard*, Uniontown, June 14, 1955. Leach's niece Patricia Jean's graduation, Commencement, Horace Mann High School, Gary, Indiana, 1955, Collection of James Stack collection.

7. "Auto Hit as Car Hurls Rail," GPT, June 14, 1955; "4 Are Killed in Turnpike Auto Crash," *Morning Herald* (Uniontown), June 15, 1955, 1; "Matt Leach, Wife Are Killed in Pennsy [*sic*] Turnpike Crash," GPT, June 14, 1955, 1; "Matt Leach, Dillinger Era State Police Chief, Wife Killed in Crash," IS, June 15, 1955; "Local Woman, 2 Others Dead in Turnpike Crash," June 14, 1955; "City Woman, Three Others Die in Crash," *Evening Standard*, June 14, 1955.

8. Shirley Boone, Certificate of Death; Barbara Graves, Certificate of Death (their information is redacted for privacy). James Sewell, age 16, was released from Somerset Hospital on June 16 (*Somerset Daily American*, June 17, 1955). The first two pages of the *Somerset Daily American* for June 15, 1955, were missing from the ProQuest–originating newspaper-on-microfilm reels. *The Morning Herald*, Uniontown, Pennsylvania, June 15, 1955, reported that the Leach vehicle slid

down a 30-foot embankment, ending in a collision with a tree that hurled Mary and Matt Leach 25 feet through the air. *The Morning Herald*, Uniontown, June 15, 1955, reported Mrs. Graves and Shirley Boone to be sisters.

9. Injuries taken from coroner's notes, held by funeral director (shared with authors); Certificate of Death, Matt Leach, Certificate of Death, Mary Heddens Leach, Commonwealth of PA, Department of Health.

10. "In the Matter of the Estate of Mary Leach, Deceased, June 24, 1955, State of Indiana, Lake County, Petition for Issuance of Letters of Administration," Lake County Vital Records Department, Lake Superior Court.

11. Poulsen to John Leach (Matt Leach's nephew and Marshall Leach's son), 2014 telephone interview.

12. Poulsen to Stack, telephone interview; GPT, June 1955, gave an account of the funeral.

13. Poulsen telephone interview with family member of the coroner, who is not named for privacy reasons.

14. "Indianapolis SAC to Director, Articles on Matt Leach by Tubby Toms," June 23, 1955, FBI, JODIL, File No. 62-70407.

15. Toms' articles ran in the *Indianapolis News* in June 1955; quoted from "Matt Leach Traced Dillinger by Intuition," IN, June 17, 1955.

Appendix C

1. William "Tubby" Toms, "Matt Leach Fired on Demand of FBI," IN, June 18, 1955.

2. Alan Hynd, "Dillinger, Dean of the Bankbusters," *True*, Sept. 1956.

3. Al Spiers, "Dillinger, America's Scourge of the Thirties," Michigan City *News Dispatch*, n.d.

Bibliography

Books

Benjamin, Stan, and Terry Rozema. *Tucson Police Department 1871–2004.* Tucson: Arizona Lithographers, 2004.

Binder, John. *Al Capone's Beer Wars: A Complete History of Organized Crime in Chicago During Prohibition.* Amherst, NY: Prometheus, 2017.

Burrough, Bryan. *Public Enemies: America's Greatest Crime Wave and the Birth of the FBI.* New York: Penguin, 2004.

Cook, Fred J. *The FBI Nobody Knows.* New York: Macmillan, 1964.

Cromie, Robert, and Joseph Pinkston. *Dillinger: A Short and Violent Life.* New York: McGraw-Hill, 1962. Reprinted, Evanston: Chicago Historical Bookworks, 1990. (Page references are to McGraw-Hill, 1962.)

Demaris, Ovid. *The Director.* New York: Harper & Row, 1975.

Eisenhower, John S.D. *Intervention: The United States and the Mexican Revolution 1913–1917.* New York: Norton, 1993.

Emery, Richard. *Sam Cowley: Legendary Lawman.* Springville, UT: Cedar Fort, 2004.

Gentry, Curt. *J. Edgar Hoover: The Man and the Secrets.* New York: Norton, 1991.

Girardin, G. Russell, with William J. Helmer. *Dillinger: The Untold Story.* Bloomington: Indiana University Press, 1994.

Gorn, Elliott J. *Dillinger's Wild Ride: The Year That Made America's Public Enemy Number One.* New York: Oxford University Press, 2009.

Helmer, William J., with Rick Mattix. *The Complete Public Enemy Almanac: New Faces and Features on the People, Places and Events of the Gangster and Outlaw Era: 1920–1940.* Nashville: Cumberland House, 2007.

Hunt, Tom. *Wrongly Executed: The Long-Forgotten Context of Charles Sberna's 1939 Electrocution.* Whiting, VT: Seven Seven Eight, 2016.

Kavieff, Paul R. *The Purple Gang: Organized Crime in Detroit-1910–1946.* Fort Lee, NJ: Barricade, 2000.

King, Jeffery S. *The Rise and Fall of the Dillinger Gang.* Nashville: Cumberland House, 2005.

Kotlowski, Dean J. *Paul V. McNutt and the Age of FDR*. Bloomington: Indiana University Press, 2015.

Leibowitz, Irving. *My Indiana*. Englewood Cliffs, NJ: Prentice Hall, 1964.

Maccabee, Paul. *John Dillinger Slept Here: A Crook's Tour of Crime and Corruption in St. Paul, 1920–1936*. St. Paul: Minnesota Historical, 1995.

Mahoney, Tim. *Secret Partners: Big Tom Brown and the Barker Gang*. St. Paul: Minnesota Historical, 2013.

Matera, Dary. *John Dillinger: The Life and Death of America's First Celebrity Criminal*. New York: Carroll & Graf, 2004.

Nickel, Steven, and William J. Helmer. *Baby Face Nelson: Portrait of a Public Enemy*. Nashville: Cumberland House, 2002.

Olsen, Marilyn. *Gangsters, Gunfire and Political Intrigue: The Story of the Indiana State Police*. Indianapolis: .38 Special, 2001.

Potter, Claire Bond. *War on Crime: Bandits, G-Men and the Politics of Mass Culture*. New Brunswick: Rutgers University Press, 1998.

Poulsen, Ellen. *Don't Call Us Molls: Women of the John Dillinger Gang*. Little Neck, NY: Clinton Cook, 2002.

Purvis, Alston, and Alex Tresniowski. *The Vendetta: FBI Hero Melvin Purvis's War Against Crime, and J. Edgar Hoover's War Against Him*. New York: Perseus, 2005.

Purvis, Melvin. *American Agent*. Garden City, NY: Doubleday, 1936.

Stewart, Tony. *Dillinger: The Hidden Truth: Reloaded*. Bloomington: Tony Stewart, 2009.

Scee, Trudy Irene. *Public Enemy #1: The True Story of the Al Brady Gang*. Camden, ME: Down East, 2015.

Toland, John. *The Dillinger Days*. New York: Random House, 1963.

Tompkins, Frank. *Chasing Villa: The Last Campaign of the U.S. Cavalry*. Silver City, NM: High-Lonesome, 1996.

Whitehead, Don. *The FBI Story*. New York: Random House, 1956.

Welch, Neil J., and David W. Marston. *Inside Hoover's FBI*. Garden City, NY: Doubleday, 1984.

Welsome, Eileen. *The General and the Jaguar: Pershing's Hunt for Pancho Villa*. Lincoln: University of Nebraska Press in cooperation with Little, Brown,, 2006.

Magazine and Newspaper Articles

Ciganovic, Kathryn. "Through the Old Military Frontier: A Travelogue." *Serb World, U.S.A.* March/April 1993.

Dunlap, Al. "Why Dillinger's Gang Is Doomed." *Liberty Magazine*. October 27, 1934.

Harrington, Denis J. "The Hunter and the Hunted." *Indianapolis Magazine*. June 1980.

Hart, Philip D. "Becoming Americans: American Naturalization and the Great Immigration." *Serb World, U.S.A.* May/June 2002.

_____. "Captain Matt Leach: Dillinger's Nemesis. *Serb World, U.S.A.* May/June 1992.

Healy, Francis F. "I Hate Coppers: John Dillinger." *Startling Detective.* August n.d. [ca. 1934].

Hyde, Lori. "Captain Matt Leach: Founding Father of the Indiana State Police." *On the Spot Journal: The History of Crime and Law Enforcement During the Twenties and Thirties.* Winter 2006.

_____. "Harvey Bailey: Dean of the American Bank Robbers." *Oklahoma Hombres.* Winter 2009.

Hynd, Alan. "Dillinger: Dean of the Bankbusters." *True Detective.* September 1956.

_____. "The Queen of the Blackmailers." *True Detective.* 1941.

Kramberger, E., and M. Orlic. German, translated by George Kosich. "Through Lika Krbava: An 1899 Tour of the Old Military Frontier." *Serb World, U.S.A.* March/April 2001.

Leach, Matt. "The Public Enemy and Crime Suppression." *Startling Detective.* October 1936.

Nicklanovich, Michael D. "The Military Frontier: Serbs of No Man's Land 1500–1918." *Serb World, U.S.A.* March/April 1988.

Pasley, Fred. "Dillinger Issue Perils Gov. McNutt." *Daily News.* May 5, 1934.

Rankin, Victor P. "The Sheik Bandits: Trailing Indiana's Sheik Bandits." *Startling Detective.* February 1935.

Senoa, Milan.. Translated from original German, 1900, by George Kosich. "Along the Kupa River: Through the Old Military Frontier." *Serb World, U.S.A.* July/August 2002.

Shinnick, William. "A Record of Murder, Robbery, and Indiana Politics." *Chicago Sunday Tribune.* October 9, 1938.

Spiers, Al. "Dillinger: America's Scourge of the Thirties." *Michigan City News Dispatch,* n.d.

Sullivan, Edward S. "How G-Men Smashed Baby Face Nelson's Mob." *Startling Detective.* August 1935.

Wollard, C. A. "Clark! Makley! Pierpont! Dillinger! Captured!" *True Detective.* June 1934.

Pamphlets

Benjamin, Stan. "Without a Shot Fired: The 1934 Capture of the Dillinger Gang in Tucson." *The Smoke Signal,* no. 80 (December 2005).

Smyres, Richard. "Dillinger Strikes in East Chicago." A publication of the East Chicago Public Library, Pearlie Eatman, Interim Director. N.d.

Serialization Articles

Corsi, Sergeant Sal, and Raymond Ruddy. "Yellow Rats: Blasting the Brady Gang. *True Detective Mysteries*. February–October 1938.

Gallagher, Basil. "The Truth About John Dillinger." *Chicago Tribune* (and syndications). August 1934.

Lockerman, Doris. "A Girl Among Manhunters." *Chicago Tribune*. October 7–19, 1935.

Negri, Joseph. "In the Hinges of Hell." *True Detective*. January–December 1941.

Spiers, Al. "It's Like This." ISP Commemorative series of articles. N.d.

Toms, William "Tubby." "Dillinger Gang Split Instigated by Leach." *Indianapolis News*. June 15, 1955.

———. "FBI Slow to Take Up Dillinger's Trail." *Indianapolis News*. June 21, 1955.

———. "Matt Leach Fired on Demand of FBI." *Indianapolis News*. June 18, 1955.

———. "Matt Leach Traced Dillinger by Intuition." *Indianapolis News*. June 17, 1955.

Archives and Public Records Depositories

All addresses and locations for the Licanin/Lich/Leach family, as well as occupants of the various apartments listed, are listed in a collection of Gary City Directories held at the Calumet Regional Archives of IU Northwest, under the direction of the archivist, Curator Steve McShane.

American Legion Headquarters

Calumet Regional Archives, Indiana University, Northwest

Crown Point Office of County Clerk

Federal Bureau of Information FOIA

Indiana State Archives

Indiana State Library

Pennsylvania State Archives

United States Federal Census Records: http://www.Ancestry.com.

United States Library of Congress, Washington, D.C.

Immigration Records and Ship Manifests

FBI. "Freedom of Information/Privacy Act." https://www.fbi.gov/services/records-management/foipa.

The Statue of Liberty–Ellis Island Foundation, Inc. http://www.EllisIsland.org.

Personal History Collections

Collection of Marilyn Olsen.

Collection of Tom Smusyn.

Collection of James Stack.

Index

References in *bold italics* are to pages with illustrations

273